SCHOOL LEADERSHIP FOR AUTHENTIC FAMILY AND COMMUNITY PARTNERSHIPS

School leaders are increasingly called upon to pursue meaningful partnerships with families and community groups, yet many leaders are unprepared to meet the challenges of partnerships, to cross cultural boundaries, or to be accountable to the community. Alliances are needed among educators, families, and community groups that value relationship building, dialogue, and power-sharing as part of socially just, democratic schools. This book brings together research perspectives that intersect the fields of leadership and partnerships to inform and inspire more authentic collaboration.

Contributors from the fields of educational leadership, family engagement, school-community partnerships, and education for social justice come together to examine the role of educational leaders in promoting partnerships as a dimension of leadership for social justice. The volume offers a mix of empirical, conceptual, and reflective chapters with research representing qualitative, quantitative, and mixed methods approaches in urban, suburban, and rural schools. The chapter, "Conversations with Community-Oriented Educational Leaders," includes candid advice from district and school-level administrators on this under-documented aspect of leadership. Situating leadership for partnerships within the leadership literature, this book proposes a model for addressing tensions embedded in home-school relations and leading schools toward more authentic relationships with stakeholders. This collection of original scholarly articles will be a unique resource for new and aspiring administrators and for researchers in both the fields of leadership and school-family-community partnerships.

Susan Auerbach is Associate Professor in the Department of Educational Leadership & Policy Studies at California State University, Northridge.

SCHOOL LEADERSHIP FOR AUTHENTIC FAMILY AND COMMUNITY PARTNERSHIPS

Research Perspectives for Transforming Practice

Edited by Susan Auerbach

Routledge
Taylor & Francis Group
NEW YORK AND LONDON

First published 2012
by Routledge
711 Third Avenue, New York, NY 10017

Simultaneously published in the UK
by Routledge
2 Park Square, Milton Park, Abingdon, Oxon OX14 4RN

Routledge is an imprint of the Taylor & Francis Group, an informa business

Library of Congress Cataloging in Publication Data
School leadership for authentic family and community partnerships : research perspectives for transforming practice / edited by Susan Auerbach.
p. cm.
Includes bibliographical references and index.
1. School principals—Professional relationships. 2. Community and school. 3. Home and school. 4. Educational leadership. I. Auerbach, Susan.
LB2831.9.S35 2011
371.2'011—dc23
2011023770

ISBN: 978-0-415-89395-4 (hbk)
ISBN: 978-0-415-89396-1 (pbk)
ISBN: 978-0-203-81443-7 (ebk)

Typeset in Bembo and Stone Sans
by EvS Communication Networx, Inc.

Printed and bound in the United States of America on acid-free paper
by Edwards Brothers, Inc.

SUSTAINABLE FORESTRY INITIATIVE
Certified Sourcing
www.sfiprogram.org
SFI-00453

This book is dedicated to educational leaders who strive for authentic partnerships with families and communities, including those whose voices and practices are represented in this book.

May they inspire others.

CONTENTS

LIST OF TABLES

FOREWORD

Creating a Climate of Belonging in Socially Just Schools

George Theoharis

> Individuals can resist injustice, but only community can do justice.
>
> (Jim Corbett, 1976)

While scholars, school administrators, teachers, families, and the public often hold differing perspectives on education issues, there is consensus that school leaders are one of a few essential components in creating more equitable and socially just schools. Leaders intent on delivering on this promise require a wealth of knowledge, skills, and commitments or dispositions. These cannot be separate from the challenge that Corbett (1976) raises that in order to "do justice," one cannot work alone; one needs a community approach. This necessitates a belief in democratic process, the skills to bring people together even at times of discord, and a commitment to creating a climate of belonging.

Defining social justice leadership is integral to understanding and then developing more such leaders. The definition I have proposed is that these leaders advocate, lead, and keep at the center of their practice and vision issues of race, class, gender, disability, sexual orientation, and other historically marginalizing factors that are found in U.S. society (Theoharis, 2009). This definition necessitates inclusive schooling practices for students with disabilities, English Language Learners, and other students traditionally separated or segregated within schools, as well as connecting with their families. This definition also necessitates that social justice leadership not be seen as a fixed or static position. It requires ongoing struggle and ongoing reflection (Bogotch, 2002).

Leaders who have lived this definition in their work as school principals and district administrators have achieved, in general, three broad steps as they advanced social justice in their school. First, they have increased access for all students to the core teaching and learning in the school, and in particular, for students from marginalized backgrounds. Second, they have worked collaboratively with teachers to significantly improve the curriculum and instruction, as well as the context in which it takes place. Finally, they have developed a climate of belonging for all in their school community (Theoharis, 2009). It is this climate of belonging that resonates so deeply with the insightful collection of chapters that Susan Auerbach has brought together in *School Leadership for Authentic Family and Community Partnerships.*

The leaders I studied who were successful at creating more equitable and just schools positioned the creation of this climate of belonging as central to their work—not as an add-on, a perfunctory duty, or a way to superficially engage certain parents. A climate of belonging in essence meant creating schools where all involved wanted to be—students, teachers, families, and community members. This climate created a notion that this was a space where all felt valued and needed, which had significant implications for engaging and working effectively with families and community.

I have witnessed in many schools across the United States that working with families has been woefully reduced to the annual school carnival, sporadic attendance at once-a-year parent-teacher conferences, fundraising projects, and a small group of parents who run the official parent organization. As described in the chapters of this book, if a climate of belonging is to be created, a differentiated and more creative approach must be taken to develop deep and authentic relationships with families and communities.

Social justice leaders I studied maintained the necessary structures of traditional family involvement, but they engaged with families and community in new ways as well (Theoharis, 2009). Examples of this engagement included organizing parent empowerment groups so that marginalized families had their agenda heard by school administrators; adopting a less punitive and more developmental, process-oriented approach to discipline; and developing systemic ways to communicate with families in home languages other than English. These social justice leaders were visible and present in and around their communities conducting neighborhood walks, visiting students' homes, and supporting teachers to develop curriculum that was engaged and located in the community. They have hosted authentic community events, such as a wake when a student death has occurred, and led purposeful conversations for learning about race and racism. In addition, these social justice leaders demonstrated a commitment to authentic listening to families and democratic decision-making. And they did not work alone to respond to community needs. They built and maintained ongoing community partnerships with public and nonprofit agencies to connect the school, families, and community organizations.

I see these efforts as significant contributors to the climate of belonging, which cannot be viewed as separate from real school improvement. A narrow understanding of K-12 education reduces school improvement/reform to changes in curriculum and instruction. However necessary such changes may be, social justice leadership requires a much broader understanding of the complexity of schools and the levers needed for equitable improvement. That is why this book and future research on authentic family and community partnerships are essential to developing leaders who run schools that deliver on a promise to meaningfully include, educate, and nurture each and every child.

This book provides a boundary-pushing look at the leadership necessary to create authentic partnerships. Current and future school leaders cannot help but take away a series of salient lessons from this collection. First, it makes a strong case for the vital role of family and community partnerships in educational leadership. Second, it moves beyond the rhetoric of home-school-community connections to include empirical research that brings this leadership to life. Finally, Auerbach and her coauthors show how authentic partnerships are integral to social justice leadership and to a focus on equitable schools and empowered communities.

References

Bogotch, I. (2002). Educational leadership and social justice: Practice into theory. *Journal of School Leadership, 12*(2), 138–156.

Corbett, J. J. (1976). *The roar of the crowd.* Manchester, NH: Ayer.

Theoharis, G. (2009). *The leadership our children deserve: 7 keys to equity, social justice, and school reform.* New York: Teachers College Press.

ACKNOWLEDGMENTS

There are many people who have contributed to the formation of this book. First and foremost, I warmly thank all the contributing authors for their participation, as well as their patience and hard work as we finalized the manuscript. For advice on publishing, I am grateful to Catherine Cooper, Lauri Johnson, Monica Miller Marsh, John Rogers, and Tammy Turner-Vorbeck, as well as my editor at Routledge, Heather Jarrow. For assistance with editing, I wish to thank Jinyi Li and Jennifer Jellison-Holme. For the gift of time provided by a sabbatical leave and faculty research grant, I am indebted to the Michael D. Eisner College of Education at California State University, Northridge.

For insights into parent involvement, home–school relations, and leadership for partnerships, I am grateful to the many parents, students, and educators who generously shared their stories with me during research projects and outreach programs. Among the colleagues whose views have shaped my understanding of these issues in conversations over the years are Lois André-Bechely, Donna Campbell, Charlotte Castagnola, Tony Collatos, Laura Gonzalez, Angela Hasan, Kathleen Hoover-Dempsey, Jennifer Jellison Holme, Mary Johnson, Margy McClain, Pat McDonough, Valerie Muñoz, Jeannie Oakes, John Rogers, Sylvia Rousseau, Irene Serna, Danny Solorzano, Bill Tierney, Tere Viramontes-Gutierrez, Amy Stuart Wells, Camille Wilson, and members of the Family-School-Community Partnerships Special Interest Group of the American Educational Research Association. For first immersing me in these issues 20 years ago, I am grateful to my fellow travelers in the Community Coalition for Quality Public Schools and the Pasadena Education Summit, as well as to then-leaders of the Pasadena Unified School District—Vera Vignes, Bruce Matsui, and Thelma Melendez—who welcomed community participation in urban school reform.

Last but far from least, I greatly appreciate the support of my husband, Bryan Langholz, in bringing this book to light and the forbearance of my children, Ben and Noah Langholz, in their younger years when I was trying to figure out my role in their education. And to my late parents, Irwin and Shirley Auerbach, whose vocations as civil rights activist and creative educator opened pathways that led me to this work, I will always be profoundly grateful.

PART I

Leadership for Partnerships

Delineating the Field

1

INTRODUCTION

Why Leadership for Partnerships?

Susan Auerbach

> *If it's not the principal leading the charge [to engage families and communities in schools], then it's not going to happen; we're just giving it lip service.*

> *If you really have a vision of what you want to accomplish [as a leader], you can't do it without the parents. And you can't do it by telling them what to do. You have to work in community with them.*

> *Families are the heartbeat of the school.... As principal, my job is to support them. This is their school; I need to understand them.... I hear the parents' stories and make a connection at such a human level.*

These quotes from three Los Angeles principals (Auerbach, 2007, 2009, 2010) reveal the passion of school leaders who have dedicated much of their practice to working closely with families and community organizations. Voices like theirs do not often surface in the literature on leadership, in the literature on parent and community involvement, or in leadership preparation programs geared to more traditional approaches. This book opens the way to more such voices and to a better understanding of this underdeveloped aspect of leadership.

Why leadership for partnerships? Administrators have tended to buffer the school from outside influence, but in the past 25 years they have been expected to serve as bridges to, and most recently partners with the community. There have been repeated calls for schools to pursue meaningful partnerships with families and community groups and for school leaders to take the initiative in such efforts. Widely adopted standards for administrative candidates stipulate that leaders should collaborate with community members, respond to their diverse interests, and draw on their resources, as well as understand the social, cultural, and economic context of the school (Council of Chief State School Officers, 2008). Federal and state legislation, as well as guidelines for many grants and comprehensive school reform programs, direct schools to have policies and programs in place for involving parents in student learning and school decision-making. Yet many educational leaders are unprepared to meet the challenges of family and community partnerships, especially in diverse schools and districts with a legacy of distrust and marginalization (Bryk & Schneider, 2002; Epstein & Sanders, 2006; López, Gonzalez, & Fierro, 2006).

Traditionally, researchers and practitioners have valued parent and community involvement mainly as a tool for improving achievement (Epstein, 1990; Henderson & Mapp, 2002; Henderson, Mapp, Johnson, & Davies, 2007). The well-documented positive association between family engagement and student achievement is now a taken-for-granted, commonsense aspect of education (Pushor, 2010; Tollefson, 2008), though there are still gaps in our knowledge of precisely how this indirect influence operates (Jordan, Orozco, & Averett, 2002). Enhancing student learning is, of course, an essential task for partnerships, and many worthwhile programs address this goal (see, for example, the Web sites of the National Network of Partnership Schools, Harvard's Family Involvement Network of Educators, and the Coalition for Community Schools). However, if the focus is solely on raising achievement, partnerships are framed narrowly as instrumental in service of the school's agenda, as Chapter 3 explains. When educators learn from stakeholders and engage in dialogue, multiple purposes for partnership can emerge (Cooper & Christie, 2005; Pushor, 2010; Warren, Hong, Rubin, & Uy, 2009).

This book suggests that partnerships which benefit schools, families, and communities are more than instrumental; they are inherently valuable as an expression of relationship. For schools to engage in such partnerships is to honor the democratic principles of American education, to assert a commitment to the common good, and to seek ways to better serve the public—in other words, to pursue aspects of social justice. Anderson (2009) calls for "authentic social spaces" in schools in which these "cherished, but currently neglected goals" are affirmed (p. 6). Similarly, Riehl (2000) suggests that building strong school-community connections is one of three major tasks of "inclusive administrative practice," which is "rooted in values of equity and social justice" (p. 55). "The fundamental purpose for engaging the community is not to educate parents, improve test scores, or meet specific accountability criteria," write López and colleagues (2006), "but to mobilize the community—both socially and politically—toward self-empowerment and self-reliance" (p. 68).

Leadership for social justice has gained popularity in the literature and in some leadership preparation programs in the past decade (Gaetane, Normore, & Brooks, 2009). Social justice leaders are advocates for children, families, and communities that challenge the status quo, address inequities, question power imbalances, and actively intervene to transform schooling (Marshall & Oliva,

2006). Even the revised standards for administrative candidates acknowledge the ethical duties of school leaders to "safeguard the values of democracy, equity, and diversity" and to "promote social justice" (Council of Chief State School Officers, 2008, p. 15). Leaders who are committed to social justice reach out to families and communities as a central part of their leadership practice, not for instrumental reasons but because it is the right thing to do (Theoharis, 2007). Just as there is a moral imperative for leaders to counter forms of oppression, so, too, should leaders nurture democratic community, a climate of belonging, and authentic participation by families and communities (Anderson, 1998, 2009; Auerbach, 2010; Furman & Starratt, 2002; Riehl, 2000; Theoharis, 2009).

This book examines the role of educational leaders in nurturing authentic partnerships with families and communities. Authentic partnerships are defined as respectful alliances among educators, families, and community groups that value relationship building, dialogue across difference, and sharing power in pursuit of common purpose in socially just, democratic schools (Auerbach, 2010). Such collaborations go beyond the limited type of partnerships typically seen in North American schools and beyond managerial approaches to leadership for partnerships that control and contain outside stakeholders.

Authentic partnerships are most urgently needed in low-income communities of color that have been poorly served by urban schools and the shrinking social safety net. Indeed, the critical literature on family and community engagement and on social justice leadership generally focuses on marginalized communities. But marginalization and oppression are not unique to urban schools; demographic change and economic crisis, for example, have increasingly brought equity challenges to suburban and rural schools as they confront new immigrant populations, levels of poverty, or intergroup tensions. Relations with the families of students with special needs remain fraught with misunderstanding and conflict in a variety of school contexts. Middle-class parents, in spite of their relative privilege, may also experience conflict with educators and uncertainty about acceptable roles when they press for change (Graue, Kroeger, & Prager, 2001; Sanders, 2010). There is a place for promoting authentic partnerships in all school communities, regardless of demographics, as a moral obligation of leadership. Readers interested in partnerships in suburban, rural, or middle-class communities will find pertinent information here in Chapters 3, 7, 8, 10, and 13.

Despite expanding expectations for school leaders in working with parents and community organizations, there are few empirical studies of leadership for partnerships (Crowson, Goldring, & Haynes, 2010; Driscoll & Goldring, 2005; Griffith, 2001; Riehl, 2000; Van Voorhis & Sheldon, 2004). Indeed, there is a disconnect among the literatures on school leadership, family-community engagement, and social justice (Auerbach, 2007; Cooper, Riehl, & Hassan, 2010). This book brings together scholars from these fields to encourage cross-pollination of ideas and to address gaps in the literature. In so doing, we hope to raise the profile of partnerships generally as a dimension of leadership and to point the way toward more authentic forms of collaboration that can inform and inspire leadership preparation, practice, and research.

Plan of the Book

The book opens with two conceptual chapters that delineate the field of leadership for partnerships, situating it in the leadership literature (Chapter 2) and the family and community engagement literature (Chapter 3). This pairing symbolizes the coming together of the two fields in this volume. In Chapter 2, Carolyn Riehl reviews recent analytic and empirical research within the contrasting discourses of leadership for school effectiveness and leadership for social justice. She proposes ways to bridge these discourses in future research to build greater understanding of leadership for partnerships. In Chapter 3, I draw on the partnerships literature to establish a rationale for more authentic school-family-community connections. I then present a continuum of leadership for partnerships, comparing leadership for authentic partnerships with leadership that prevents partnerships (rare but still existing), leadership for nominal partnerships (business as usual), and leadership for traditional partnerships (more collaborative and responsive).

Understanding the difference that difference makes, confronting issues of power, and proactively addressing inequities are hallmarks of leadership for social justice. Part II highlights perspectives on diversity and leading partnerships across difference in race, class, culture, and ability/disability. Inspired by a visionary leader 100 years ago, John Rogers, Rhoda Freelon, and Veronica Terriquez in Chapter 4 analyze results from a survey of urban principals on parent engagement beliefs and strategies, suggesting that most fall short of pursuing democratic ideals and robust involvement. They contrast higher and lower socioeconomic status (SES) schools to explain varying levels of parent participation in school activities and governance and the role of administrators in supporting parent participation. In Chapter 5, April Ruffin-Adams and Camille Wilson infuse Black feminist theory, critical race theory, and Foucault's conception of power into an analysis of relations between school officials and African American mothers of students with disabilities, focusing on the marginalization of these parents and the "politics of containment" in the special education placement process. They note the dire effects of inappropriate special education placement for African American male students, calling on leaders to promote advocacy-oriented partnerships attuned to families' goals for their children. In Chapter 6, Edward Olivos questions appropriate roles and legitimate forms of involvement for bicultural parents, illustrating tensions between Latino parents and school officials with examples from his work in California and Oregon. He offers a framework for school leaders to work through these tensions as they move from "accomodationist" parent involvement to "transformative" engagement with bicultural communities.

Two key functions for educational leaders in partnerships, as in other arenas, are developing policy and programs. Part III examines the dynamics of these efforts in varied contexts in the United States and Canada. Chapters 7 (Joseph Flessa and Hélène Grégoire) and 8 (Molly Gordon) examine how Ontario provincial and U.S. district parent and community engagement policies are interpreted by leaders at the school level, with a focus on factors that promote or hinder meaningful partnerships. Flessa and Grégoire explore the assumptions that underlie policy aspirations and the dilemmas of implementing them, while Gordon documents the challenges of creating organizational cultures of engagement at both the district and school level. In Chapter 9, Janet Chrispeels assesses the work of two intermediary organizations that offer parent education programs in schools and compares their theories of action and their impact on immigrant parents' human, social, and intellectual capital. She recommends that school leaders partner with intermediary organizations to build parents' leadership capacity and improve home-school relations. Catherine Hands's case study of two Canadian high schools in Chapter 10 shifts the focus to teacher leadership, describing how teacher leaders initiated and sustained a wide variety of school-community partnerships to address students' needs. The school administrators' role was to support teachers' work in developing these opportunities for community-based learning.

Among newer, more controversial contexts for leadership for partnerships are community organizing initiatives, charter schools, and district-level reform initiatives, which are covered in Part IV. A pioneering essay in Chapter 11 by Sara McAlister, Heinrich Mintrop, Seenae Chong, and Michelle Renée explores the tensions and possibilities in relations between community organizing groups and school leaders. They draw on the work of the Annenberg Institute for School Reform with community organizing to show how these initiatives harness parent power to bring additional resources to schools and present more of an opportunity than a threat to school leaders who choose to work in alliance with them. In Chapter 12, Marc Stein, Ellen Goldring, and Claire Smrekar report on a study of the dynamics of parent involvement at charter schools in Indianapolis. They analyze parents' perceptions of school invitations for parent involvement, relating this to principal expectations, the school climate for partnerships, and the potential of small schools of choice to build positive relationships with families. Chapter 13, "Conversations with Community-Oriented Leaders," presents the voices of two principals, one district reformer, one superintendent, and one assistant superintendent for family engagement from across the United States who reflect on their experience leading a wide range of partnerships. Their candid observations on the challenges of community relations and advice to administrators who aspire to greater collaboration with stakeholders echo themes raised throughout the book.

Finally, the Conclusion in Chapter 14 brings together researchers' perspectives from this collection with the issues raised by the practitioners in Chapter 13 to suggest lessons presented in the book for current and aspiring school leaders, leadership preparation programs, and future research on leadership for partnerships.

References

Anderson, G. (1998). Toward authentic participation: Deconstructing the discourses of participatory reforms in education. *American Educational Research Journal, 35*(4), 571–603.

Anderson, G. L. (2009). *Advocacy leadership: Toward a post-reform agenda in education*. New York: Routledge.

Auerbach, S. (2007). Visioning parent engagement in urban schools: Role constructions of Los Angeles administrators. *Journal of School Leadership, 17*(6), 699–735.

Auerbach, S. (2009). Walking the walk: Portraits in leadership for family engagement in urban schools. *School Community Journal, 19*(1), 9–32.

Auerbach, S. (2010). Beyond Coffee with the Principal: Toward leadership for authentic school-family partnerships. *Journal of School Leadership, 20*(6), 730–759.

Bryk, A. S., & Schneider, B. (2002). *Trust in schools: A core resource for improvement*. New York: Russell Sage Foundation.

Cooper, C. W., & Christie, C. A. (2005). Evaluating parent empowerment: A look at the potential of social justice evaluation in education. *Teachers College Record, 107*(10), 2248–2274.

Cooper, C. W., Riehl, C., & Hasan, L. (2010). Leading and learning with diverse families in schools: Critical epistemology amid communities of practice. *Journal of School Leadership, 20*(6), 760–790.

Council of Chief State School Officers. (2008). *Educational leadership policy standards: ISLLC 2008*. Washington, DC: Author.

Crowson, R. L., Goldring, E. B., & Haynes, K. T. (2010). *Successful schools and the community relationship: Concepts and skills to meet 21st century challenges*. Richmond, CA: McCutchan.

Driscoll, M. E., & Goldring, E. B. (2005). How can school leaders incorporate communities as contexts for student learning? In W. Firestone & C. Riehl (Eds.), *A new agenda for research in educational leadership* (pp. 61–80). New York: Teachers College Press.

Epstein, J. L. (1990). School and family connections: Theory, research and implications for integrating sociologies of education and family. In D. G. Unger & M. B. Sussman (Eds.), *Families in community settings: Interdisciplinary perspectives* (pp. 99–126). New York: Haworth Press.

Epstein, J. L., & Sanders, M. (2006). Prospects for change: Preparing educators for school, family, and community partnerships. *Peabody Journal of Education, 81*(2), 81–120.

Furman, G. C., & Starratt, R. J. (2002). Leadership for democratic community in schools. In J. Murphy (Ed.), *The educational leadership challenge: Redefining leadership for the 21st century: 101st Yearbook of the National Society for the Study of Education, Part I* (pp. 105–133). Chicago, IL: University of Chicago Press.

Gaetane, J. M., Normore, A. H., & Brooks, J. S. (2009). Leadership for social justice: Preparing 21st century school leaders for a new social order. *Journal of Research on Leadership Education, 4*(1), 1–31.

Graue, M. E., Kroeger, J., & Prager, D. (2001). A Bakhtinian analysis of particular home-school relations. *American Educational Research Journal, 38*(3), 467–498.

Griffith, J. (2001). Principal leadership of parent involvement. *Journal of Educational Administration, 39*(2), 162–186.

Henderson, A. T., & Mapp, K. L. (2002). *A new wave of evidence: The impact of school, family and community connections on student achievement*. Austin, TX: Southwest Educational Development Laboratory.

Henderson, A. T., Mapp, K. L., Johnson, V. R., & Davies, D. (2007). *Beyond the bake sale: The essential guide to family-school partnerships.* New York: New Press.

Jordan, C., Orozco, E., & Averett, A. (2002). *Emerging issues in school, family and community connections: Annual synthesis 2001.* Austin, TX: Southwest Educational Development Laboratory.

López, G. R., Gonzalez, M. L., & Fierro, E. (2006). Educational leadership along the U.S.-Mexico border: Crossing borders/embracing hybridity/building bridges. In C. Marshall & M. Oliva (Eds.), *Leadership for social justice: Making revolutions in education* (pp. 64–84). Boston, MA: Pearson.

Marshall, C., & Oliva, M. (2006). Building the capacities of social justice leaders. In C. Marshall & M. Oliva (Eds.), *Leadership for social justice: Making revolutions in education* (pp. 1–15). Boston, MA: Pearson.

Pushor, D. (2010). Are schools doing enough to learn about families? In M. Miller Marsh & T. Turner-Vorbeck (Eds.), *(Mis)Understanding families: Learning from real families in our schools* (pp. 4–16). New York: Teachers College Press.

Riehl, C. (2000). The principal's role in creating inclusive schools for diverse students: A review of normative, empirical, and critical literature on the practice of educational administration. *Review of Educational Research, 70*(1), 55–81.

Sanders, M. (2010). Parents as leaders: School, family, and community partnerships in two districts. In P. D. Houston, A. M. Blankstein, & R. W. Cole (Eds.), *Leadership for family and community involvement* (pp. 13–32). Thousand Oaks, CA: Corwin.

Theoharis, G. (2007). Social justice educational leaders and resistance: Toward a theory of social justice leadership. *Educational Administration Quarterly, 43*(2), 221–258.

Theoharis, G. (2009). *The school leaders our children deserve: Seven keys to equity, social justice, and school reform.* New York: Teachers College Press.

Tollefson, K. (2008). *Volatile knowing: Parents, teachers, and the censored story of accountability in America's public schools.* Lanham, MD: Rowman & Littlefield.

Van Voorhis, F., & Sheldon, S. (2004). Principals' roles in the development of U.S. programs of school, family, and community partnerships. *International Journal of Educational Research, 41,* 55–70.

Warren, M., Hong, S., Rubin, C. L., & Uy, P. S. (2009). Beyond the bake sale: A community-based relational approach to parent engagement in schools. *Teachers College Record, 111*(9), 2209–2254.

2

EDGING IN

Locating a Focus on School-Family-Community Partnerships within the Scholarship of Educational Leadership

Carolyn Riehl

The research on school partnerships with families and communities presents convincing evidence that school leaders are important for establishing and facilitating these institutional and interpersonal relationships. Whether they lead formal partnerships like the Comer Project (Haynes, 1998) or less structured efforts to involve families in schools (e.g., Abrams & Gibbs, 2000; Martin, Fergus, & Noguera, 2010; Porras Hein, 2003), leaders establish priorities, set the tone, and provide the means for involving families and communities in education or for keeping them at bay. At the present time, however, most research on school-family-community partnerships, including those studies that address the role of leadership, is located outside of the domain of educational leadership research. How can this research topic—leadership for partnerships—establish a place for itself within the large and growing body of research on leadership? In this chapter, I take a closer look at two important domains within leadership research—research on leadership for organizational effectiveness and student learning and research on leadership for social justice and equity. I do this in order to examine whether these domains might be compatible with and hospitable to research on leadership for family and community partnerships. I review representative and recent work to identify points of potential convergence within these domains, and I make suggestions for ways in which these subfields can be cultivated to establish a solid knowledge base on leadership for partnerships.

Research on Leadership for Organizational Effectiveness and Student Learning

The search for school effects on learning has been called an "international preoccupation" (Lewis & Murphy, 2008). With increasing intensity, policymakers and the public are challenging practitioners in the educator sector to produce results from their efforts and expenditures and to be held accountable for outcomes. Educational researchers are following closely behind, seeking to demonstrate and explain the impact of various structures, resources, processes, and people on learning and achievement. Research on leadership is increasingly caught up in this activity. In part, this seems to be a genuine effort to expand causal models of school effects on learning to include leadership as a determining factor. This could, in part, represent an attempt by the leadership research domain to stay relevant during a time when only those educational practices and people with a demonstrable impact on learning seem to find legitimacy and support. On the other hand, the focus on leadership could also be a new version of the "romance of leadership" (Meindl, Ehrlich, & Dukerich, 1985), reflecting our culture's long-standing infatuation with leadership and the tendency to attribute to leadership powers and consequences that may properly belong somewhere else. It also could be due to more cynical purposes, such as an interest on the part of research funders or others to denigrate teachers and elevate administrators, or to "blame and shame" both teachers and leaders and thereby justify harsh remedies such as the removal of principals and staff in school turnaround efforts (Gunter & Fitzgerald, 2008). It is important for the leadership research field to consider how these subtle impulses might be influencing their efforts. Nonetheless, the search for leadership effects continues.

Organizationally Focused Theories and Research

Most current research on leadership effects on learning builds out from conceptual models that can be identified as organizationally focused theories. These models tend to specify what leaders do to keep their organizations functioning smoothly. Impact on the school organization's bottom line of learning is implied but not often articulated carefully or tested empirically, especially in early models that were adapted from business and industry. Many organizationally focused models incorporate some version of the idea that leaders must focus on the two dimensions of managing tasks and managing social relationships in organizations (Owens & Valesky, 2007). Following Burns's (1978) seminal work on leadership, new theories emerged that emphasized how leaders promote vision, meaning, and strategic directions in their organizations, how they respond to change and practice adaptive rather than merely technical leadership (Heifetz, 1994). Again, these models are mostly concerned with describing smooth organizational functioning, not organizational outcomes.

Of the many conceptual models in this line of work, one of the most prominent has been transformational leadership, a theory that elevates the leader's role in directing an organization's pursuit of its vision and purposes (e.g., Jantzi & Leithwood, 1996; Leithwood, 1994). Another conceptual model, that of constructivist leadership (Lambert, 2003), focuses on the leader's role in helping others make meaning, develop knowledge, and learn, on the assumption that organizations are grounded in the meanings they embody. Models of distributed leadership emphasize how leadership functions are spread across formal roles, individuals, tasks, and tools (Spillane, Halverson, & Diamond, 2001). Similarly, collaborative leadership models seek to explain how leaders work with others to develop organizations (Hallinger, 2005). Change leadership and turnaround leadership models attend primarily to the special challenges of organizational change, whether ongoing and incremental or more punctuated and disruptive. And not surprisingly, many models of instructional leadership or learning-focused leadership (Hallinger, 2005; Knapp, Copland, Honig, Plecki, & Portin, 2010; Marks & Printy, 2003) pay special attention to the actions leaders take for strengthening the central task of teaching in schools.

These frameworks sometimes seem positioned to compete with one another as models cut from whole cloth that must be adopted intact. But when examined more closely, most seem to incorporate some fairly consistent components related to the older emphasis on task-person and the newer emphasis on values and purposes. Leadership is characterized as a goal-directed influence process, enacted through a set of basic functions that help to mobilize the organization and its people toward desired ends (Leithwood & Riehl, 2005). The basic functions have to do with constructing meanings and setting directions, working with people, working with organizational structures and processes, and, in education, managing the core competency of the instructional program (e.g., Leithwood, Louis, Anderson, & Wahlstrom, 2004; Leithwood & Riehl, 2005; Louis, Dretzke, & Wahlstrom, 2010; Robinson, Lloyd, & Rowe, 2008).

Many of these frameworks implicitly or explicitly include family and community in their conceptualizations. In some models, family and community characteristics are considered part of the contextual background of education; they influence what students are like and present opportunities or constraints that impact the work of adults in schools and must therefore be addressed by leaders (e.g., Bossert, Dwyer, Rowan, & Lee, 1982; Pitner, 1988). Other leadership theories that use an open systems framework emphasize the need for leaders to work with external stakeholders for at least three reasons: so that schools can better reflect the needs and interests of their clients and consumers, so that external agents will accept and support the school and ensure its legitimacy, and so that leaders can keep overly powerful or intrusive stakeholders at a safe distance (e.g., Crowson, 1998; Day, Leithwood, & Sammons, 2008; Hallinger, 2005; Horvat, Curci, & Partlow, 2010). And still other organizationally focused leadership theories view families and communities as important partners and resources for student learning and development, suggesting ways in which leaders enhance family and community effectiveness as learning partners; for example, by sponsoring parent education programs or by finding ways to incorporate family knowledge and culture into the school program (e.g., Leithwood

& Riehl, 2005). For the most part, each posited relationship between leaders and external stakeholders envisions leaders' work with families or communities as a means that leads toward the ends of smooth organizational functioning and enhanced student learning (Auerbach, 2010). But some approaches are not merely instrumental; they are also expressive of respect for families and communities and seek to empower and involve them in genuine ways.

Attention to families and communities is not prominent in all theories of organizationally focused leadership, however. Some current models that focus heavily on the leader's role in instructional improvement seem to assume that all of the resources needed to support student learning are found within the confines of the school (e.g., Correnti & Rowan, 2007; Knapp et al., 2010; Rowan, Correnti, & Miller, 2002). In part, this may be a deliberate departure from earlier models of school effects that attributed large proportions of the variation in student learning to factors outside of the school, such as community demographics or students' family backgrounds. These external factors sometimes seem to have been convenient explanations of student learning differences because they were easier to measure than whatever factors might be found within the "black box" of the school's instructional program. Raudenbush (2009) defends the strategy of looking only to school factors as a pragmatic choice, claiming that "the children who depend most on good schooling for academic growth are the least likely to receive it" (p. 171). Whatever other problems stand in students' way, reasons Raudenbush, if we can increase the amount and quality of schooling for these children, inequity would be reduced. That is a compelling argument, but leadership theories that leave families and communities out of the model also reflect a particular point of view; namely, that principals are the heads of schools, not the heads of relationships among schools, families, and communities. In the end, by omitting these relationships from theories of leadership, researchers might fail to explore important opportunities for leaders to make a difference.

In sum, organizationally focused conceptual models of leadership do open space for considering family and community partnerships and it seems that research on leadership for partnerships could find a hospitable home in this domain. Unfortunately, the empirical research derived from these models tells a somewhat different story. Researchers have not yet produced many comprehensive and credible analyses of leadership effects on student outcomes, and the few that exist say relatively little about how leaders work with families and communities to impact learning. Reasons for this are plentiful: There are problems generating empirical models that fully reflect the theories behind them; problems enacting sophisticated research designs that enable longitudinal and reciprocal effects to emerge; problems finding ways to gather data on complex and nuanced processes in large and representative samples; and problems utilizing analytic methods that find meaningful causal patterns, not just statistically significant associations.

Leadership Effects on Student Learning

As noted above, organizationally focused research on leadership has been slow in documenting effects on student learning. As Pitner (1988) explained in an important early synthesis of research on leadership effects, many conceptual models posit that leadership has an indirect effect on school outcomes, working through various other people, processes, and conditions to impact learning. Some models also include antecedent conditions that influence leadership itself. In the empirical research Pitner examined, however, most researchers utilized analytic strategies that measured the direct effects of leadership on student outcomes, if they measured outcomes at all. Some researchers designed their studies to explore possible indirect effects, but then measured only process variables and did not follow through to outcomes. Many studies measured leadership through survey instruments such as the Leader Behavior Description Questionnaire (LBDQ) and the Principal Instructional Management Rating Scale (PIMRS), neither of which included items related to families or communities. Not surprisingly, then, the early wave of research Pitner summarized had weak and unconvincing findings about effects on learning and said virtually nothing about leaders working with external stakeholders.

A decade later, in another influential review of studies linking leadership to student learning outcomes, Hallinger and Heck (1998) reported that research methodologies had evolved away from direct effects models, although many studies were still plagued by inadequate methodological approaches and limited data. They found small effects of leadership on learning that operated mainly through goal setting in schools. In all of the research they reviewed, only one contextual effect was noted: when demographic variables were factored in, leadership effects on student outcomes seemed to wash out in high socioeconomic status (SES) contexts but not in low SES contexts, suggesting that leadership is more important in low-income contexts. Also, in schools that were more effective, principals seem to have encouraged more parent involvement, although the direction of causality was quite unclear.

Since the Hallinger and Heck review, school systems have dramatically expanded the data they collect on students' educational histories and performance in school. Much of these data, stored as electronic administrative records, could be used in studies of leadership effects on learning. This is a major advance over the days when researchers had to generate student-level data by combing through paper records on students. Administrative datasets also include information on school leaders' backgrounds and qualifications, although there is still not much information on what they do, leaving leadership practice in the proverbial black box. But researchers are exploring new ways to document leaders' actions, through measures such as questionnaires and logs of activity (e.g., Camburn, Huff, Goldring, & May, 2010; Camburn, Spillane, & Sebastian, 2010). Large federally sponsored research datasets continue to provide arrays of information on students, schools, and learning outcomes, although their variables pertaining to leadership are still fairly rudimentary. Researchers in the leadership field are also using more sophisticated analytic tools such as hierarchical linear modeling (e.g., Marks & Printy, 2003). Thus, the capacity for studying leadership and generating credible and important findings about its impact on learning is increasing.

But once again, there are few studies that incorporate data on families and communities, or leaders' work with them, in examinations of leadership effects. Heck, Larsen, and Marcoulides (1990) examined how principals enacted a set of 34 instructional leadership behaviors in high- and low-achieving schools and concluded that the impact of parent engagement was not significantly different across schools, although there was a significant effect in what principals did to buffer teachers from intrusions in high-achieving schools. Drawing on data from teachers in 24 schools involved in a nationwide study of school restructuring, Marks and Printy (2003) showed moderate effects of an integrated form of leadership (combining both shared instructional leadership and transformational leadership) on several measures of authentic learning in math and social studies; however, nothing at all was mentioned about leaders' roles or involvement with parents and community partnerships. In a meta-analysis of research that has been widely cited (Waters, Marzano, & McNulty, 2003), 21 key leadership responsibilities were examined for their relationship to student outcomes; the only one that referred to parents was "outreach," defined as "is an advocate and spokesperson for the school to all stakeholders." Witziers, Bosker, and Kruger (2003) conducted a meta-analysis of 37 multinational studies, all of which used a direct effects model (which seems to have enjoyed a longer lifespan in Europe than in the United States). They not surprisingly found only small effects for leadership and nothing pertaining to leaders' work with families or communities. Clark, Martorell, and Rockoff (2009) also reverted to a direct effects model to study the impact of leadership on student attendance and learning. Although their analysis benefited from having rich administrative data on students, they essentially used a black box approach to leadership, relying mostly on variables measuring leader demographics and experience, and thus had nothing to report about what leaders did with family and community partnerships.

In contrast, Horng, Klasik, and Loeb (2010) sought a more nuanced picture of leadership effects. They gathered objective measures of how high school principals in a large urban district use their time and studied whether time spent on different tasks was associated with a range of outcomes for students. The tasks were grouped into six categories: administrative (e.g., budgets, personnel); organization management; day-to-day instruction; instructional program; internal relations; and external relations. In this framework, attention to work with families and community was minimal: Tasks under "external relations" included working with local community members or organizations and fundraising, while under "internal relations" tasks included communicating with parents and counseling students and parents. The only category that had a relationship to student performance was organizational management.

Robinson et al. (2008) conducted a series of meta-analyses of leadership research, taking pains to aggregate properly across studies that are in fact quite different, theoretically and methodologically. They inductively derived five dimensions of leadership practice in 12 studies: establishing goals and expectations; resourcing strategically for instruction; planning, coordinating, and evaluating teaching and curriculum; promoting and participating in teacher learning and development; and ensuring an orderly and supportive environment. The authors concluded that "the closer educational leaders get to the core business of teaching and learning, the more likely they are to have a positive impact on students' outcomes" (p. 664). The only finding they reported relative to families and communities was that leaders in high-performing schools protected teachers from undue pressure from other administrative levels and from parents.

Many researchers study leadership using qualitative methods, which enable nuances and contingencies of leadership actions and processes to come into view more clearly, even though causal conclusions are harder to establish (Leithwood & Riehl, 2005; Robinson et al., 2008). There is some evidence from such studies that working with families and communities is indeed an important component of effective leadership practice, and that it is not always easy to do. For example, in a study of British schools that had shown 3 years of sustained improvement in student outcomes, Penlington, Kington, and Day (2008) found head teachers to be important in establishing a culture centered on a vision for success. Heads in the more disadvantaged schools did not use students' backgrounds as an excuse, but instead intensified their efforts to get parents involved in the school. Other studies show similar commitments from leaders to work with parents of students who have not experienced success, even though it was difficult achieve (e.g., Good, 2008; Khalifa, 2010).

Overall, in the organizationally focused leadership research domain, there is clear room for conceptualizing leaders' work with families and communities as a key component of effective practice. It is more of a challenge to add this emphasis to empirical studies, especially those that connect leadership to student learning. It will require careful efforts to measure or document leadership with families and communities in ways that are sensitive to contextual variations (e.g., some families' need for more assistance to become involved) and that account for two-way effects (i.e., leaders' impact on families and communities and vice versa) and effects over time. The impact of concerted efforts with families, for example, might take time to translate into student learning gains.

Two examples of recent work may be harbinger of good things to come. Leithwood, Patten, and Jantzi (2010) present a model of leader effects on student learning in which leadership is theorized to impact learning through four organizational pathways: Rational, Emotions, Organizational, and Family. Each path is populated by sets of conditions that can be influenced by leadership and that in turn impact learning. The Rational path relates mostly to instruction, the technical core of schooling. The Emotions path includes factors related to teacher efficacy, morale, engagement, and trust. The Organizational path covers those factors traditionally considered central to organizational functioning, including aspects of organizational structure and culture. The Family path includes aspects of students' families that, from the school's perspective, could be alterable, including family educational culture. In this first empirical test of the conceptual model, Leithwood et al. utilized a survey design and a sample of respondents from nearly 200 elementary schools. They measured leadership using teacher responses to several questions about leaders' influence, constructed a few variables to represent each of the four pathways, and developed a composite measure of student achievement. Not surprisingly, since the empirical design did not pretend to cover each pathway fully, the researchers did not find strong leadership effects. But they drew an interesting conclusion from the analysis: "Indeed, engaging the school productively with parents, if this has not been a focus, may well produce larger effects on student learning in the short run than marginal improvements to already at least satisfactory levels of instruction" (p. 698).

Similarly, in their recent presentation of lessons learned from years of research by the Consortium on Chicago School Research, Bryk, Sebring, Allensworth, Luppescu, and Easton (2010) analyzed a voluminous amount of data to show that strong family and community ties to schools formed an essential subsystem of support that led to stronger instructional work in schools and ultimately to higher student performance. These ties not only created safer and more orderly schools, they also helped parents support their children's learning; enabled teachers to learn more about their students' home culture and community and incorporate that knowledge into their instruction; and brought supplemental community services to students with high needs. Because this research was longitudinal in nature, Bryk et al. were able to demonstrate the importance of school leadership as a driver of change, leveraging increased family and community involvement to benefit schools and students. A key mechanism in this was the development of relational trust, and again the longitudinal nature of the data enabled the researchers to show that efforts to build trust increased parent involvement just as parent involvement increased relational trust (cf. Auerbach, Chapter 3, this volume; McAlister, Mintrop, Chong, & Renée, Chapter 11, this volume). This comprehensive and well-executed research can serve as a strong guide for future research on leadership for school-family-community partnerships in the service of better outcomes for students.

Research on Leadership for Social Justice and Equity

A second, growing segment of leadership research takes a different approach in linking leadership to learning outcomes, by eschewing most traditional concerns for organizational functioning and effectiveness and instead pursuing a value orientation toward inclusion, equity, and social justice. These values are ends in themselves, defining the kinds of educational organizations being envisioned, but they are also means to the goal of raising student achievement, especially for marginalized students who have been poorly served by the educational system. Perhaps more accurately, pursuing student success is an inherent aspect of social justice and equity, not just an end result.

This emerging body of research, like the leaders whose practice has inspired it, has pushed a large rock uphill. Until recently, most educational leaders have been perceived as more comfortable maintaining rather than challenging the status quo (Riehl, 2000). Both the public and educational leaders themselves prefer thinking of their role as managers instead of advocates and "troublemakers" (Marshall & Ward, 2004, cited in Theoharis, 2010). This may be changing as new programs for leadership preparation place greater emphasis on recruiting individuals with a passion for change (e.g., Maxwell, 2007). But for the most part, leadership for social justice, equity, or inclusion signals a principled, sometimes defiant standpoint that is, if not a rebuke, then at least a challenge to traditional models.

As with models of organizationally focused leadership, some conceptual models of leadership in this domain seem to be frameworks cut from whole cloth. Scholars have described models for transformative leadership (Quantz, Cambron-McCabe, & Dantley, 1991; Shields, 2010); democratic leadership (Begley & Zaretsky, 2004; Fuhrman & Starratt, 2002; Starratt, 2001); and social justice leadership (Brown, 2004; Cambron-McCabe & McCarthy, 2005; Larson & Murtadha, 2002; Theoharis, 2010, 2007). Others take a more general approach, conceptualizing how the main functions of leadership are accomplished with a specific focus on desired goals such as inclusion or equity (e.g., Foster, 1989; Riehl, 2000; Scheurich & Skrla, 2003; Skrla & Scheurich, 2001). While these conceptual models have distinctive nuances, most share a similar ethic that emphasizes a critique of the status quo and a pursuit of transformative justice. For example, Theoharis (2007) describes social justice leaders as those who "advocate, lead, and keep at the center of their practice and vision issues of race, class, gender, disability, sexual orientation, and other historically and currently marginalizing conditions in the United States" (p. 222). Shields (2010) offers a similar description of transformative leadership:[1]

> Transformative leadership begins with questions of justice and democracy; it critiques inequitable practices and offers the promise not only of greater individual achievement but of a better life lived in common with others. Transformative leadership, therefore, inextricably links education and educational leadership with the wider social context within which it is embedded.
>
> *(p. 559)*

Shields considers transformative leadership to hold "the most promise and potential to meet both the academic and the social justice needs of complex, diverse, and beleaguered education systems" (p. 562). She asserts that although leaders working from an organizationally focused lens and those working from a social justice perspective can both pursue academic quality as well as social responsibility, "there are clear distinctions between the ways in which leaders subscribing to each theory conceptualize, interpret, and approach these tasks" (p. 570).

This domain of leadership research is highly compatible with a focus on leaders' work with families and communities, both in its conceptual models and empirical studies. At the moment, most empirical research on transformative or social justice leadership tends to be qualitative and descriptive, based on closely observed case studies of leaders who demonstrate a knowledge of and commitment to this form of leadership and who work in schools that have had a positive impact on student achievement, especially for marginalized students. As these studies report, such principals strive to create new meanings and knowledge around diversity and inequity, disrupting deficit thinking and encouraging their staff to learn more about their students (Riehl, 2000; Shields, 2010). This extends to families and communities as well; principals take steps to help their staff perceive families and communities differently. They take their teachers into the community for neighborhood walks, home visits, and school meetings off site; they have their teachers ride buses with students so they can meet parents (Scheurich, 1998; Theoharis, 2010). They are open and frank about discussing difficult issues around race, ethnicity, and social class, actively resisting "pathologizing silences" and challenging deeply held beliefs (Shields, 2004).

Leaders who pursue social justice "perform cultural work" (Cooper, 2009) by empowering diverse and marginalized families and students in different ways, including them in decisions, and providing educational assistance such as family literacy programs (Ross & Berger, 2009). They establish partnerships with community groups and businesses, drawing as many resources and services into the school as they can, and they give back to the community as well, by, for example, having students participate in community projects that not only provide a service but also teach students how to be advocates (e.g., Auerbach, Chapter 13, this volume). This work is not always easy and leaders do not always succeed in being transformative, especially when they fall back on habitual top-down behaviors or struggle against "the enormity of the daily work of the principalship, the momentum of the status quo, obstructive staff attitudes and beliefs, and insular/privileged parental expectations" (Theoharis, 2009, p. 339; cf. Carr, 1997). In Cooper's (2009) study, elementary school principals were stymied by tensions between families and educators. Even when they professed to be enlightened themselves, they sometimes engaged in stereotyping and disempowering actions, practicing what Cooper called "inclusive rhetoric and exclusive treatment" (cf. Olivos, Chapter 6, this volume).

These theories and empirical descriptions of transformative leadership for social justice tend to treat families and communities not just as clients or consumers of educational services, but as real partners in learning. The work of helping families and communities becomes part of the school's mission, and the resources they can bring to the learning process are valued. Transformative leadership models assume that leaders cannot pursue social justice only within the walls of the school but must also reach out to families and communities to ameliorate inequities in resources and opportunities available to children and youth.

In many of these theories, trust and social capital function as core mechanisms connecting families and communities to school. Leaders who work proactively with families and communities help to develop trust by affirming the value of families, reducing vulnerability and risk by shrinking the "relational gap" between families and schools and creating new beliefs about parents and students (Adams, Forsyth, & Mitchell, 2009). They also help to enact changes in their schools so that the social and cultural capital different kinds of students bring to school is valued and incorporated into culturally responsive instruction (Leithwood & Riehl, 2005).

Although theories and empirical research on transformative leadership for inclusion and social justice incorporate work with families and communities into the core of their frameworks, not everything has to do with such partnerships. Transformative leaders work to improve the same school processes and conditions that organizationally focused leaders do. They ensure that students have access to high quality, ambitious curriculum and competent instruction (Riehl, 2000; Ross & Berger, 2009). They help teachers maintain high expectations for students (Brown, Benkovitz, Muttillo, & Urban, 2011). They monitor student progress on high stakes assessments and make sure that students are prepared to do well, even while acknowledging the limits of many accountability structures for students and schools.

In short, this domain of educational leadership research provides very fertile ground for research on leadership for school-family-community partnerships. Because so much of the empirical work on transformative leadership is qualitative in nature, efforts to establish causal linkages among leadership, partnerships, and student performance are just developing and have to rely on logics that are not persuasive to all audiences (Shields, 2010). But many conceptual building blocks are in place that can support new empirical investigations. As the actions of transformative leaders are described with greater clarity in case studies, this knowledge can inform the construction of research tools that can document the practices and impact of larger samples of leaders.

Areas of Convergence and Possibilities for Further Cultivation

As research on educational leadership continues to develop, it will be important to make progress on establishing the causal connections among leadership, organizational functioning, and desired outcomes for students, including social justice and equitable achievement (Firestone & Riehl, 2005). We need fully articulated conceptual models of leadership that reflect the dynamic nature of leadership practice and the interdependencies among contextual conditions, leadership actions, the thoughts and actions of followers and others, and the outcomes they generate. Many of the models I have discussed in this chapter are quite promising. To achieve their full potential, however, conceptual models will need to incorporate more thoroughly the leader's role in promoting healthy and productive relationships between schools and the families and communities they serve, because those relationships have been associated with positive benefits for students and their learning. And even more, empirical studies of leadership will need to provide data and analyses that show fidelity to the conceptual models from which they are derived. Weak measures of leadership practice and research designs that cannot capture realistic longitudinal, reciprocal, indirect effects will not be useful.

It may be possible to improve the explanatory power of conceptual models of leadership, incorporate leaders' work with families and communities into them, and even draw organizationally focused theories and transformative theories closer, in several ways. A first pathway toward greater convergence could be for researchers to pay more attention to the boundary spanning and border crossing roles of educational leaders. The concept of boundary spanning is familiar in many technical-functional accounts of organizations. Persons in boundary spanning roles help to strengthen organizations by representing the organization to other organizations and institutions within its wider context, and vice versa, thereby increasing shared understandings, shared purposes, and institutional legitimacy (Daft, 1992; Scott & Davis, 2007). They also strengthen organizations by drawing resources from the environment into the organization. Those organizations that have healthy boundary spanning functions have productive exchanges with partners in their environments, which allow them to thrive. Individuals forge useful bridges across organizational-environmental boundaries through the relationships they develop with others, and also through the use of boundary objects or tools, such as common languages or technologies, and by engaging in boundary-spanning social practices or routines (Coldren & Spillane, 2007). Boundary spanning is a dynamic process, contingent on many characteristics of organizations and their environments. If educational leadership were conceptualized as a practice that combined internal management of an organization with boundary spanning functions, it would be easy to integrate partnerships, whether formal or informal, as an important element in models of leaders' work.

Boundary spanning has an analog in cultural studies of education, which explore the border crossing roles of teachers and others (including students themselves) who traverse the cultural boundaries of home, community, and school, erasing misunderstandings and distrust and eliciting efforts toward shared goals (Garza, 2007; Giroux, 2005; MacBeath, 2006; Ogbu, 1990; Weis & Fine, 2000). As I noted above, transformative school leaders engage in this cultural work when they forge connections between schools and the diverse families and communities they serve. Border crossing bears connotations of disruptive political work, but it is not so far removed from the concept of boundary spanning. Hence, conceptualizing leadership in terms of border crossing and boundary spanning might be a way to draw traditional and transformative leadership theories closer together.

A second approach to greater convergence would be to incorporate the emotional aspects of leadership practice more fully into leadership theories. Theorists have suggested that leaders' emotional intelligence and positive use of emotions help to activate other nodes along causal pathways between leadership and desired outcomes (Goleman, Boyatzis, & McKee, 2002). For example, when leaders provide emotional support, teachers may be more inclined to embrace change and more motivated to pursue new goals (Leithwood & Riehl, 2005). Similar emotional mechanisms might also be important in building trusting and productive relationships between families and educators. Jeynes (2010) has suggested that

> the key qualities necessary for schools to foster parental involvement may also be subtle. That is, whether teachers, principals, and school staff are loving, encouraging, and supportive to parents may be more important than the specific guidelines and tutelage they offer to parents.
>
> *(p. 748)*

Many openings would be provided for including and documenting the emotional and substantive work of leading partnerships, if leadership models were framed so as to divide the work of leadership into internal organizational management and boundary spanning/border crossing functions, and if that work were further elaborated in terms of its practical actions and emotional components.

Most theories about leadership effects on student learning trace a web of actions and conditions that at some point travel through the school's instructional program, because teaching is thought to have the closest and deepest impact on student learning. Many models focus on what leaders do with teachers to help strengthen instruction and support learning; only some models define families and communities as partners in the instructional program and pay attention to leaders' roles with those partners. A third way in which conceptual theories of leadership for partnerships could converge with traditional and transformative theories of leadership effects is likely to emerge as more attention is given to the personalization of instruction. If, in the future, the successful principal will be one who is able to help drive the design of learning environments and instructional programming down to the level of individual students, the leader's role may very well include working with families and communities in new ways. In emerging personalized learning systems, many of which are rich in technology, parents will be important partners in determining student needs and monitoring the learning that students do out of school, via virtual classrooms or even instruction delivered through smartphones. Community partners may be serving as mentors for students, providing apprenticeships and opportunities for problem-based learning. These new realities will place new demands on leaders, and they will need to be factored into comprehensive models of leadership.

Finally, the concept of distributed leadership presents a fourth possible avenue for cultivating linkages between general theories of leadership and theories of leadership for partnerships. Several empirical studies have suggested that partnerships are more easily managed when responsibilities for them are shared with individuals other than the school principal, including teachers, school counselors, psychologists, and representatives from community agencies (Abrams & Gibbs, 2000; Hands, Chapter 10, this volume; Leithwood & Jantzi, 2006; Martin et al., 2010; Warren, Hong, Rubin, & Uy, 2009). Others have documented the potential of parent leadership development for furthering school reform, as well as enriching home-school relations (Chrispeels, Chapter 9, this volume; McAlister Mintrop, Chong, & Renée, Chapter 11, this volume). The more that theories of traditional or transformational leadership evolve away from an emphasis on the formal position of the school leader and focus more on a wide range of leadership functions distributed among many different individuals, the easier it will be to locate and describe leadership for partnerships and assess its impact in supporting student learning.

In addition to these suggestions for strengthening conceptual models of leadership so they can incorporate leadership for partnerships, methodological advances are needed in order to produce empirical work that can reflect, test, and refine these expanded understandings of leadership. I have already noted that empirical models of leadership, whether they are qualitative or quantitative, must continue to utilize indirect effect designs, unlocking the black box of leadership practice to describe dynamic, interactive processes that play out over time through other persons and processes. Leadership actions and consequences will need to be recorded in sensitive, objective ways. It is not very helpful to measure leadership for partnerships in terms of simplistic variables such as a count of how many meetings with parents a principal attends, or to ask a principal herself about the impact of her leadership on teachers. Detailed descriptions of leadership from single or multiple case studies can be used as the basis for designing survey instruments that can provide snapshots of the leadership practice of large and diverse samples of leaders. Statistical modeling will be needed to describe the nested effects of leadership practiced by multiple actors. In these and other ways, empirical research can rise to the challenge of measuring complex interactions posited by conceptual theories.

Conclusion

Both the more traditional domain of research on leadership for organizational effectiveness and student learning and the more emergent domain of research on leadership for social justice and equity have room for conceptualizing the role of families and communities in promoting learning as well as leaders' role in partnerships. Success in developing and converging these lines of research will depend on our collective ability to articulate clear theories and then on our ability to find ways—using qualitative and quantitative methods—to document the conditions and processes of interest and measure their effects on student learning. The relationships among leadership, family and community partnerships, teacher actions and perceptions, and student actions and outcomes are complex. Piecemeal research efforts make a contribution, but the leadership research field would do well to hold out for comprehensive models and persuasive evidence. This may require researchers to adopt common definitions, methods, and metrics. The loss of uniqueness of individual studies will be more than compensated for by the expected power of findings and insights.

There is always a lurking danger that research will unwittingly strengthen the hegemony of subtle, sanctioned structures of power. Gunter and Fitzgerald (2008) argue that current trends in leadership practice and research may be producing a "centralized and branded" form of leadership under which many aspects of the school are itemized, monitored, and judged to respond to external accountabilities (p. 263). Under this regime, "School leaders become trapped within the logic of leading reform, where they are expected to swap professional discretion and quality located in pedagogic expertise and research for professional acclaim as reforming heads" (p. 264).

Similarly, Nicols and Griffith (2009) claim that this shift has implications for families:

> The current managerial turn in public education coordinates the everyday activities of local schooling and parenting. As parents and educators learn to speak this new managerial discourse, their understanding of schooling shifts away from local concerns and toward the extra-local concerns of political accountability.
>
> *(p. 241)*

Though these authors are writing in a United Kingdom context, the same arguments could be made in the United States. These tendencies toward scripted and inauthentic leadership that obscure its real purposes may be easier to resist if traditional, organizationally focused leadership research were placed in closer juxtaposition to leadership for social justice and transformative equity, so that scholarship could "challenge and irritate the status quo" (Gunter & Fitzgerald, 2008, p. 263). The quest for ways to incorporate family and community partnerships into educational leadership practice provides a rationale for pursuing that juxtaposition. It is likely that we cannot fully understand leadership for partnerships unless we examine it with both a traditional and a transformative lens. This project—advancing knowledge about leadership for partnerships—might thereby help prevent leadership research from becoming a mere instrument of the status quo.

Note

1. Although the terminology is similar, the model of transformational leadership articulated by Leithwood and colleagues is quite different from Shields's model of transformative leadership. "Transformational" leadership aims to achieve reform by helping persons enact a new vision for the organization; "transformative" leadership targets social relationships and inequities in organizations because they reflect broader, fundamental patterns in society.

References

Abrams, L. S., & Gibbs, J. T. (2000). Planning for school change: School-community collaboration in a full-service elementary school. *Urban Education, 35*(1), 79–103.

Adams, C. M., Forsyth, P. B., & Mitchell, R. M. (2009). The formation of parent-school trust: A multilevel analysis. *Educational Administration Quarterly, 45*(1), 4–33.

Auerbach, S. (2010). Beyond coffee with the principal: Toward leadership for authentic school-family partnerships. *Journal of School Leadership, 20*(6), 728–757.

Begley, P. T., & Zaretsky, L. (2004). Democratic school leadership in Canada's public school systems: Professional value and social ethic. *Journal of Educational Administration, 42*(6), 640–655.

Bossert, S. T., Dwyer, D. C., Rowan, B., & Lee, G. V. (1982). The instructional management role of the principal. *Educational Administration Quarterly, 18*(3), 34–64.

Brown, K. M. (2004). Leadership for social justice and equity: Weaving a transformative framework and pedagogy. *Educational Administration Quarterly, 40*(1), 77–108.

Brown, K. M., Benkovitz, J., Muttillo, A. J., & Urban, T. (2011). Leading schools of excellence and equity: Documenting effective strategies in closing achievement gaps. *Teachers College Record, 113*(1), 57–96.

Bryk, A. S., Sebring, P. B., Allensworth, E., Luppescu, S., & Easton, J. Q. (2010). *Organizing schools for improvement: Lessons from Chicago.* Chicago, IL: University of Chicago Press.

Burns, J. M. (1978). *Leadership.* New York: Harper & Row.

Cambron-McCabe, N., & McCarthy, M. M. (2005). Educating school leaders for social justice. *Educational Policy, 19*(1), 201–222.

Camburn, E. M., Huff, J. T., Goldring, E. B., & May, H. (2010). Assessing the validity of an annual survey for measuring principal leadership practice. *Elementary School Journal, 111*(2), 314–335.

Camburn, E. M., Spillane, J. P., & Sebastian, J. (2010). Assessing the utility of a daily log for measuring principal leadership practice. *Educational Administration Quarterly, 46*(5), 707–737.

Carr, A. A. (1997). Leadership and community participation: Four case studies. *Journal of Curriculum and Supervision, 12*(2), 152–168.

Clark, D., Martorell, P., & Rockoff, J. (2009). *School principals and school performance* (CALDER Working Paper No. 38). Washington, DC: Urban Institute.

Coldren, A. F., & Spillane, J. P. (2007). Making connections to teaching practice: The role of boundary practices in instructional leadership. *Educational Policy, 21*(2), 369–396.

Cooper, C. W. (2009). Performing cultural work in demographically changing schools: Implications for expanding transformative leadership frameworks. *Educational Administration Quarterly, 45*(5), 694–724.

Correnti, R., & Rowan, B. (2007). Opening up the black box: Literacy instruction in schools participating in three comprehensive school reform programs. *American Educational Research Journal, 44*(2), 298–339.

Crowson, R. L. (1998). *School-community relations, under reform* (2nd ed.). Berkeley, CA: McCutchan.

Daft, R. L. (1992). *Organizational theory and design* (3rd ed.). St. Paul, MN: West.

Day, C., Leithwood, K., & Sammons, P. (2008). What we have learned, what we need to know more about. *School Leadership & Management, 28*(1), 83–96.

Firestone, W. A., & Riehl, C. (Eds.). (2005). *A new agenda for research in educational leadership.* New York: Teachers College Press.

Foster, W. (1989). The administrator as a transformative intellectual. *Peabody Journal of Education, 66*(3), 5–18.

Fuhrman, G. C., & Starratt, R. J. (2002). Leadership for democratic community in schools. In J. Murphy (Ed.), *The educational leadership challenge: Redefining leadership for the 21st century: 101st Yearbook of the National Society for the Study of Education* (pp. 105–133). Chicago, IL: University of Chicago Press.

Garza, E. (2007). Becoming a border pedagogy educator: Rooting practice in paradox. *Multicultural Education, 15*(1), 2–7.

Giroux, H. A. (2005). *Border crossings: Cultural workers and the politics of education* (2nd ed.). New York: Routledge.

Goleman, D., Boyatzis, R., & McKee, A. (2002). *Primal leadership: Realizing the power of emotional intelligence.* Boston, MA: Harvard Business School Press.

Good, T. L. (2008). In the midst of comprehensive school reform: Principals' perspectives. *Teachers College Record, 110*(11), 2341–2360.

Gunter, H. M., & Fitzgerald, T. (2008). The future of leadership research? *School Leadership & Management, 28*(3), 261–279.

Hallinger, P. (2005). Instructional leadership and the school principal: A passing fancy that refuses to fade away. *Leadership and Policy in Schools, 4*(3), 221–239.

Hallinger, P., & Heck, R. H. (1998). Exploring the principal's contribution to school effectiveness: 1980–1995. *School Effectiveness and School Improvement, 9*(2), 157–191.

Haynes, N. M. (1998). Lessons learned. *Journal of Education for Students Placed at Risk (JESPAR), 3*(1), 87–99.

Heck, R. H., Larsen, T. J., & Marcoulides, G. A. (1990). Instructional leadership and school achievement: Validation of a causal model. *Educational Administration Quarterly, 26*(2), 94–125.

Heifetz, R. A. (1994). *Leadership without easy answers.* Cambridge, MA: Harvard University Press.

Horng, E. L., Klasik, D., & Loeb, S. (2010). Principal's time use and school effectiveness. *American Journal of Education, 116*(4), 491–523.

Horvat, E. M., Curci, J. D., & Partlow, M. C. (2010). Parents, principals, and power: A historical case study of "managing" parental involvement. *Journal of School Leadership, 20*(6), 702–727.

Jantzi, D., & Leithwood, K. (1996). Toward an explanation of variation in teachers' perceptions of transformational school leadership. *Educational Administration Quarterly, 32*(4), 512–538.

Jeynes, W. H. (2010). The salience of the subtle aspects of parental involvement and encouraging that involvement: Implications for school-based programs. *Teachers College Record, 112*(3), 747–774.

Khalifa, M. (2010). Validating social and cultural capital of hyperghettoized at-risk students. *Education and Urban Society, 42*(5), 620–646.

Knapp, M. S., Copland, M. A., Honig, M. I., Plecki, M. L., & Portin, B. S. (2010). *Learning-focused leadership and leadership support: Meaning and practice in urban systems.* Seattle, WA: Center for the Study of Teaching and Policy, University of Washington.

Lambert, L. (2003). Leadership redefined: An evocative context for teacher leadership. *School Leadership & Management, 23*(4), 421–430.

Larson, C. L., & Murtadha, K. (2002). Leadership for social justice. In J. Murphy (Ed.), *The educational leadership challenge: Redefining leadership for the 21st century: 101st Yearbook of the National Society for the Study of Education* (pp. 134–161). Chicago, IL: University of Chicago Press.

Leithwood, K. (1994). Leadership for school restructuring. *Educational Administration Quarterly, 30*(4), 498–518.

Leithwood, K., & Jantzi, D. (2006). *A critical review of the parent engagement literature. Final report for the Ontario Ministry of Education, Parent Engagement Office.* Toronto, CA: Ontario Institute for Studies in Education.

Leithwood, K., Louis, K. S., Anderson, S., & Wahlstrom, K. (2004). *How leadership influences student learning: Review of Research.* New York: Wallace Foundation.

Leithwood, K., Patten, S., & Jantzi, D. (2010). Testing a conception of how school leadership influences student learning. *Educational Administration Quarterly, 46*(5), 671–706.

Leithwood, K., & Riehl, C. (2005). What do we already know about educational leadership? In W. Firestone & C. Riehl (Eds.), *A new agenda for research in educational leadership* (pp. 12–27). New York: Teachers College Press.

Lewis, P., & Murphy, R. (2008). New directions in school leadership. *School Leadership & Management, 28*(2), 127–146.

Louis, K. S., Dretzke, B., & Wahlstrom, K. (2010). How does leadership affect student achievement? Results from a national U.S. survey. *School Effectiveness and School Improvement, 21*(3), 315–336.

Macbeath, J. (2006). Finding a voice, finding self. *Educational Review, 58*(2), 195–207.

Marks, H. M., & Printy, S. M. (2003). Principal leadership and school performance: An integration of transformational and instructional leadership. *Educational Administration Quarterly, 39*(3), 370–397.

Marshall, C., & Ward, M. (2004). "Yes, but...": Education leaders discuss social justice. *Journal of School Leadership, 14*(5), 530–563.

Martin, M., Fergus, E., & Noguera, P. (2010). Responding to the needs of the whole child: A case study of a high-performing elementary school for immigrant children. *Reading & Writing Quarterly, 26*(3), 195–222.

Maxwell, L. A. (2007). Real-world lessons. *Education Week, 27*(3), 13–15.

Meindl, J. R., Ehrlich, S. B., & Dukerich, J. M. (1985). The romance of leadership. *Administrative Science Quarterly, 30*(1), 78–102.

Nichols, N., & Griffith, A. I. (2009). Talk, texts, and educational action: An institutional ethnography of policy in practice. *Cambridge Journal of Education, 39*(2), 241–255.

Ogbu, J. U. (1990). Understanding diversity: Summary comments. *Education and Urban Society, 22*(4), 425–429.

Owens, R. G., & Valesky, T. C. (2007). *Organizational behavior in education: Adaptive leadership and school reform (*9th ed.). Boston, MA: Pearson.

Penlington, C., Kington, A., & Day, C. (2008). Leadership in improving schools: A qualitative perspective. *School Leadership & Management, 28*(1), 65–82.

Pitner, N. J. (1988). The study of administrator effects and effectiveness. In N. J. Boyan (Ed.), *Handbook of research on educational administration* (pp. 99–122). New York: Longman.

Porras Hein, N. (2003). Mexican American parent participation and administrative leadership. *Journal of Latinos and Education, 2*(2), 109–115.

Quantz, R. A., Cambron-McCabe, N., & Dantley, M. (1991). Preparing school administrators for democratic authority: A critical approach to graduate education. *Urban Review, 23*(1), 3–19.

Raudenbush, S. W. (2009). The "Brown" legacy and the O'Connor challenge: Transforming schools in the images of children's potential. *Educational Researcher, 38*(3), 169–180.

Reynolds, C. H., & O'Dwyer, L. M. (2008). Examining the relationships among emotional intelligence, coping mechanisms for stress, and leadership effectiveness for middle school principals. *Journal of School Leadership, 18*(5), 472–500.

Riehl, C. J. (2000). The principal's role in creating inclusive schools for diverse students: A review of normative, empirical, and critical literature on the practice of educational administration. *Review of Educational Research, 70*(1), 55–81.

Robinson, V. M., Lloyd, C. A., & Rowe, K. J. (2008). The impact of leadership on student outcomes: An analysis of the differential effects of leadership types. *Educational Administration Quarterly, 44*(5), 635–674.

Ross, J. A., & Berger, M. (2009). Equity and leadership: Research-based strategies for school leaders. *School Leadership & Management, 29*(5), 463–476.

Rowan, B., Correnti, R., & Miller, R. J. (2002). What large-scale, survey research tells us about teacher effects on student achievement: Insights from the "prospects" study of elementary schools. *Teachers College Record, 104*(8), 1525–1567.

Scheurich, J. J. (1998). Highly successful and loving, public elementary schools populated mainly by low-SES children of color: Core beliefs and cultural characteristics. *Urban Education, 33*(4), 451–491.

Scheurich, J. J., & Skrla, L. (2003). *Leadership for equity and excellence: Creating high-achievement classrooms, schools, and districts.* Thousand Oaks, CA: Corwin Press.

Scott, W. R., & Davis, G. F. (2007). *Organizations and organizing: Rational, natural, and open system perspectives.* Upper Saddle River, NJ: Pearson Education.

Shields, C. M. (2004). Dialogic leadership for social justice: Overcoming pathologies of silence. *Educational Administration Quarterly, 40*(1), 109–132.

Shields, C. M. (2010). Transformative leadership: Working for equity in diverse contexts. *Educational Administration Quarterly, 46*(4), 558–589.

Skrla, L., & Scheurich, J. J. (2001). Displacing deficit thinking in school district leadership. *Education and Urban Society, 33*(3), 235–259.

Spillane, J. P., Halverson, R., & Diamond, J. B. (2001). Investigating school leadership practice: A distributed perspective. *Educational Researcher, 30*(3), 23–28.

Starratt, R. J. (2001). Democratic leadership theory in late modernity: An oxymoron or ironic possibility? *International Journal of Leadership in Education, 4*(4), 333–352.

Theoharis, G. (2007). Social justice educational leaders and resistance: Toward a theory of social justice leadership. *Educational Administration Quarterly, 43*(2), 221–258.

Theoharis, G. (2009). *The school leaders our children deserve: Seven keys to equity, social justice, and school reform.* New York: Teachers College Press.

Theoharis, G. (2010). Disrupting injustice: Principals narrate the strategies they use to improve their schools and advance social justice. *Teachers College Record, 112*(1), 331–373.

Warren, M. R., Hong, S., Rubin, C. H., & Uy, P. S. (2009). Beyond the bake sale: A community-based relational approach to parent engagement in schools. *Teachers College Record, 111*(9), 2209–2254.

Waters, T., Marzano, R. J., & McNulty, B. (2003). *Balanced leadership: What 30 years of research tells us about the effect of leadership on student achievement* (Working Paper). Aurora, CO: Mid-Continent Research for Education and Learning.

Weis, L. & Fine, M. (Eds). (2000). *Construction sites: Excavating race, class and gender among urban youth.* New York: Teachers College Press.

Witziers, B., Bosker, R. J., & Kruger, M. L. (2003). Educational leadership and student achievement: The elusive search for an association. *Educational Administration Quarterly, 39*(3), 398–425.

3

CONCEPTUALIZING LEADERSHIP FOR AUTHENTIC PARTNERSHIPS

A Continuum to Inspire Practice

Susan Auerbach

The idea that schools should create partnerships with families and community groups has become a commonsense, taken-for-granted aspect of education (Pushor, 2010; Tollefson, 2008). Yet there is a wide gap between the rhetoric and reality of partnerships in American schools (Davies, 2002; Gordon & Louis, 2009), with a lack of comprehensive approaches (Epstein & Sanders, 2006; Van Voorhis & Sheldon, 2004), or partnerships based on parity and common purpose (Cooper & Christie, 2005; López & Stoelting, 2010; Warren, Hong, Rubin, & Uy, 2009). This conceptual chapter problematizes the term *partnerships,* presents an alternative definition of authentic partnerships, and introduces a continuum of leadership for partnerships to inform practice.

Authentic partnerships are defined here as respectful alliances among educators, families, and community groups that value relationship building, dialogue across difference, and sharing power in pursuit of a common purpose in socially just, democratic schools (Auerbach, 2010). I draw on the family and community involvement literature to examine this definition, demonstrate how authentic partnerships differ from more limited approaches to collaboration, and outline the role of school leaders in this process. After I briefly trace the historical roots of partnerships, I discuss the conceptual basis for authentic partnerships in theories of authentic participation and relational trust. Then I use the literature to examine three components of authentic partnerships: respectful alliances, relationship building, and power sharing. Though much of the discussion focuses on school-family partnerships in urban schools, reflecting the emphasis of the critical literature, perspectives on suburban schools, middle-class parents, and school-community partnerships[1] are also included. Finally, I present a model of leadership for partnerships and illustrate four stages along a continuum (leadership preventing partnerships, leadership for nominal partnerships, leadership for traditional partnerships, and leadership for authentic partnerships). The emphasis is on the role of leaders in nurturing partnerships; given their positional authority and direct influence on school climate, they must take the initiative in reaching out to stakeholders and modeling welcoming, collaborative behaviors (Hoover-Dempsey et al., 2005; Riehl, 2000; Sanders & Sheldon, 2009).

Historical and Conceptual Understandings of Partnerships

Historical Roots

The role of parents[2] and communities in schools has shifted from insiders to outsiders to purported partners over the past 150 years. Though 19th century American public schools were hubs of community life with families at the center, increasing centralization and professionalization in the 20th century began to separate the community from the "closed system" of the school as administrators buffered the school from outside influence (Cutler, 2000). The system became more open in the 1960s and 1970s with legislation and social movements that pressed schools to become more responsive to the needs of parents and communities and administrators acting as "boundary spanners" with stakeholders (Crowson, Goldring, & Haynes, 2010). The Education for All Handicapped Children Act of 1976 marked a watershed in parents' right to a voice in educational decisions (Sarason, 1995), and the effective schools movement hailed both parent involvement and school leadership as keys to student achievement and school improvement (Driscoll & Goldring, 2005).

In the 1980s, decentralization, restructuring, and site-based management opened schools to greater stakeholder participation while calls intensified for more collaborative forms of leadership. The landmark 1988 Chicago school reforms gave parents and community members a majority stake on Local School Councils with the power to hire and fire principals (since rescinded). Businesses, organizations, and universities began to partner systematically with schools, and the service coordination or full-service schools movement brought health and social services to schools in poor communities. The walls between schools and communities were breaking down, with administrators spending more time managing the external environment of the school (Crowson et al., 2010; Rallis & Goldring, 2000). Meanwhile, the work of Joyce Epstein and colleagues (Epstein, 1990; Epstein et al., 2002) on parent involvement and student achievement framed the discourse on school-family partnerships, greatly influencing policy, program development, and research.

In recent years, the idea that schools should engage in partnerships to improve achievement became a commonsense "mantra" (Davies, 2002). Parent involvement became politically constructed as a tool for boosting test scores, an "instrumental view of participation in which parents become the means to an end that they did not author" (Tollefson, 2008, p. 46). Partnerships geared to achievement goals generally reflect school agendas, which may not fit with the priorities of families and community groups (Cooper & Christie, 2005; Miretsky, 2004; Warren et al., 2009). This raises questions about who sets partnership agendas and what counts as family and community involvement.

Problematizing Partnerships

In common parlance, *partnership* means a relationship of cooperation, shared responsibility, mutual benefit, and voluntary participation. In education, it is a "diffuse concept" meant to "invoke a warm glow of equality and joint endeavor" (Vincent, 1996, p. 466), as seen in school mission statements that reference it. The term has come to be used uncritically as a synonym for family and community involvement. If schools bring child care services to the site or teach parents how to play math games, they are often said to be engaging in partnerships. Yet joint activity is not always collaborative in spirit (Anderson, 1998; Gordon & Louis, 2009; Henry, 1996) and schools often promote parent involvement to comply with regulations (Auerbach, 2007a; Epstein, Galindo, & Sheldon, 2010). Although partnership implies parity, "in practice, these partnerships seldom break with the traditional school-centered and activity-based model of parent involvement" in which schools set the agenda and parents support the school (Warren et al., 2009, p. 2244). For example, critical scholars and activists have noted the limitations of Epstein's (1990) partnership framework in addressing issues of parent voice, culture, advocacy, and power (Cooper, 2009; Johnson, in press; López & Stoelting, 2010; Olivos, 2006).

It is misleading to use a prescriptive term that connotes a mutually beneficial relationship to describe a range of activities and interactions that may have little to do with the spirit of partnership (cf. Graue, Kroeger, & Prager, 2001). Henderson, Mapp, Johnson, and Davies (2007) stress that certain core beliefs must be present for "meaningful partnerships" to exist, such as the conviction that all families have something to contribute and that parents and educators should be equal partners in education. These beliefs are by no means a given in schools, as will be seen.

The term *partnership* is also problematic due to its association with dominant culture values and practices. Some cultures hold a view of more separate spheres of responsibility for families and educators, like the Haitian immigrants in Doucet's (in press) study who resisted school outreach in order to protect their privacy and Mexican immigrants who traditionally stress teaching moral values rather than academics at home (Reese, Balzano, Gallimore & Goldenberg, 1995). Middle-class parents are more likely than poor or working-class parents to see home and school as interconnected and aligned with their values and practices (Lareau, 1989). This was evident in the middle-class African American parents discussed in Diamond and Gomez (2004), whose positive attitudes toward the school led them to reinforce learning at home, unlike more alienated lower-class parents. Thus, middle-class parents are more likely to have what Walker and colleagues (2005) call a partnership-focused role construction, or orientation to responsibility for education, as opposed to a parent-focused or school-focused orientation (Crowson et al., 2010).

Partners or Supporters and Resources?

Despite the rhetoric of partnership, the literature suggests that many educators do not want parents or community groups as equal partners with agency and voice. Smrekar and Cohen-Vogel (2001) suggest that institutional norms create "highly defined, socially constructed scripts" for home-school relations; "parents learn over time the circumscribed role they are expected to assume" as helpers and supporters rather than partners and collaborators (pp. 75, 87). Similarly, Hargreaves (2000) found that Canadian teachers were most comfortable with parents offering "support-at-a-distance" or "silent partnerships." Even well-educated, middle-class parents in Graue et al. (2001) had to figure out the school's boundaries for acceptable parent behavior; teachers were displeased when parents questioned kindergarten policies.

Just as schools tend to see parents as supporters and helpers, they see community groups mainly as service providers and resources to help the school with its own goals rather than as fellow organizations with which to collaborate (Brooks, 2009; Schutz, 2006). For example, Kahne and colleagues (2001) found a one-sided relationship in a Chicago youth development initiative in which principals dominated meetings with community partners and tried "to maintain as much control as they can over their environment and the products of partnerships" (p. 445). Entering into partnerships with community organizations departs from business as usual for administrators and calls for the renegotiation of roles, responsibilities, and policies in the process of "crossing boundaries" (Cordiero & Kolek, 1996; Honig, 2003; Smrekar & Mawhinney, 1999). In practice, however, community partnerships are often treated as add-ons that do not require changes in school culture or operations (Riehl, 2000; Smylie, Crowson, Chou, & Levin, 1994). Schools tend to favor a service provision model of partnerships rather than empowering parent and community leaders to work with the school to develop programs (Ordoñez-Jasis & Jasis, 2004; Warren, 2005).

Critical scholars have increasingly called for authentic forms of partnership that go beyond these limited institutional scripts. For example, Cooper and Christie (2005) and Doucet (in press) refer to "true partnerships" between home and school that share power and offer mutual support rather than one-sided parent support of the school's agenda. Warren et al. (2009) describe "authentic collaboration" that results from eliciting parents' concerns in community organizing initiatives, and Theoharis (2009) documents "authentic connections" that ensue under social justice leadership. To understand how the scripts might be rewritten for partnerships and leadership for partnerships, it is helpful to consider theories of authentic participation and relational trust.

Authentic Participation and Relational Trust

The concept of authentic partnerships is indebted to Anderson's (1998, 2009) work on authentic participation, which questions whether participatory reforms in education have changed the status quo or power relations. Like *partnerships*, *participation* is a vague term meant to evoke positive feelings and thus should be examined critically (Vincent, 1996). Anderson (1998) asks who actually participates, under what conditions, and to what ends. He argues that structures for increased participation in schools have done little to enfranchise marginalized groups and have instead solidified entrenched power. He contrasts corporate-influenced site-based decision-making to authentic participation geared to enhanced learning and social justice, where leaders "facilitate the opening up of democratic spaces" (p. 593). "Once schools claim to make community participation one of their cherished ideals," he warns, "communities can take them at their word and demand authentic forms of participation, even where these might not have been intended" (p. 582). Thus, stakeholders can hold schools accountable for treating them as equal partners (Cooper, Riehl, & Hasan, 2010; Oakes, Rogers, & Lipton, 2006; Johnson, in press).

The authentic participation and advocacy leadership envisioned by Anderson (2009) are attuned to what Sergiovanni called the *lifeworld* of schools—values, beliefs, and interactions—as opposed to the policies and rules of the *systemworld*. While the latter tends to dominate schools, the lifeworld is often neglected. For Anderson (2009), "Any attempt to thoughtfully reform schools will have to address the creation of schools as authentic social spaces in which students, their parents, school professionals, and the surrounding community are deeply understood, respected, and empowered" (p. 10).

Trust is both a precondition for and a result of authentic participation in partnerships. Bryk and Schneider (2002), referencing social capital theory, suggest that relational trust is a property of organizations and a "critical resource" for school reform. Relational trust is based on perceived respect, competence, integrity, and personal regard for others, and depends on reciprocity. Noting patterns of distrust and power imbalance in urban home-school relations, Bryk and Schneider charge leaders with taking "actions that reduce parents' sense of vulnerability in these exchanges" and demonstrate genuine caring (p. 28).

Principals have a direct influence on shaping a school climate of trust and belonging through "boundary-spanning interactions" with families (Adams, Forsyth, & Mitchell, 2009; Riehl, 2000, Chapter 2 this volume; Theoharis, 2009). Hoover-Dempsey and colleagues (2005) consider the building of school-family trust essential to conveying a "school invitation to involvement," which is, in turn, key to motivating parent involvement (see Stein, Goldring, & Smrekar, Chapter 12, this volume). Adams et al. (2009) found that parents' trust in schools differed depending on each school's organizational norms and was strongly associated with parents' sense of their influence at school and students' sense of belonging.

The foundational concepts of authentic participation and relational trust are intertwined with elements of the definition of authentic partnerships described below.

Elements of Authentic Partnerships

As noted, authentic partnerships are respectful alliances that value relationship building, dialogue, and sharing power as part of socially just schools. The following sections draw on the literature to unpack elements of this definition and contrast it to more traditional views of school partnerships with families and community organizations.

Respectful Alliances v. Deficit Discourses on Parent Involvement

The first key element in authentic partnerships is a foundation of respect. Schools with respectful alliances promote a "joining process" in which they welcome families and community groups and honor their contributions (Mapp, 2003). They affirm families' cultures and "allow parent life experience and culture to inform schools' cultural worlds" (Pérez Carreón, Drake, & Barton, 2005, p. 468). They see the school as part of the broader community with a stake not only in student achievement but in "the multiple dimensions of students' lives," including family well-being, community revitalization, and social justice (Coalition for Community Schools, 2006; Theoharis, 2009; Warren et al., 2009). Offering coordinated social services, for example, can be a response to the "moral imperative to address these historically nonschooling issues" (Beck & Murphy, 1993, p. 192).

Respect for families is often invoked by educators, but parents do not always perceive that they are respected in schools. Low-income parents and parents of color are keenly sensitive to signs of disrespect and rebuff. They feel dismissed and devalued by overly bureaucratic procedures; front office staff who ignore them or do not speak their language; teachers who expect little of their children; parenting classes that aim to "fix" their childrearing; governance councils that expect rubber-stamp approval; and other oppressive practices (see e.g., André-Bechely & Bernstein, 1998; Auerbach, 2007b; Cooper, 2009; Cooper et al., 2010; Fine, 1993; Johnson, in press; Noguera, 2001; Oakes et al., 2006; Olivos, 2006, Chapter 6, this volume; Ruffin-Adams & Wilson, Chapter 5, this volume). Educators may not be aware of these reactions and may need to assess their own beliefs and practices in this area.

A major barrier to respectful alliance is the persistence of deficit thinking in schools about poor, minority, and immigrant families and communities. Low-income neighborhoods are assumed to be rife with crime and dysfunction; poor families of color are considered uncaring and uninvolved, symbolized by low attendance at school events (Cooper et al., 2010; Noguera, 2001; Smrekar & Cohen-Vogel, 1999). These parents' presumed deficiency in knowledge or skills to help their children leads to a one-way "school-to-home transmission" model of involvement (Swap, 1993). A narrow range of behaviors count as legitimate involvement—generally school-based involvement that supports the school—with little recognition of other forms of parent care or support (Auerbach, 2007b; Cooper, 2009; López, 2001).

Traditionally, the discourse on parent involvement has reflected unexamined deficit thinking and favored some parents over others. Poor and minority parents are conceived as objects rather than subjects, "empty vessels" in need of training by the school (Lightfoot, 2004). Parents are framed as both the problem and the solution, depending on whether their practices reinforce school culture and practices (López & Stoelting, 2010; Prins & Toso, 2008). Binary oppositions construct "the good parent" as "one who takes the lead of the school, is involved but not too involved, and who supports but does not challenge" (Nakagawa, 2000, p. 456). Parents who question school practices are seen as confrontational or inappropriate (Cooper, 2009; Diamond & Gomez, 2004; Fine, 1993; Olivos, Chapter 6, this volume). Higher socioeconomic status (SES) parents are often feared and resented, seen as demanding, intrusive, and entitled (Lareau & Lopes Muñoz, 2009; Lewis & Forman, 2002). Thus, we are caught in a too little-too much view of parent involvement, in which educators are critical of and frustrated by both parents who they see as not involved enough (poor and minority parents) and those who they see as too involved (demanding parents of higher SES and activists). The only acceptable middle ground for many educators is involvement as deferential support (Cooper, 2009), a stance that demeans parents' agency as partners.

In respectful alliances, school leaders reject deficit thinking and reexamine their own beliefs and assumptions in this arena as part of refining their leadership platform. They reach out to stakeholders with the understanding that "parents can be your best allies" (Auerbach, 2007a) and that grassroots organizations know their community best (Schutz, 2006). They validate families as knowledgeable and caring, with legitimate goals for their children (Cooper et al., 2010), and they lead by example to model this respect for faculty and staff.

Building Relationships and Dialogue across Difference

Another component of authentic partnerships is relationship building, which opens the way to dialogue. Warren et al. (2009) suggest that with traditional approaches centered on school goals and activities, we forget that partnerships are essentially about relationships. They propose a relational approach to parent involvement in which educators take time to get to know families and elicit their interests and concerns for collective action. Relationship building, whether with fellow families or educators, enhances social capital for marginalized groups, increasing their access to information and opportunities (Auerbach, 2007b; Noguera, 2001).

Schools that value relationships are often described by educators and parents as being like a family in which people know, care about, and support one another in a comfortable atmosphere. For example, a principal in Beck and Murphy's (1999) case study spoke of students as "our children," created a homelike environment in the parent center, and allowed parents and teachers to bring their preschool-age children on campus. In that setting, "Professional and personal roles were sometimes blurred and...being a parent was viewed as honorable and important" (p. 99). Instead of ritual events in which educators and families meet as "polite strangers," schools can bring families from the periphery to the center and "re-story" one-way activities like Meet the Teacher Night as reciprocal, participatory Meet the Family Night (Pushor, 2010).

Relationship building begins with understanding parents' preferred ways of relating to schools. Parents often favor more personal, informal forms of communication, involvement, and parent programs than schools typically provide (Auerbach, 2004, 2007b; Delgado-Gaitan, 2004; Scribner, Young, & Pedroza, 1999). For example, Auerbach (2004, 2009) found that when educators in small classroom meetings spoke about their experience growing up in immigrant families, Latino parents became more comfortable sharing their own stories. While the personalized approach is especially important to bridge cultural gaps with marginalized populations, middle-class parents also seek greater flexibility and warmth in their dealings with administrators (Lareau & Lopes Muñoz, 2009). Indeed, parents of diverse backgrounds are easily alienated by the bureaucratization of schooling with its formal procedures and contractual relationships; these function as barriers to collaboration and community building (Furman & Merz, 1996; Henry, 1996; Sarason, 1995; Smrekar & Mawhinney, 1999). They gravitate instead to school cultures that nurture the lifeworld of schools—people's beliefs, experience, and relationships. Leaders attentive to this find opportunities to "listen for the deeper dreams and hopes the school community holds for its future" (Deal & Peterson, 1999, p. 203).

Building relationships also involves understanding parents' educational orientations, which may differ from those of the school (Diamond & Gomez, 2004; Doucet, in press). Parents come to school with values, priorities, and practices that have been shaped by their positionality as well as by individual biography and past experience with schools (Graue et al., 2001). Compared to educators focused on achievement, parents and community leaders may take a more holistic, communitarian view of child, adult, and community development (Auerbach & Collier, in press; Cooper & Christie, 2005; Miretsky, 2004;

Oakes et al., 2006; Scribner et al., 1999). When schools plan partnership programs without considering these orientations, they risk privileging the school agenda.

If educators are to know and understand families, they need to create safe spaces for dialogue across difference. Through dialogue, stakeholders can co-construct the purposes of partnerships and their respective roles while promoting mutual understanding (Delgado-Gaitan, 2004; Fine, 1993; Pushor, 2010; Rosenberg, Lopez, & Westmoreland, 2009). Dialogue, storytelling, and inquiry are central to the "reciprocal learning" that Cooper et al. (2010) propose for partnerships, in which participants see each other as both teacher and learner, challenge the status quo, and jointly create communities of practice. Productive dialogue calls for attention to what Miretsky (2004) calls the "communication needs" of democratic schools, including the cultivation of trust, respect, honest communications, and mutual goals. The process of co-constructing the school is difficult and time-consuming, but as one principal commented, that is part of "the promise of public schools" (Auerbach, 2010).

School leaders demonstrate their concern with relationships when they create a climate of belonging for all stakeholders and a family-friendly atmosphere that minimizes bureaucracy (Constantino, 2003; Theoharis, 2009). They seek ways to enhance families' social capital and "nurture families' educational cultures" with culturally responsive parent involvement rather than imposing the school's agenda (Leithwood & Riehl, 2003; Tillman, 2003). They ensure that parent activities at school include time for informal interaction among parents and with educators, and for the sharing of hopes and dreams for their children (Auerbach, 2004; Henderson et al., 2007). They listen attentively to parents' stories and share their own in authentic rather than scripted encounters (Auerbach, 2009; Pushor, 2010). Guided by an ethic of care, they see "teachers, students, parents, and others as colleagues, partners, co-learners, and friends" building a community of learners (Beck & Murphy, 1993, p. 195). Inspired by ideals of democratic community, they create processes and structures that promote "intentional civic participation with a deep respect for difference" (Furman & Starratt, 2002, p. 116).

Sharing Power in Socially Just Schools

Perhaps the most challenging component of authentic partnerships for educators is sharing power with families and community groups, especially regarding core issues of teaching and learning, personnel, or scarce resources. Socially just, democratic schools confront power relations in schools and society, rejecting hierarchical relations and positional authority and moving toward flatter structures with shared power among participants in pursuit of the common good (Anderson, 1998, 2009; Dantley & Tillman, 2006). Unlike managing the external environment, sharing power in socially just schools means inviting stakeholders to the table as full partners, working in coalition with them, and empowering them to share leadership.

"Parents enter the contested public sphere of public education typically with neither resources nor power," Michelle Fine (1993) wrote in a seminal article still relevant today. She predicted they would always be resented, silenced, and contained by educators in urban schools unless they organized to exert a collective voice. Despite growing parent activism and calls for collaborative leadership, power differentials between educators and parents remain the norm, especially in marginalized communities.

"Educators who fear parent power are operating out of a unilateral power framework of winners and losers," according to Warren et al. (2009, p. 2213). The alternative to a traditional "power over" approach with subordinate parents is the relational approach of "power to" work together toward common goals. Relational power has been popularized both through community organizing movements and the leadership literature. For example, Sergiovanni (1992) and Murphy (2005) urge administrators to exchange unilateral "power over" teachers in transactional approaches for the "power to" of shared or servant leadership. Similarly, Beck and Murphy (1993) discuss learning to lead from within a web of relationships by empowering rather than controlling others. "Power to" with stakeholders can be pursued through democratic approaches to communications, interactions, and outreach, as well as formal decision-making.

Structures and policies for shared governance are necessary but not sufficient for sharing power with stakeholders (e.g., Anderson, 1998; Beck & Murphy, 1999; Fine, 1993; Gordon, Chapter 8, this volume; Gordon & Louis, 2009; Smylie et al., 1994). For example, studies have found that parents on advisory councils deferred to professionals on matters of substance while administrators used council meetings to co-opt parents and socialize them to school norms (Beck & Murphy, 1999; Rallis & Goldring, 2000). Administrators who were otherwise active in leadership for partnerships were so frustrated with the regulations of mandated advisory councils that they considered shared governance irrelevant to school goals (Auerbach, 2007a).

Parent leadership development is essential if families are to have a meaningful seat at the decision-making table, especially in marginalized communities. This begins with training in curriculum, operations, and policy that "minimize[s] the knowledge gap between educators and family and community members" (Sanders, 2009, p. 1709). As a veteran parent activist observed, "Only when parents know the rules of engagement, particularly the language of education, can they hold the system accountable" (Johnson, in press). Parent leadership programs that promote advocacy and organizing skills are relatively rare, initiated by outside organizations, and often unwelcome in schools (see Chrispeels, Chapter 9, this volume; McAlister et al., Chapter 11, this volume). Such programs empowered parents to speak up at school and press for change, or to take greater control of their own lives; reports are mixed on how schools responded (e.g., André-Bechely & Bernstein, 1998; Bolivar & Chrispeels, 2008; Cooper & Christie, 2005; Oakes et al., 2006; Warren et al., 2009). Developing parent leaders as part of shared leadership is a long-term process that calls for commitment by all parties and relevant training for both educators and parents (Sanders, 2009).

Power relations in middle-class and upper middle-class settings present other challenges. Clearly, higher SES parents come to school with more forms of capital to negotiate institutions, customize their children's education, and make demands that may advantage their children and disadvantage others (Brantlinger, 2003; Horvat, Weininger, & Lareau, 2003; Lareau, 1989; Wells & Serna, 1996). They may become mired in conflict with school authorities with the threat of exit or political pressure if they are not appeased (Lareau & Lopes Muñoz, 2009; Lewis & Forman, 2002). There is a double standard by which administrators apply different rules to different groups of parents, denying power to marginalized groups and ceding it to dominant groups. Like the too little-too much view of parent involvement, this double standard tips the playing field for home-school relations and prevents authentic partnerships. An alternative can be seen in principals' "constant, often friendly, negotiation of power and control" with parents at an urban school that became increasingly White and middle class over 30 years; principals recognized parents' power and attempted to leverage it to meet shared goals, like creating a new arts program (Horvat, Curci, & Parlow, 2010).

The literature on collaborative and transformational leadership typically focuses on professionals inside the school rather than including the broader community in the "messy work" of sharing leadership (Chrispeels, 2004; Giles, 2006). The convergence in recent years of calls for shared power in partnerships and collaborative forms of school leadership (Gordon & Louis, 2009) suggests potential for leadership for authentic partnerships. To the extent that schools develop respectful, caring alliances with stakeholders, learn from and with them in dialogue, and include their voices in setting agendas, there will be progress toward sharing power. With a more level playing field based on critical examination of home-school relations, educators can be recast as learners alongside parents rather than experts, and leaders learn to colead with others (Cooper et al., 2010).

How do school leaders move toward authentic partnerships? Having elaborated a rationale for, components of, and barriers to this type of collaboration, I now turn to a model of leadership for partnerships that I developed to inspire practice.

A Continuum of Leadership for Partnerships

When promoting change in practice, it is useful to delineate stages along the way to a goal with a continuum. This acknowledges that change takes time, that people may be at different stages, and that what matters is progress toward the goal. For example, Lindsey and colleagues' continuum of leadership for cultural proficiency progresses from cultural destructiveness and blindness to cultural competence and proficiency (Lindsey, Robins, & Terrell, 2002). Likewise, Henderson et al.'s (2007) continuum of school-family partnerships moves from isolated fortress schools and "come if we call" schools to "open door" and finally partnership schools. I offer a continuum of leadership for partnerships as a tool for analysis to help administrators identify what is and what could be as they work with families and community groups.

On this continuum, *leadership for authentic partnerships* is conceived as the destination toward which leaders and their schools should strive, associated with relational and empowerment approaches to partnerships, and transformative and inclusive approaches to leadership (Auerbach, 2010; Cooper et al., 2010; Riehl, 2000; Warren et al., 2009). At the opposite end of the continuum is *leadership preventing partnerships*, highlighting beliefs and practices that separate schools from communities, with leaders buffering the school from outside influences (Crowson et al., 2010; Goldring & Hausman, 2001). The next category, *leadership for nominal partnerships*, begins to bridge the divide with limited outreach and activities conducted on the school's terms in a public relations or service approach (Ordoñez-Jasis & Jasis, 2004; Rallis & Goldring, 2000). This is followed by *leadership for traditional partnerships* with more extensive outreach, joint activities, and a focus on two-way communications, as in the Epstein (1990) model. With its stress on shared responsibility for children's education and well-being, this stance opens the way to authentic partnerships but may remain service-oriented and centered on school agendas (Cooper et al., 2010; López & Stoelting, 2010; Warren et al., 2009).

Table 3.1 summarizes key characteristics of the four categories. The categories progress from administrators having the greatest power; parents and community groups having the least voice; and deficit views having the most influence to administrators sharing power; parents and community groups having the greatest voice; and an emphasis on community assets. Schools become progressively more family friendly, community oriented, and democratic as they become more open to authentic participation. Goals for partnerships broaden from a narrow achievement orientation that reflects school agendas to a range of goals including achievement that reflects mutual concerns. Parents and community organizations expand their roles from clients, supporters, and resources to partners, advocates, and leaders. As with other continua, the categories are conceptually distinct but somewhat fluid, recognizing the potential for overlap. Each category is described below with related models and examples from the literature.

TABLE 3.1 Characteristics of the Leadership for Partnerships Continuum

	Leadership Preventing Partnerships	*Leadership for Nominal Partnerships*	*Leadership for Traditional Partnerships*	*Leadership for Authentic Partnerships*
Goals	-Maintain control -Protect school from outside influence	-Maintain control -Comply with mandates -Improve achievement	-Improve achievement and school climate -Meet family and community needs	-Various goals based on mutual interests -Equity, social justice, dialogue, empowerment
Position of families	-Outsiders -Deficit view	-Clients, visitors, supporters -Deficit view	-Supporters, allies, limited partners -Mix of deficit & assets views	-Full partners, advocates, leaders -Assets view
Position of community organizations	-Outsiders	-Resources, services	-Resources, services, limited partners	-Full partners, advocates, leaders
Related models/types of school leadership, role of leaders*	-Transactional -Leader as buffer	-Transactional -Leader as buffer, potential bridge -Traditional PR approach	-Mix of transactional and collaborative -Leader as bridge, listener -Two-way PR approach	-Collaborative -Transformative -Inclusive -Social justice
Related models/types of family and community engagement and school-community relations*	-Protective -Fortress -Closed system	-School-to-home transmission -"Come if we call" -Service -Public relations -Cooperation with community partners	-"Open door" -Partnerships (Epstein, Swap, Henderson et al.) -Family-friendly - Service -Coordination with community partners (e.g. full service schools)	-Relational -Two-way accommodation, mutual learning -Empowerment -Partnerships (Henderson et al.) - Collaboration with community partners
Power relations with families and community groups	-Unilateral "power over" -Large power differential	-Unilateral "power over" -Large power differential	-Mix of unilateral "power over" and relational "power to" -Moderate power differential	-Relational "power to" -Minimized power differential

*For references to related models or types of school leadership and family/community engagement, see explanations of the continuum in the body of the paper.

Leadership Preventing Partnerships and Leadership for Nominal Partnerships

The first stage on the continuum, leadership preventing partnerships, is associated with the buffering role of administrators in a closed system separating community and school, or what Swap (1993) calls the protective approach and Henderson et al. (2007) call fortress schools. Administrators in this category are not geared to partnerships but rather to maintaining order and protecting the school from outside influence. This extreme position is characterized by the most extreme top-down transactional leadership, unilateral "power over" stakeholders, and deficit beliefs, like those of a principal who felt immigrant parents were incapable of helping their children learn (Auerbach, 2010). Though this stance is increasingly rare and outdated, some educators still convey the message "don't cross the yellow line" and expect parents to leave education to the experts (Auerbach, 2007a). Parents and community groups are positioned as outsiders, intruders, or problems that make educators' work more difficult. This applies not only in lower SES communities but in some more affluent schools, where staff distance themselves from parent interference (Lewis & Forman, 2002). Leaders in this category use formal relations and bureaucracy to erect a wall between school and community.

With the second stage on the continuum, leadership for nominal partnerships, schools are compelled to communicate more with stakeholders in a more open system under mandates for parent and community involvement (Auerbach, 2010; Crowson et al., 2010; Driscoll & Goldring, 2005). This category is related to Swap's (1993) school-to-home transmission model of home-school interaction, Henderson et al.'s (2007) "come-if-we call" school, and Ordoñez-Jasis and Jasis's (2004) service model in which the school provides limited information and services to families. Leadership remains transactional with hierarchical relations and unilateral "power over" stakeholders (Beck & Murphy, 1993; Warren et al., 2009). However, there is now a combination of buffering and bridging strategies as leaders attempt to garner parent support (Goldring & Hausman, 2001; Rallis & Goldring, 2000). Parents, still seen through deficit lenses, are framed as clients and supporters who accept the school's authority.

Leadership for nominal partnerships may be the norm in American schools today (see Sanders & Sheldon, 2009). Schools must respond to policies calling for partnerships, yet many educators remain wary of parents and community members and retain deficit beliefs. For example, district officials associated low student achievement with "dysfunctional" families (Auerbach & Collier, in press), and urban principals said parents who advocated for their children were "out of their place" (Cooper, 2009; Diamond & Gomez, 2004; Olivos, 2006). Administrators often express a need to maintain control over parents, like a principal who said that unless a parent program was "structured and purposeful," parents might be there to "stir up trouble" (Auerbach & Collier, in press).

Outreach efforts by such leaders exemplify the discourse of the school as giver of knowledge and parents as passive recipients (Lightfoot, 2004).

School leaders often claim to support partnerships while attempting to maintain control and devoting minimal resources to partnership activities (Auerbach, 2007a, 2010; Davies, 2002; Epstein & Sanders, 2006; Epstein et al., 2010). Public relations is the most common approach used by principals to manage the external environment (Rallis & Goldring, 2000), like the principals in Osterman, Crow, and Rosen (1997) who focused on being visible, communicating clearly, and containing conflict. Public relations functions as buffering with its focus on school needs and "controlling participation" to suit the school's agenda (Schutz, 2006). Indeed, survey studies report that most principals had a traditional management orientation that protected the school from external publics; they favored traditional activities like volunteering and resisted sharing power (Goldring & Hausman, 2001; Griffith, 2001; Osterman et al. 1997; Rogers, Freelon, & Terriquez, Chapter 4, this volume).

Leadership for Traditional Partnerships

The third stage on the continuum, leadership for traditional partnerships, opens the school to greater stakeholder participation and shared responsibility for student learning. These partnerships are mainly geared to improving student achievement but also aim to enhance home-school communications, school climate, and family health and well-being, as in full-service schools. This approach is grounded in Epstein's (1990) framework for parent and community involvement and is akin to Constantino's (2003) vision of family-friendly schools, Henderson et al.'s (2007) "open door" model, and aspects of their partnership model. Compared to nominal partnerships, traditional partnerships provide more services and activities to families with more varied community connections. Public relations become more two-way and proactive with leaders seeking greater stakeholder input. Rather than merely cooperating with community organizations, as in nominal partnerships, the school coordinates with them in joint planning and implementation (Decker, Decker, & Brown, 2007). The school sets the agenda but with more opportunities for collaboration, power differentials are somewhat reduced (Sanders, 2009). Parents and community groups are framed as supporters and resources but also as allies and limited partners (Auerbach, 2007a).

Studies of leadership for traditional partnerships by Epstein and colleagues draw on the extensive sample of member schools in the National Network of Partnership Schools.[3] These studies highlight traditional management tasks that support partnerships, such as principals' allocation of funding, teacher release time, and dedicated staff positions as well as districts' provision of professional development and opportunities for sharing across schools (Epstein, Galindo, & Sheldon, 2010; Epstein et al., 2002; Van Voorhis & Sheldon, 2004). Surveys of action teams found positive associations between high ratings of principal support for partnerships and the quality of outreach programs, as well as between strong district leadership for partnerships and implementation of school programs (Epstein, Galindo, & Sheldon, 2010; Van Voorhis & Sheldon, 2004). This parallels research on leadership of traditional partnerships with community groups, which was most effective when administrators identified staff to coordinate partnerships who understood both the culture of the school and that of outside organizations and gave coordinators authority to lead (Cordeiro & Kolek, 1996; Honig, 2003).

Other studies illustrating leadership for traditional partnerships stress administrators' focus on raising achievement, mobilizing resources, and making themselves accessible. Griffith's (2001) survey of principals' parent involvement practices found that those who were most effective engaging parents in low-income schools identified either with the instructional leader role or with a "missionary" role that prioritized school climate and collaboration. Leaders in Auerbach's (2007a) case study mainly valued family engagement in the form of academic training for parents. They took symbolic steps to show respect and listen to parent concerns, allocating resources and delegating tasks as they did managing other aspects of school operations.

Leadership for Authentic Partnerships

The final stage on the continuum, leadership for authentic partnerships, represents the most open, least hierarchical approach to school-community relations with efforts to reduce power differentials. In this approach, goals are jointly constructed based on mutual interests of educators and other stakeholders; they reflect social justice ideals and democratic processes and may include, but are not limited to, improving achievement (Auerbach, 2010; Furman & Starratt, 2002). These partnerships demonstrate relational approaches to parent involvement and two-way accommodation in which educators and families seek common ground for the common good (Anderson, 2009; Delgado-Gaitan, 2004; Pushor, 2010; Rosenberg et al., 2009; Warren et al., 2009). With a flatter organization and belief in relational power, authentic partnerships empower families and community organizations as full partners, advocates, and leaders rather than compliant supporters or service providers (Johnson, in press; Oakes et al., 2006; Ordonez-Jasis & Jasis, 2004; Warren, 2005). This type of partnership is linked to transformative leadership, leadership for social justice, and inclusive leadership, which question the status quo in power relations, strive for equity and cultural responsiveness, and reach out to marginalized families (Auerbach, 2010; Cooper et al., 2010; Giles, 2006; Marshall & Oliva, 2006; Riehl, 2000). Leaders for social justice use their "position and influence to create caring and/or emancipatory spaces for students, parents, teachers, and other constituents" (López et al., 2006, p. 67).

Some literature documents the existence of social justice oriented leaders who "had a drive to connect with the community" (Auerbach, 2009; Theoharis, 2009, p. 140). For example, an African American principal turned a low-performing fortress school into a thriving partnership school by making home visits, offering advocacy training, opening up governance structures, and making teachers accountable to parents at the same time that she cultivated relationships with local businesses and agencies (Brooks, 2009; Giles, 2006). Similarly, the principals in Theoharis's (2009) study changed how marginalized families were seen and treated at their schools by modeling welcoming behavior, making time to listen to parents, altering front office procedures, and creating separate support groups for diverse parents. López, Gonzalez, and Fierro (2006) describe a White principal of a low-SES Latino school near the Texas-Mexican border who became a community ally and advocate of improved living conditions, resisting district pressure to control parents. He worked with community organizers to train parents in political skills, started a dual language program, and promoted critical dialogue between teachers and parents. "Schools need leaders who are willing to stand in the interstices of two worlds (the school and the community) and who can function seamlessly in both for the collective benefit of everyone," according to López et al. (2006, p. 78). Such leaders are well positioned to interact more authentically with families and community groups in a genuine spirit of partnership.

Conclusion

This chapter drew on the literature to explain key elements of authentic partnerships and to illustrate stages along a continuum of leadership for partnerships. It showed how authentic partnerships are facilitated by leaders' joining in respectful alliances with families and community organizations, building relationships, and sharing power in a relational approach. By contrast, authentic partnerships are hindered by mental models among educators such as deficit thinking and binary views of parent involvement; practices such as buffering the school from outside influence and privileging the school's agenda; and approaches such as transactional leadership marked by unilateral power relations. Table 3.1 summarized these and other contrasts in four categories of leadership for partnerships.

Some may question the feasibility of leadership for partnerships, much less for authentic partnerships, given the many roles, heavy workload, budget cuts, and competing pressures of multiple reforms that school leaders face today. The challenges are magnified in urban schools beset with low achievement, high-stakes accountability pressures, and high staff and administrator turnover. Clearly, local contexts and conditions shape the possibilities and dynamics of partnerships and their leadership (Auerbach, 2007a, Chapter 13, this volume; Honig, 1998). Honig (1998) noted the challenges of scaling up leadership for school-community connections beyond a small number of committed, charismatic leader "wizards," in part because each context calls for different leadership capacities and responses.

I believe that administrators need more exposure to the wizards in the literature and in their midst as role models for what is possible (Auerbach, 2007a, 2009, 2010; López et al., 2006; Theoharis, 2009). We need more case studies of leadership for partnerships, including leaders' beliefs, strategies, and challenges and the response of school staff, students, parents, and community members to their efforts in diverse contexts. In particular, we need more in-depth examinations of the impact of ongoing dialogue between parents and educators, of experiments in democratizing power relations, and of school-community relations during political conflict. We also need other types of research beyond case studies to solidify the empirical base for understanding leadership for partnerships and the intersection between family-community engagement and social justice (Riehl, 2000, Chapter 2, this volume).

Educators, parents, community members, and researchers will likely differ in their assessment of what specific situations constitute authentic partnerships; the line between traditional and authentic partnerships in the continuum, for example, is particularly fluid and subject to debate. If the continuum of leadership for partnerships spurs reflection and debate among educators and researchers on the nature, goals, and strategies of partnerships, it will have served its purpose to inform and inspire practice in this arena. What matters is the recognition of authentic participation as a central goal of partnerships and attempts to move schools and leaders in that direction.

This chapter has emphasized the role of educators in moving toward authentic relations with families and communities in the belief that once schools open the way, stakeholders will join with them in the true spirit of partnership. But of course, the growth of authentic participation in schools is not an easy task or a foregone conclusion. Reculturing schools is an ongoing, unfinished process; new waves of families, community groups, faculty, and staff must be constantly welcomed into partnership, enculturated in its norms, and empowered to further shape it. Like Dewey's (1938/1988) concept of democracy in education as something to be reinvented by each generation, visions of partnership must be continually renegotiated through dialogue in each school community. That is the possibility and the challenge of leadership for authentic partnerships.

Notes

1. I use the term *school-community partnerships* to denote cooperative arrangements between schools or districts and businesses, corporations, public agencies, nonprofit organizations, media, universities, and other local groups and institutions, as opposed to school-family partnerships that specifically reach out to families within the school.
2. I use the term *parent* throughout this article to refer to any primary adult caregiver of children, including grandparents, aunts and uncles, guardians, foster parents, and so on.

Similarly, I use the terms *parent involvement, parent engagement, family involvement,* and *family engagement* to encompass all adult caregivers and family members of students.

3. The National Network of Partnership Schools' more than 1,000 member institutions have made a commitment to apply Epstein's model to the development of parent involvement policies, plans, and programs. They receive information and technical assistance on parent and community involvement from the national organization. While studies of these schools are useful, they should be viewed in light of this unusual context of commitment to and support for partnerships.

References

Adams, C. M., Forsyth, P. B., & Mitchell, R. M. (2009). The formation of parent-school trust: A multilevel analysis. *Educational Administration Quarterly, 45*(4), 4–33.

Anderson, G. (1998). Toward authentic participation: Deconstructing the discourses of participatory reforms in education. *American Educational Research Journal, 35*(4), 571–603.

Anderson, G. L. (2009). *Advocacy leadership: Toward a post-reform agenda in education.* New York: Routledge.

André-Bechely, L. N., & Bernstein, S. (1998). *Building parent leadership in curriculum reform through school/university collaboration.* Paper presented at the annual meeting of the American Educational Research Association, San Diego, CA.

Auerbach, S. (2004). Engaging Latino parents in supporting college pathways: Lessons from a college access program. *Journal of Hispanic Higher Education, 3*(2), 125–145.

Auerbach, S. (2007a). Visioning parent engagement in urban schools: Role constructions of Los Angeles administrators. *Journal of School Leadership, 17*(6), 699–735.

Auerbach, S. (2007b). From moral supporters to struggling advocates: Reconceptualizing parent roles in education through the experience of working-class families of color. *Urban Education, 42*(3), 250–283.

Auerbach, S. (2009). Walking the walk: Portraits in leadership for family engagement in urban schools. *School Community Journal, 19*(1), 9–32.

Auerbach, S. (2010). Beyond coffee with the principal: Toward leadership for authentic school-family partnerships. *Journal of School Leadership, 20*(6), 730–759.

Auerbach, S., & Collier, S. (in press). Bringing high stakes from the classroom to the parent center: Lessons from an intervention program for immigrant families. *Teachers College Record, 114*(3).

Beck, L. G., & Murphy, J. (1993). *Understanding the principalship: Metaphorical themes, 1920s–1990s.* New York: Teachers College Press.

Beck, L. G., & Murphy, J. (1999). Parental involvement in site-based management: Lessons from one site. *International Journal of Leadership in Education, 2*(2), 81–102.

Bolivar, J., & Chrispeels, J. H. (2008). *Enhancing parent leadership through building social and intellectual capital.* Paper presented at the annual meeting of the American Educational Research Association, New York.

Brantlinger, E. (2003). *Dividing classes: How the middle class negotiates and rationalizes school advantage.* New York: RoutledgeFalmer.

Brooks, S. M. (2009). A case study of school-community alliances that rebuilt a community. *School Community Journal, 19(2),* 59–80.

Bryk, A. S., & Schneider, B. (2002). *Trust in schools: A core resource for improvement.* New York: Russell Sage Foundation.

Chrispeels, J. (2004). The dynamics of sharing and distributing leadership. In J. Chrispeels (Ed.), *Learning to lead together: The promise and challenge of sharing leadership* (pp. 3–20). Thousand Oaks, CA: Sage.

Coalition for Community Schools. (2006). *Community and family engagement: Principals share what works* (Executive Summary). Washington, DC: Author.

Constantino, S. (2003). *Engaging all families for student success: Creating a positive school culture by putting research into practice.* Lanham, MD: Scarecrow Education.

Cooper, C. W. (2009). Parent involvement, African American mothers, and the politics of educational care. *Equity & Excellence in Education, 42(4)*, 379–394.

Cooper, C. W., & Christie, C. A. (2005). Evaluating parent empowerment: A look at the potential of social justice evaluation in education. *Teachers College Record, 107*(10), 2248–2274.

Cooper, C. W., Riehl, C. J., & Hasan, L. (2010). Leading and learning with diverse families in schools: Critical epistemology amid communities of practice. *Journal of School Leadership, 20*(6), 758–788.

Cordeiro, P., & Kolek, M. (1996). Connecting school communities through educational partnerships. In P. A. Cordeiro (Ed.), *New directions for school leadership: Vol. 2. Boundary crossings: Educational partnerships and school leadership* (pp. 1–14). San Francisco, CA: Jossey-Bass.

Crowson, R. L., Goldring, E. B., & Haynes, K.T. (2010). *Successful schools and the community relationship: Concepts and skills to meet 21st century challenges.* Richmond, CA: McCutchan.

Cutler, W. W., III. (2000). *Parents and schools: The 150-year struggle for control in American education.* Chicago, IL: University of Chicago Press.

Dantley, M., & Tillman, L. (2006). Social justice and moral transformative leadership. In C. Marshall & M. Oliva (Eds.), *Leadership for social justice: Making revolutions in education* (pp. 16–30). Boston: Pearson.

Davies, D. (2002, January). The 10th school revisited: Are school, family, community partnerships on the reform agenda now? *Phi Delta Kappan, 83*(5), 388–392.

Deal, T. E., & Peterson, K. D. (2000). Shaping school culture. In Jossey-Bass (Ed.), *The Jossey-Bass reader on educational leadership* (pp. 202–216). San Francisco, CA: Jossey-Bass. (Original work published 1999)

Decker, L. E., Decker, V. A., & Brown, P. M. (2007). *Diverse partnerships for student success: Strategies and tools to help school leaders.* Lanham, MD: Rowman & Littlefield Education.

Delgado-Gaitán, C. (2004). *Involving Latino families in schools: Raising student achievement through home-school partnerships.* Thousand Oaks, CA: Corwin.

Dewey, J. (1988). Democracy and education in the world of today. In J. A. Boydston (Ed.), *John Dewey: The later works, 1925–1953: Vol. 13. 1938–1939* (pp. 294–303). Carbondale, IL: Southern Illinois University Press. (Original work published 1938)

Diamond, J. D., & Gomez, K. (2004). African American parents' educational orientations: The importance of social class and parents' perceptions of schools. *Education & Urban Society, 36*(4), 383–427.

Doucet, F. (in press). (Re)constructing home and school: Immigrant parents, agency, and the (un) desirability of bridging multiple worlds. *Teachers College Record, 113*(12).

Driscoll, M. E., & Goldring, E. B. (2005). How can school leaders incorporate communities as contexts for student learning? In W. Firestone & C. Riehl (Eds.), *A new agenda for research in educational leadership* (pp. 61–80). New York: Teachers College Press.

Epstein, J. L. (1990). School and family connections: Theory, research and implications for integrating sociologies of education and family. In D. G. Unger & M. B. Sussman (Eds.), *Families in community settings: Interdisciplinary perspectives* (pp. 99–126). New York: Haworth Press.

Epstein, J. L., Galindo, C. L., & Sheldon, S. B. (2010). *Levels of leadership: Effects of district and school leaders on the quality of school programs of family and community involvement.* Paper presented at the triennial meeting of the International Roundtable on School, Family, and Community Partnerships Network of Scholars (INET), Denver, CO.

Epstein, J. L., & Sanders, M. (2006). Prospects for change: Preparing educators for school, family, and community partnerships. *Peabody Journal of Education, 81*(2), 81–120.

Epstein, J. L., Sanders, M. G., Simon, B. S., Salinas, K. C., Jansorn, N. R., & Van Voorhis, F. L. (2002). *School, family and community partnerships: Your handbook for action* (2nd ed.) Thousand Oaks, CA: Corwin Press.

Fine, M. (1993). [Ap]parent involvement: Reflections on parents, power, and urban public schools. *Teachers College Record, 94*(4), 682–709.

Furman, G. C., & Merz, C. (1996). School and community connections: Applying a sociological framework. In J. Cibulka & W. Kritek (Eds.), *Coordination among schools, families, and communities: Prospects for educational reform* (pp. 323–348). Albany, NY: State University of New York Press.

Furman, G. C., & Starratt, R. J. (2002). Leadership for democratic community in schools. In J. Murphy (Ed.), *The educational leadership challenge: Redefining leadership for the 21st century: 101st Yearbook of the National Society for the Study of Education, Part I* (pp. 105–133). Chicago, IL: University Chicago Press.

Giles, C. (2006). Transformational leadership in challenging urban elementary schools: A role for parent involvement? *Leadership and Policy in Schools, 5*, 257–282.

Goldring, E. B., & Hausman, C. (2001). Civic capacity and school principals: The missing links for community development. In R. Crowson (Ed.), *Community development and school reform* (pp. 193–210). Oxford, UK: Elsevier Science.

Gordon, M. F., & Louis, K. S. (2009). Linking parent and community involvement with student achievement: Comparing principal and teacher perceptions of stakeholder influence. *American Journal of Education, 116* (November), 1–31.

Graue, M. E., Kroeger, J., & Prager, D. (2001). A Bakhtinian analysis of particular home-school relations. *American Educational Research Journal, 38*(3), 467–498.

Griffith, J. (2001). Principal leadership of parent involvement. *Journal of Educational Administration, 39*(2), 162–186.

Hargreaves, A. (2000). Professionals and parents: Personal adversaries or public allies? *Prospects, 30*(2), 201–213.

Henderson, A. T., Mapp, K. L., Johnson, V. R., & Davies, D. (2007). *Beyond the bake sale: The essential guide to family-school partnerships.* New York: New Press.

Henry, M. E. (1996). *Parent-school collaboration: Feminist organizational structures and school leadership.* Albany, NY: State University of New York Press.

Honig, M. (1998). *Opportunity to lead for school-community connections.* Paper presented at the annual meeting of the American Educational Research Association, San Diego, CA.

Honig, M. (2003). Building policy from practice: District central office administrators' roles and capacity for implementing collaborative educational policy. *Educational Administration Quarterly, 39*(3), 292–338.

Hoover-Dempsey, K. V., Walker, J., Sandler, H., Whetsell, D., Green, C., Wilkins, A., & Closson, K. (2005). Why do parents become involved? Research findings and implications. *Elementary School Journal, 106*(2), 105–130.

Horvat, E. M., Curci, J. D., & Partlow, M. C. (2010). Parents, principals, and power: A historical case study of "managing" parent involvement. *Journal of School Leadership, 20*(6), 704–729.

Horvat, E. M., Weininger, E. B., & Lareau, A. (2003). From social ties to social capital: Class differences in the relations between schools and parent networks. *American Educational Research Journal, 40*(2), 319–351.

Johnson, M. (in press). A 21st century model for bicultural parent engagement from a parent advocate perspective. In E. M. Olivos, O. Jiménez-Castellanos, & A. M. Ochoa (Eds.), *Bicultural parent engagement: Advocacy and empowerment.* New York: Teachers College Press.

Kahne, J., O'Brien, J., Brown, A., & Quinn, T. (2001). Leveraging social capital and school improvement: The case of a school network and a comprehensive community initiative in Chicago. *Educational Administration Quarterly, 37*(4), 429–461.

Lareau, A. (1989). *Home advantage: Social class and parental intervention in elementary education.* New York: Falmer Press.

Lareau, A., & Lopes Muñoz, V. (2009). *"You stabbed her in the back and twisted the knife": Structural conflicts between the principal and the PTO at a suburban public elementary school.* Paper presented at the annual meeting of the American Educational Research Association, San Diego.

Leithwood, K. A., & Riehl, C. (2003). *What do we already know about successful school leadership?* Paper presented at the annual meeting of the American Educational Leadership Association, Chicago.

Lewis, A. E., & Forman, T. A. (2002). Contestation or collaboration? A comparative study of home-school relations. *Anthropology and Education Quarterly, 33*(1), 60–89.

Lightfoot, D. (2004). "Some parents just don't care": Decoding the meanings of parental involvement in urban schools. *Urban Education, 39*(1), 91–107.

Lindsey, R. B., Robins, K. N., & Terrell, R. D. (2003). *Cultural proficiency: A manual for school leaders* (2nd ed.). Thousand Oaks, CA: Corwin Press.

López, G. (2001). The value of hard work: Lessons on parent involvement from an (im)migrant household. *Harvard Educational Review, 71*(3), 416–437.

López, G. R., Gonzalez, M. L., & Fierro, E. (2006). Educational leadership along the U.S.-Mexico border: Crossing borders/embracing hybridity/building bridges. In C. Marshall & M. Oliva (Eds.), *Leadership for social justice: Making revolutions in education* (pp. 64–84). Boston, MA: Pearson.

López, G. R., & Stoelting, K. (2010). Disarticulating parent involvement in Latina/o impacted schools in the Midwest. In M. Miller Marsh & T. Turner-Vorbeck (Eds.), *(Mis)Understanding families: Learning from real families in our schools* (pp. 31–48). New York: Teachers College Press.

Mapp, K. M. (2003). Having their say: Parents describe why and how they are engaged in their children's learning. *School Community Journal, 13*(1), 35–64.

Marshall, C., & Oliva, M. (2006). Building the capacities of social justice leaders. In C. Marshall & M. Oliva (Eds.), *Leadership for social justice: Making revolutions in education* (pp. 1–15). Boston, MA: Pearson.

Miretsky, D. (2004). The communication requirements of democratic schools: Parent-teacher perspectives on their relationships. *Teachers College Record, 106*(4), 814–851.

Murphy, J. (2005). Unpacking the foundations of ISLLC standards and addressing concerns in the academic community. *Educational Administration Quarterly, 41*(1), 154–191.

Nakagawa, K. (2000). Unthreading the ties that bind: Questioning the discourse of parent involvement. *Education Policy, 14,* 443–472.

Noguera, P. (2001). Transforming urban schools through investments in the social capital of parents. In M. Warren (Ed.), *Social capital in poor communities* (pp. 189–212). New York: Russell Sage Foundation.

Oakes, J., Rogers, J., & Lipton, M. (2006). *Learning power: Organizing for education and justice.* New York: Teachers College Press.

Olivos, E. M. (2006). *The power of parents: A critical perspective of bicultural parent involvement in public schools.* New York: Lang.

Ordoñez-Jasis, R., & Jasis, P. (2004). Rising with De Colores: Tapping into the resources of la comunidad to assist under-performing Chicano-Latino students. *Journal of Latinos and Education 3*(1), 53–64.

Osterman, K. F., Crow, G. M., & Rosen, J. L. (1997). New urban principals: Role conceptions at the entry level. *Urban Education 32*(3), 373–393.

Pérez Carreón, G., Drake, C., & Barton, A.C. (2005). The importance of presence: Immigrant parents' school engagement experiences. *American Educational Research Journal 42*(3), 465–600.

Prins, E., & Toso, B. W. (2008). Defining and measuring parenting for educational success: A critical discourse analysis of the Parent Education Profile. *American Educational Research Journal, 45*(3), 555–596.

Pushor, D. (2010). Are schools doing enough to learn about families? In M. M. Marsh & T. Turner-Vorbeck (Eds.), *(Mis)Understanding families: Learning from real families in our schools* (pp. 4–18). New York: Teachers College Press.

Rallis, S. F., & Goldring, E. B. (2000). *Principals of dynamic schools: Taking charge of change* (2nd ed.). Thousand Oaks, CA: Corwin Press.

Reese, L., Balzano, S., Gallimore, R., & Goldenberg, C. (1995). The concept of *educación*: Latino family values and American schooling. *International Journal of Educational Research, 23*(1), 57–81.

Riehl, C. (2000). The principal's role in creating inclusive schools for diverse students: A review of normative, empirical, and critical literature on the practice of educational administration. *Review of Educational Research, 70*(1), 55–81.

Rosenberg, H., Lopez, M. E., & Westmoreland, H. (2009). Family engagement: A shared responsibility. Family Involvement Network for Educators (FINE) Newsletter (November). Cambridge, MA: Harvard Family Research Project. Retrieved from www.hfrp.org/publications-resources/browse-our-publications

Sanders, M. (2009). Collaboration for change: How an urban school district and a community-based organization support and sustain school, family, and community partnerships. *Teachers College Record, 111*(7), 1693–1712.

Sanders, M. G., & Sheldon, S. B. (2009). *Principals matter: A guide to school, family, and community partnerships*. Thousand Oaks, CA: Corwin.

Sarason, S. B. (1995). *Parental involvement and the political principle*. San Francisco, CA: Jossey-Bass.

Schutz, A. (2006). Home is a prison in the global city: The tragic failure of school-based community engagement strategies. *Review of Educational Research, 76*(4), 691–744.

Scribner, J. D., Young, M. D., & Pedroza, A. (1999). Building collaborative relationships with parents. In P. Reyes, J. D. Scribner, & A. Paredes Scribner (Eds.), *Lessons from high-performing Hispanic schools: Creating learning communities* (pp. 36–60). New York: Teachers College Press.

Sergiovanni, T. J. (1992). *Moral leadership: Getting to the heart of school improvement*. San Francisco, CA: Jossey-Bass.

Smrekar, C., & Cohen-Vogel, L. (2001). The voices of parents: Rethinking the intersections of family and school. *Peabody Journal of Education, 76*(2), 75–100.

Smrekar, C. E., & Mawhinney, H. B. (1999). Integrated services: Challenges in linking schools, families, and communities. In J. Murphy & K. S. Louis (Eds.), *Handbook of research on educational administration* (2nd ed., pp. 443–461). San Francisco, CA: Jossey-Bass.

Smylie, M., Crowson, R. L., Chou, V., & Levin, R. (1994). The principal and community-school connections in Chicago's radical reform. *Educational Administration Quarterly, 30*(3), 342–364.

Swap, S. M. (1993). *Developing home-school partnerships: From concept to practice*. New York: Teachers College Press.

Theoharis, G. (2009). *The school leaders our children deserve: Seven keys to equity, social justice, and school reform*. New York: Teachers College Press.

Tillman, L. C. (2004). African American parental involvement in a post-Brown era: Facilitating the academic achievement of African American students. *Journal of School Public Relations, 25*(spring), 161–176.

Tollefson, K. (2008). *Volatile knowing: Parents, teachers, and the censored story of accountability in America's public schools*. Lanham, MD: Rowman & Littlefield.

Van Voorhis, F., & Sheldon, S. (2004). Principals' roles in the development of U.S. programs of school, family, and community partnerships. *International Journal of Educational Research, 41*, 55–70.

Vincent, C. (1996). Parental empowerment? Collective action and inaction in education. *Oxford Review of Education, 22*(4), 4656–4682.

Walker, J. M., Wilkins, A. S., Dallaire, J., Sandler, H. M., & Hoover-Dempsey, K. V. (2005). Parental involvement: Model revision through scale development. *Elementary School Journal, 106*(2), 85–104.

Warren, M. R. (2005). Communities and schools: A new view of urban education reform. *Harvard Educational Review, 75*(2), 133–173.

Warren, M., Hong, S., Rubin, C. L., & Uy, P. S. (2009). Beyond the bake sale: A community-based relational approach to parent engagement in schools. *Teachers College Record, 111*(9), 2209–2254.

Wells, A. S., & Serna, I. (1996). The politics of culture: Understanding local political resistance to detracking in racially mixed schools. *Harvard Educational Review, 66*(1), 93–118.

PART II

Leading Partnerships across Difference

Navigating Race, Class, Culture, and Power

4

ENLISTING COLLECTIVE HELP

Urban Principals' Encouragement of Parent Participation in School Decision-Making

John Rogers, Rhoda Freelon, and Veronica Terriquez

In 1917, Angelo Patri published *A Schoolmaster of the Great City,* a memoir about his work as a principal in a working-class, immigrant community in New York City. Patri described a variety of strategies for getting parents to "feel the power that comes through united effort" (p. 154). He identified and met with neighborhood leaders to hear their hopes and concerns; established after-school forums for parents and teachers to discuss issues of parenting and pedagogy; and linked parents with public officials who could bring additional resources to the school and its surrounding community. To bring in the hard-to-reach parents who "needed us most," Patri and his teachers created a schedule of public lectures, concerts, and plays (p. 97). The social events served as a bridge to other participation. At intermission, Patri would rise and say, "My friends, I have brought you here to enlist your collective help in the work of the school" (p. 100).

A century after Patri first became a principal, it has become commonplace that school leaders should involve parents, particularly low-income parents, in the life of the school. Administrator organizations and credentialing bodies identify collaboration with parents and community as a core competency for principals.[1] National educational reform models include parent involvement as an essential component of quality schooling.[2] Perhaps most significantly, the No Child Left Behind Act (NCLB; 2002) highlights the centrality of parent involvement to school improvement efforts. The federal law mentions parent involvement more than 100 times (Puriefoy, 2005). The U.S. Department of Education's nonregulatory guidance begins with then-Secretary Rod Paige's declaration that, "[S]chools can't improve without the help of parents" (U.S. Department of Education, 2004, p. 1). These calls for enhanced parent involvement all highlight the importance of engaging low-income parents to create more inclusive and equitable schooling.

Drawing on survey data from elementary school principals in the Los Angeles Unified School District (LAUSD), this chapter examines the extent to which principals take action to realize prevailing policy rhetoric about the importance of fostering engaged parents. We begin with a brief discussion of selected literature on school leaders and parent participation, highlighting arguments for why parents should be engaged in school governance. The next section describes our survey methods. We then report on principals' parent and community engagement practices, considering whether these practices differ in schools that enroll low and high proportions of low-income students. In the fourth section, we identify factors associated with high parent participation in school decision-making. The chapter closes with a discussion of our findings and the implications for practice and further research.

School Leaders and Parent Participation

Empirical study of principals' actions is important because normative expectations do not necessarily translate into practice. The qualitative studies of Susan Auerbach (2007, 2010) and others have documented dramatic differences in the vision and commitment that principals bring to their work with parents generally, but specifically with low-income parents of color and immigrant parents (Hein, 2003; Lopez, Scribner, & Mahitivanichcha, 2001).

Although quantitative studies explore how school leaders work with parents (Epstein, Galindo, & Sheldon, 2010; Griffith, 2001; Osterman, Crow, & Rosen, 1997; Sheldon & Van Voorhis, 2004; Van Voorhis & Sheldon, 2004), they have yet to systematically account for the inequalities identified by qualitative researchers. Van Voorhis and Sheldon (2004) examined how a sample of 320 principals supported partnerships with the community and specifically explored how program quality is related to increased levels of parent involvement, including participation in school decision-making committees, but an analysis across different social demographic profiles of the schools was not discussed. Similarly, Epstein et al. (2010) did not highlight differences in context in their exploration of how principal and school district commitments to family and school-community relationships enhance the quality of parent and community involvement programs. Hence, in spite of these contributions, we know little about the prevalence of different forms of principal practice and principal beliefs across different school and community contexts. For example, do principals serving schools that enroll high concentrations of low-income students engage parents differently from principals with more affluent student bodies? Do principals serving different constituencies provide the same opportunities for parents to enact power through participation in decision-making bodies?

Studies of parent participation find that parent income is associated with some, but not all, forms of parent engagement. According to data from the National Household Education Survey of 2007 (National Center for Education Statistics [NCES], 2008), more than 9 in 10 parents reported attending a general school meeting and parent-teacher conferences, with little difference in participation by family income. The vast majority of parents also reported participating in school events and fundraising, and a slight majority reported volunteering. Here we see a stronger relationship between family income and participation. A far smaller proportion of parents participated in decision-making. Only 17% of parents reported participating in school committees: Parents in families with incomes of more than $100,000 were roughly three times as likely as parents in families earning less than $50,000 to serve on school committees.

Why do we see these divergent patterns of parent participation and what do these patterns tell us about the practice of school leaders? The differences in parents' level of participation by family income may be related to individual factors such as family work schedule. Or, given the high level of economic segregation in public schools, it is possible that schools with high concentrations of low-income students afford different opportunities for parent engagement than schools with few low-income students. What is interesting about these patterns is that family income is not related to certain forms of parent participation, but it is strongly related to parent engagement in decision-making.

Stark differences between parent participation on committees and participation in other school activities belie public declarations on the meaning of parent involvement. Normative expectations for school leaders emphasize the importance of encouraging parents to participate in school committees and play a significant role in school improvement and governance. The No Child Left Behind Act bluntly states: "Parents should be involved in decision-making" (NCLB, 2002, Section 1118 c (4) C). Moreover, research-based frameworks have been incorporated into parent involvement policies in many states. Several states have adopted Epstein's model (1990, 1995), which identifies participation in school decision-making as one of six important types of parent involvement. In part, the low rate of parent participation on school committees reflects the weak legislative language of NCLB's parent involvement provisions. "Should" does not mean "must," and hence the law's rhetorical commitment to having educators treat parents as "full partners in their children's education…and decision-making" has rarely been enforced by state or district officials (Rogers, 2006).

There is a significant difference between encouraging parents to participate in the school's agenda and inviting parents to join as equal partners in making decisions about the school's work (Barton, Drake, Perez, St. Louis, & George, 2004; Giles, 2006). The latter path poses challenges for principals—for some because of deeply held beliefs about the relative value of professional expertise and community knowledge, for others because they lack the time or skills to enact more inclusive leadership, and for still others because a high-stakes policy environment creates pressure to assert tight control over school improvement efforts. Certainly, some school leaders champion the participation of parents in school decision-making. But many other school leaders who welcome parent involvement at their schools are unwilling, reluctant, or unable to wholeheartedly embrace Angelo Patri's (1917) call for parents to enter school as a "collective force" (p. 97).

In this chapter, we draw on survey data to examine the efforts of Los Angeles elementary school principals to promote parent participation. Specifically, we examine whether principals' efforts to engage parents differ in schools with low and high proportions of low-income students. Our analysis aims to inform general understandings of the parent involvement practices of elementary school principals across diverse school contexts. We focus particular attention on parent participation in decision-making, considering how this relates to other forms of parent involvement, to school context, and to principals' attributes, beliefs, and practices.

Why Parent Participation in Decision-Making Matters

There has been a great deal of scholarship documenting the value of parent involvement; much less has been written about the importance of engaging parents in decision-making. Parent participation in school decision-making matters because it forges a sense of legitimacy, increases the problem-solving capacity of schools, and fosters civic engagement and democracy. For each of these purposes, parent participation in decision-making is particularly important for low-income parents of color and immigrant parents.

Diverse and inclusive participation in decision-making improves parent-school relations and brings new ideas into the problem-solving process (Marschall, 2006). Participation holds potential cognitive benefits for the school as a whole. The unique experiences and perspectives of parents can inform decisions about how best to allocate limited resources or how to shape educational programs. In school improvement efforts, it is particularly important for schools to engage parents whose children have experienced difficulty, as these parents can communicate the salience of the problem as well as insights into how it might be addressed.

In addition to benefitting schools, parent participation in decision-making can enhance democracy and civic life. Recent decades have witnessed a broad pattern of decline in civic engagement. Since 1970, the United States has experienced falling voting rates and diminished participation in voluntary associations (Galston, 2007; Putnam, 2000). Public schools offer unique possibilities for reengaging the broader public in civic life. They are local institutions, of great importance to community members, and carry a long tradition of public participation (Shirley, 2010). Further, opportunities to participate in decision-making in public schools may be of particular importance to immigrant parents because when they become involved in school committees they can learn about American political culture (Rogers, Saunders, Terriquez, & Velez, 2008; Terriquez & Rogers, forthcoming). Further, parents who lack citizenship status can participate in school governance even though their participation in other civic realms is limited (Garcia-Bedolla, 2006).

In spite of these benefits, there are challenges associated with increasing parent participation in school decision-making. Malen (1999) documents how school-based committees often limit the power of parents, even as educators espouse a rhetorical commitment to shared governance. In these settings, educators frequently set the agenda and relegate parents to support roles, thus undermining authentic parent participation in school-decision making (Anderson, 1998; Malen, 1999; Nakagawa, 2000; Rogers, 2004).

To promote student learning, it is critical for schools to share common cause with parents and the surrounding community. Yet, historical patterns of unresponsive school personnel or poor school performance can alienate parents. Mark Warren (2005) has noted that this lack of legitimacy on the part of school personnel has been a particular concern for low-income urban communities. As far back as 1968, Charles Hamilton noted that a renewed sense of legitimacy can be established as parents are granted power to make significant decisions about the school. By participating meaningfully in decision-making committees, parents become stakeholders in the work of the school.

Los Angeles Principals' Parent Involvement Survey

In spring 2008, we invited all school site administrators in the Los Angeles Unified School District (LAUSD) to participate in a 10- to 15-minute online survey on parent involvement.[3] Principals were told that the study aimed to inform understandings of the role of principals in parent involvement—there were no incentives for participating in the study. More than 200 principals completed the survey, 141 of whom were elementary school principals.

The survey asked schools leaders: (a) how much time they devoted to parent involvement; (b) how many parents and community members they interacted with, as well as their level of participation in the local neighborhood; (c) goals for parent involvement at their school; (d) the strategies they used to engage parents; and (e) the number of parents who participated in different activities including decision-making. In order to assess how principal attributes or school characteristics affect parent involvement, school leaders were asked to report on their school's size, level, and student demographics.

Our analysis in this chapter draws on survey responses from the elementary school principals.[4] The 141 elementary school principals in our study represent 26% of the 542 elementary principals serving in the LAUSD in the 2007-2008 school year. Typical response rates for traditional mail surveys to a general population can range from 30 to 45%. Our response rate is on a par with Web-based surveys that tend to have lower response rates than traditional paper surveys (Cook, Heath, & Thompson, 2000; Kaplowitz, Hadlock, & Levine, 2004). Further, our sample is fairly reflective of principal and school demographics in LAUSD. It included a slightly smaller proportion of males (27 to 36%) than the district as a whole, with the racial/ethnic background of principals similar to the district as a whole, though an exact comparison is difficult because 21% of principals declined to specify their race or ethnicity (see Table 4.1).

We asked principals about the size of their school, the proportion of students receiving free or reduced price meals, and the proportion of students desig-

TABLE 4.1 Principal and School Characteristics

	Survey Respondents	*LAUSD Elementary Principals*
Number of Respondents	141	542
Gender		
Male	27%	36%
Female	73%	63%
Racial/Ethnic Background		
African American	13%	17%
Asian	4%	8%
Latino	25%	30%
White	37%	43%
Native American/Mixed Race	1%	1%
Did not specify	21%	
School Population Size		
500 or less	34%	42%
501–1000	52%	47%
1001–2000	15%	12%
% Free or Reduced Price Meals		
Less than 25%	8%	11%
25–49%	9%	13%
50–74%	11%	15%
75–100%	73%	61%
% English Language Learners		
Less than 15%	10%	18%
15–30%	17%	14%
31–45%	12%	14%
45% or more	61%	53%

Note: Totals may not add up to 100% due to rounding.

nated as English Learners. LAUSD elementary schools are much larger and enroll far more low-income students and English Learners than the nation as a whole. Our sample includes a slightly higher percentage of principals from very large elementary schools than is true of the district as a whole. It also includes a slightly higher percentage of principals serving schools with the most low-income students (designated by free or reduced price meals status) and English Learners (see Table 4.1). These differences are quite modest and suggest that our sample of principals work in schools that are reflective of the district.

Parent Participation and Principals' Parent Involvement Practices

While educators and policymakers universally invoke the importance of parent involvement, not all schools act with the same commitment and care toward parents. Parents are least likely to feel welcome in schools that serve large numbers of low-income students and students of color (Auerbach, 2007; Lott, 2001). Low-income parents who had poor experiences themselves as students may experience public schools as intimidating spaces, thereby undermining their desire for greater involvement. Yet, this pattern is not inevitable; some schools serving predominantly low-income students of color promote wide-scale parent participation. When schools establish welcoming environments, provide avenues for structured involvement, and initiate contact with families, parents are more likely to be involved in the life of the school (Auerbach, 2007; Hoover-Dempsey & Sandler, 1997).

Parent Participation in School Activities and Decision-Making

To get a sense of how many parents participate in school-based activities, we asked the principals to report the number of parents that attend Open House, sporting events, and parent meetings. Table 4.2 presents data on the number of parents attending various events in elementary schools with high and low concentrations of students from low-income families. The data reveal some differences in the number of parents participating in school events between schools where more than half the students receive free or reduced price meals and schools where less than half the student body receive free or reduced price meals. Nearly 63% of principals in high-poverty schools reported that fewer than 25 parents attend meetings where parents discuss community action on some school or community issue, whereas 33% of principals from low-poverty schools reported having 100 or more parents at such meetings.[5]

Table 4.2[6] also compares high and low-poverty schools by parent participation in school decision-making. Principals from high-poverty schools were more likely to report fewer parents involved in decision-making than principals of low-poverty schools. At high-poverty schools, 19% of principals reported 50

TABLE 4.2 Principals' Report of Parent Participation in School Activities by Free or Reduced Price Meals Concentration

Activity	*% Free or Reduced Price Meals*	*Number of Parents*				
		None	*1–25*	*26–99*	*100+*	*N*
Open House	Less than 50%	0%	0%	5%	95%	*21*
	More than 50%	2%	2%	8%	88%	*107*
Back to School Night	Less than 50%	0%	0%	5%	95%	*21*
	More than 50%	5%	1%	11%	83%	*107*
Parent-teacher conferences	Less than 50%	5%	0%	5%	90%	*21*
	More than 50%	1%	0%	5%	94%	*107*
Sporting events	Less than 50%	43%	14%	19%	24%	*21*
	More than 50%	56%	20%	16%	8%	*107*
Fundraising activities	Less than 50%	0%	0%	10%	90%	*21*
	More than 50%	10%	6%	28%	56%	*107*
School festivals or social events	Less than 50%	0%	0%	24%	76%	*21*
	More than 50%	4%	2%	19%	76%	*107*
School plays/ musical performances/art events	Less than 50%	0%	0%	14%	86%	*21*
	More than 50%	5%	1%	13%	81%	*107*
Workshops on parenting	Less than 50%	0%	33%	52%	14%	*21*
	More than 50%	2%	36%	48%	14%	*107*
Meetings to promote community action on some school or community issue	Less than 50%	5%	14%	48%	33%	*21*
	More than 50%	27%	36%	26%	10%	*107*
Parent meetings to discuss test scores	Less than 50%	0%	14%	62%	24%	*21*
	More than 50%	2%	29%	46%	23%	*107*
		<15	*15–24*	*25–49*	*50+*	*N*
Parents involved in decision-making	Less than 50%	0%	29%	29%	43%	*21*
	More than 50%	25%	27%	29%	19%	*107*

or more parents were involved in school decision-making compared to 43% of principals from low-poverty schools. This data mirrors similar trends found in the National Household Education Survey noted above.

To explore the role of principals in fostering environments for increased parent involvement, we examined the principals' self-reported actions and beliefs. We were interested in differences based on the socioeconomic status of the school's student body. Administrative data allow us to compare schools with low and high proportions of students who qualified for free or reduced priced meals—families whose income was less than 175% of the federal poverty level. While eligibility for free or reduced price meals provides no information on family affluence and limited information on the degree of poverty experienced within a school community, it is the best proxy available to account for socio-economic status (Harwell & LeBeau, 2010).

Principal Actions to Promote Parent Engagement

Our survey results show that principals at schools serving few low-income families spent more time on parent involvement activities. Among elementary schools in which fewer than half of students received free or reduced price meals, 38% of principals spent an average of 11 or more hours per week on parent involvement activities. By comparison, only 13% of principals in schools with more than half of the student body receiving free or reduced price meals committed comparable hours to parent involvement activities. Table 4.3 shows that 62% of principals in high-poverty schools reported spending five hours or less each week on parent engagement, compared with only 14% of principals in schools serving fewer low-income families. The findings do not necessarily mean that principals of low-poverty schools are more committed to parent involvement than principals of high-poverty schools. They may suggest that the principals at low-poverty schools must respond to increased demands for their time from families in their schools.

The number of families that a principal has personally met or the number of parents that a principal knows by name provides an indication of a principal's level of commitment to working with parents. Our data show that principals at low-poverty schools reported meeting higher numbers of families than principals from high-poverty schools. More than half of principals at low-poverty schools met more than 250 families during the school year, compared with less than one-quarter of principals in high-poverty schools. Sixty percent of principals in high-poverty schools had personally met fewer than 150 families while only 33% of principals in low-poverty schools reported meeting so few family members. The tendency for principals in low-poverty schools to meet more families may have consequences for parent involvement. Principals that are more visible and connected to families might discover that they have more support from parents for school-based volunteering efforts, such as fundraising, classroom assistance, and service on decision-making bodies.

Similar patterns emerge for the number of parents that principals knew by name (see Table 4.3). Principals at low-poverty schools reported knowing more parents by name than principals in high-poverty schools. Two-thirds of principals in low-poverty schools reported knowing at least 100 parents by name, compared with only one-quarter of principals serving high-poverty schools. Almost three times (41 to 14%) as many principals of high-poverty schools

TABLE 4.3 Principals' Actions to Promote Parent Engagement

Average Hours/Week Principals Spend on Parent Involvement						
% Free or Reduced Price Meals	*0–1*	*2–5*	*6–20*	*11+*		*N*
Less than 50%	0%	14%	48%	38%		**21**
50–100%	4%	58%	25%	13%		**107**
All Elementary Principals	3%	51%	29%	17%		**128**
Number of Families Principals Have Met						
% Free or Reduced Price Meals	*<50*	*50–99*	*100–149*	*150–250*	*>250*	*N*
Less than 50%	5%	14%	14%	14%	52%	**21**
50–100%	9%	30%	21%	15%	24%	**107**
All Elementary Principals	9%	27%	20%	15%	29%	**128**
Number of Parents Principals Know by Name						
% Free or Reduced Price Meals	*<50*	*50–99*	*100–149*	*>150*		*N*
Less than 50%	14%	19%	24%	43%		**21**
50–100%	41%	33%	14%	12%		**107**
All Elementary Principals	37%	31%	16%	17%		**128**

reported knowing fewer than 50 parents' names as principals of low-poverty schools.

Community Connections

Weiss, Kreider, Lopez, and Chatman-Nelson (2009) argue that school leaders should seek out opportunities to learn more about the community settings surrounding their schools as these experiences may reinforce the importance of parent engagement and allow principals to connect with difficult-to-reach parents. We asked principals about their contacts with the community to get a sense of how embedded they were in the broader neighborhood where the school is located.

Table 4.4 indicates that principals from low-poverty schools shopped in their school community more often than principals of high-poverty schools. Three-quarters of principals from low-poverty schools reported shopping more than once a week in the community surrounding their school compared to one-quarter of principals in high-poverty schools. This finding could be related to the paucity of retail outlets in low-income communities that cause principals to shop elsewhere. Moreover, shopping in the community may be a limited proxy for the concept of community embeddedness. To examine this concept further, we explored how often elementary school principals attended civic, recreational, and religious events in the community. Principals in low-poverty

TABLE 4.4 Elementary Principals' Contact with the Community by Free or Reduced Price Meals Concentration

% Free or Reduced Price Meals	*Never*	*Less than once a month*	*2–3 times a month*	*Once a week or more*	*N*
Shop in community					
Less than 50%	0%	10%	14%	76%	**21**
50–00%	9%	21%	44%	26%	**107**
All Elementary Principals	8%	19%	39%	34%	**128**
Attend civic, cultural, religious, or recreational activities in community					
Less than 50%	10%	38%	38%	14%	**21**
50–100%	24%	51%	20%	5%	**107**
All Elementary Principals	22%	49%	23%	6%	**128**
Meet with community members					
Less than 50%	5%	52%	38%	5%	**21**
50–100%	17%	69%	12%	2%	**107**
All Elementary Principals	15%	66%	16%	2%	**128**
Meet with representatives of community-based organizations and agencies for children and youth					
Less than 50%	10%	48%	38%	5%	**21**
50–100%	17%	64%	20%	0%	**107**
All Elementary Principals	16%	61%	23%	1%	**128**

schools were twice as likely (52 to 25%) as principals of high-poverty schools to report attending such events at least two or three times a month. Similar patterns held for principals reporting meetings with community members or representatives of community organizations. While such meetings were not common for most principals, they were more common in schools enrolling few low-income students.

Explaining Variation in Parent Participation in Decision-Making

We argue above that broad parent participation in school decision-making is not common in American public schools. This may be related to the fact that most principals do not foreground decision-making as a goal for parent involvement efforts. As noted in Table 4.2, only 19% of principals serving low-income schools reported having 50 or more parents involved in school decision-making. Table 4.5 reveals elementary school principals' top goals for working with parents. About one in five principals stated their goal for working with families was to encourage more parents to help children with homework. Similarly, one

TABLE 4.5 Principals' Goals for Working with Parents

	#1 Goal	*Top 3 Goal*
Provide parents with strategies for healthy child development	20%	45%
Encourage more parents to help their children with homework	22%	38%
Increase the number of parent volunteers at the school	12%	30%
Involve more parents in making decisions about school policy and budget	5%	28%
Involve parents as advocates for securing better conditions and more resources for the school	6%	29%
Create an environment where teachers and staff feel supported by parents	18%	48%
Create an environment where teachers and staff know they must meet parents' high expectations	9%	28%
Provide parents with information on how to help their children attend college	2%	13%
Provide parents with access to the social services they need to support their family	6%	38%
Number of respondents	**141**	**141**

in five also stated that a top goal was to provide parents with strategies about healthy child development. Principals assigned a lower priority to goals about involving more parents in critical decisions about school policy and organizing parents for advocacy. Only 5% of principals selected these as top goals for working with parents.

Sharing information with parents is an important responsibility of schools and serves as one of many ways that principals may bridge gaps in knowledge about key school practices, outcomes, and opportunities. In contrast to the differences in the practices of principals serving low- and high-poverty schools, we found no discernable difference between these groups of principals in the information they provided parents. Table 4.6 reports the percentage of elementary school principals that share information with parents in writing. Most elementary school principals in our sample appear to be providing information to parents on a range of topics. However, less than half of principals reported providing information to parents about learning conditions at their school in comparison to other schools, and only 45% reported providing information about how parents can shape policy at the district or state level. These findings suggest that principals in our sample were least likely to provide parents with information that could be used to make decisions or prompt policy change.

While parent participation in decision-making may not be the most salient form of parent engagement for many principals, we found evidence of it across

TABLE 4.6 Information Schools Share with Parents in Writing

Goals	*Principals*
Your school's test results	89%
Your school's improvement plan	78%
Your school's philosophy of learning	79%
List of contacts for help	82%
Learning conditions in your school compared with other schools	48%
The qualifications of your school's faculty	74%
How parents can help children with homework	94%
After-school programs for students	93%
How parents can participate in school decision-making	93%
How parents can shape policy at district or state level	45%
Expectations school holds for parents and guardians	91%
Number of respondents	**141**

all schools. What varies is the number of parents participating in decision-making. Roughly equal numbers of principals reported that less than 15, 15 to 24, 25 to 50, or more than 50 parents participated in decision-making. Given the importance of parent participation in decision-making to school improvement and the practice of democracy, we are interested in using our principal survey data to explore why principals reported such different levels of engagement in decision-making. Below, we develop a model to examine what conditions are associated with high numbers of parents participating in school decision-making.

Constructing the Model

To determine the factors that are related to high levels of parent participation in decision-making among the elementary schools in our sample, we examined several principal and parent actions. The basic empirical model we explored suggests that the number of parents involved in decision-making is a function of school characteristics, principal characteristics, parent participation in other school-sanctioned events, and principal beliefs and actions. The dependent variable in the model is the number of parents that principals reported were involved in decision-making at their school—an ordinal variable with four levels (less than 15, 15–24, 25–50, or 50 or more). We employed an ordinal logistic regression technique because our dependent variable is categorical and the use of traditional ordinary least squares was not appropriate (Long, 1997; Winship & Mare, 1984). Table 4.7 provides descriptive statistics on each of the variables included in the model followed by descriptions of each variable.[7]

TABLE 4.7 Descriptive Statistics for Variables Used in Ordered Logistic Regression Model

Variables	*%*	*Mean*	*SD*	*Range*
Dependent Variable: Number of Parents Involved in School Decision-Making‡				
Less than 15	22%			
15–24	27%			
25–50	29%			
50 or more	21%			
Independent Variables				
School size‡		1.81	0.68	1–3
% Free or reduced price meals ‡		3.48	0.95	1–4
Asian		0.04	0.19	0–1
African American		0.13	0.34	0–1
Latino		0.25	0.43	0–1
Decline to state		0.21	0.41	0–1
Female		0.73	0.44	0–1
Fluent in Spanish		0.39	0.48	0–1
Can communicate in Spanish		0.36	0.48	0–1
Years as principal‡		2.56	1.07	1–4
Principal Actions				
Goal to increase number of parents in decision-making		0.28	0.45	0–1
Hours devoted to parent involvement‡		2.56	0.80	1–4
Number of parents principal knows by name‡		2.08	1.09	1–4
Principal provides parents with information about shaping district/state policy		0.71	0.45	0–1
Principal provides parents with information about how to participate in decision- making		0.93	0.26	0–1
Community contact*		1.09	0.54	0–2.7
Parent Actions				
Parents participate in general school events*		2.83	0.35	1.7–3
Parents participate in social activities		0.86	0.34	0–1
Number of parents attending fundraising activities		3.38	0.93	1–4
Parent volunteers*		0.97	0.55	0–2.6

Notes: *Composite variables; ‡ Ordinal variables

Two key features of the school were used as important control variables in this study: student enrollment and percentage of students receiving free or reduced price meals. School size was an important variable to control for because we were attempting to explain the quantity of parents engaged in decision-making at a school site, and the number of students enrolled should be positively related to this outcome. Additionally, the percentage of students receiving free or reduced priced meals represents our indicator of families' socioeconomic level. The National Household Educational Survey shows that low-income parents are less likely to participate in school committees than more affluent parents (National Center for Education Statistics [NCES], 2008). Further, an abundance of sociological literature suggests that middle-class and affluent families have greater time, resources, and social and cultural capital valued by schools, and hence are more likely than low-income parents to be invited into decision-making roles at their children's schools (Horvat, Weininger, & Lareau, 2003; Lareau, 2003).

Our data allow us to control for various principal characteristics that may influence how many parents are engaged in decision-making at a school site. Principal race, gender, and ability to communicate in Spanish were included as dummy variables in the model. Given that a large percentage of schools in LAUSD serve primarily Spanish-speaking Latino communities, Spanish language facility may help principals more readily engage families. We also included principals' years on the job as an independent categorical variable (less than 2 years, 3–6 years, 7–10 years, or 11 or more).

The overall level of parent involvement in traditional school-sanctioned activities may be related to whether or not many parents are involved in more robust forms of parent engagement such as decision-making at the school site. To account for this, we included measures of parent participation in official parent events, social activities, volunteering, and fundraising. Using several questions from the survey, we created simple composite variables for each of these constructs, with the exception of the fundraising variable that is based on the categorical response of a single item. Parent involvement in official parent events includes participation in Open House, Back-to-School nights, and parent-teacher conferences. This construct represents a basic level of participation in school events where parents are passive participants. The variable social activity is a binary variable indicating whether or not a parent attended school festivals, plays, musical performances, and sporting events. Volunteering represents a composite variable based on principal reports of parent participation in yard supervision, office-clerical work, tutoring, classroom support, and sporting events. These events are separated from parent participation in social activities as they may represent a more sustained level of involvement during the course of the school year rather than participation and volunteering in occasional school-based social activities.

The final components of the model are related to principals' beliefs about parent involvement and the steps they take to facilitate increased involvement. As school leaders, principals are uniquely positioned to create school environments that foster increased parent participation. We explored specific principal actions and their possible relation to more democratic forms of parent involvement. We conjectured that the number of hours principals spend per week on parent engagement and the number of families they know by name may be factors that influence parent involvement in decision-making. We also considered whether principals provided parents with information about state and district policy or about how to participate in decision-making. We accounted for principals' commitment to participatory governance by including a variable that indicates whether principals prioritized involving parents in decisions about school policy and budget. Finally, a composite variable representing community embeddedness was included to capture how well principals were integrated into the local community that the school serves. This construct was comprised of survey items related to how often principals attended community events or met with local civic leaders and community-based organizations.

Results

Table 4.8[8] reports the results of the ordinal logistic regression model for the number of parents involved in decision-making at the school site. Four variables emerged as statistically significant predictors of the dependent variable.[9] The variables cover school characteristics, parent actions, and principal characteristics and actions. We used odds ratios to interpret the statistically significant results. Odds ratios were used to show the likelihood that a principal with a given set of characteristics would have higher (or lower) numbers of parents engaged in school decision-making. The higher the odds ratio for a particular variable, the greater the odds that more parents were engaged in school decisions when holding all other factors constant.

With respect to school-level characteristics, it seems reasonable to expect that the size of the student body will be positively related to the number of parents at the school involved in decision-making. This result was highly significant ($p < .001$) and suggests the odds of larger elementary schools in our sample having more parents involved in school decision-making is 3.32 times the odds of smaller elementary schools. Certainly, schools with more students have more parents to draw on in terms of participating in various school activities.[10]

Being a female principal emerged as statistically significant in the model ($p < .05$). Female principals were 2.5 times more likely than male principals to report high numbers of parents involved in decision-making. There is a body of literature that suggests that women may be prone to lead democratically, foregrounding relationships and exhibiting caring in their leadership styles (Eagly, Karau, & Johnson, 1992; Oplatka, 2003).

TABLE 4.8 Ordinal Logistic Regression Analysis Modeling the Number of Parents Involved in Decision-Making at an Elementary School (N=123)

Predictor	*B*	*SE β*	*Wald's X^2*	*P*	*Odds Ratio*
Intercept 3	-10.1649	2.5587	15.7827	<.0001	NA
Intercept 2	−8.3238	2.5204	10.9069	.0010	NA
Intercept 1	−6.3877	2.4544	6.7731	.0093	NA
School Characteristics					
School size	1.2008	0.3116	14.8455	**.0001*****	3.323
% free or reduced price meals	−0.3707	0.2625	1.9941	.1579	0.690
Principal Characteristics					
African American	0.9068	0.6093	2.2150	.1367	2.476
Asian	−0.7406	0.9920	0.5573	.4553	0.477
Latino	0.4876	0.5566	0.7675	.3810	1.628
Decline to state	0.4749	0.6412	0.5487	.4589	1.608
Female	0.9034	0.4543	3.9543	**.0468****	2.468
Fluent in Spanish	−0.0301	0.6096	0.0024	0.9606	0.970
Can communicate in Spanish	-0.2461	0.5569	0.1953	0.6585	0.782
Years as principal	0.2846	0.1762	2.6092	.1062	1.329
Principal Actions					
Top goal to increase number of parents in decision-making	0.2362	0.4176	0.3197	.5718	1.266
Hours devoted to parent involvement	0.3030	0.2708	1.2517	.2632	1.354
Number of parents principal knows by name	0.2998	0.1966	2.3260	.1272	1.350
Provide parents with information about shaping district/state policy	0.7672	0.4332	3.1366	**.0766***	2.154
Provide parents with information about school decision-making	1.0425	1.0514	0.9830	.3215	2.836
Community Contact	0.0419	0.3815	0.0120	.9126	1.043
Parent Actions					
Parents participate in general school events	0.1351	0.6538	0.0427	.8363	1.145
Parents participate in social activities	0.3467	0.7067	0.2407	.6237	1.414
Number of parents attending fundraising activities	0.3210	0.2368	1.8382	.1752	1.379
Parent volunteers	1.0018	0.4107	5.9513	**.0147****	2.723

Psuedo-R^2 = 0.4498 / *p<.10, **p<.05, ***p<.01

Among parents' other participation, volunteering emerged as a statistically significant predictor of parent participation in decision-making. This suggests that elementary schools with higher levels of parent volunteerism are 2.7 times as likely as schools with low volunteerism to have more parents involved in school decision-making. It is difficult to determine clear lines of causality in the relationship between volunteerism and decision-making. Educators may ask parents who are involved in decision-making to play a greater role as volunteers or vice versa.[11]

Finally, while we hypothesized that principal actions and beliefs are critical to fostering parent participation in decision-making, only one of the four variables we considered emerged as marginally significant ($p < .10$). Our results reveal that principals who provided parents with information about how to shape district and state policy were twice as likely as other principals to have higher numbers of parents involved in decision-making at their school. This relationship suggests that sharing information with parents may encourage them to become more engaged in school affairs as full partners in decision-making and advocacy.

Implications and Conclusion

Our analysis points to two broad findings from our survey of elementary principals in Los Angeles. First, the time and commitment that principals devoted to parent involvement and community engagement was strongly related to the proportion of low-income students enrolled in the school. On average, principals of schools with small proportions of low-income students reported that they spent far more time on parent involvement activities, participated in the community and interacted with community members more often, and knew more parents than their peers leading high-poverty schools. Second, several factors predict the number of parents who participate in decision-making in elementary schools. Large school size, schools with female principals, and schools with principals who provided parents with information about how to impact policy were all associated with higher numbers of parents participating in decision-making. We discuss the implications of each of these findings in turn.

There are many possible explanations for why principals of high-poverty schools, on average, seem to invest less time and energy on parent involvement than principals of elementary schools with fewer low-income students. First, as we note above, a number of studies have found that low-income parents have less time and resources for parent involvement. It is possible that principals of high-poverty schools conclude—consciously or unconsciously—that additional efforts to engage parents will not yield a significant payoff in the form of more parent participation. Second, in a period of high-stakes accountability, principals of high-poverty schools often face more pressure than their peers to raise test scores over a short period of time. Such pressure might prompt these principals to focus their limited time and energy on strategies that narrowly address student test performance and move away from parent involvement activities. Third, principals of high-poverty schools are much less likely than their peers to view parent involvement activities as a potential source for additional resources for their schools. While more than half of the principals of schools with small proportions of low-income students reported receiving more than $40,000 in parent donations, no principals of high-poverty schools reported donations of this size and more than one third reported no parent donations.

No matter the explanation, it is problematic that principals of high-poverty schools, on average, invested less time in parent and community involvement than their peers in schools enrolling fewer low-income students. This outcome is particularly troubling given that policymakers have targeted attention on parent involvement in high-poverty schools as a strategy for reducing the achievement gap. It suggests that policymakers might consider requiring schools to report on particular parent engagement practices as a way to monitor variation across schools serving different student populations. Such information could be incorporated into an accountability structure. If districts establish clear standards for principals' engagement activity and evaluate principals based on these standards, we would likely see changes in principal practice. These changes are likely to be most robust if principals have access to information and supports about how best to encourage parent participation in decision-making. Principal training programs and districts have a role to play in developing this understanding and capacity.

Further, policymakers may want to consider strategies for diminishing the influence of parent fundraising on principal behavior. Such strategies include equalization plans that share revenues generated from fundraising across district schools or funding mechanisms (such as the weighted student formula) that direct more resources to schools with higher proportions of low-income students.

It is also important to consider the potential role of empowered community-based groups in shaping principal's actions. Community organizing groups can galvanize low-income and working-class parents and recast the power relationships between parents and educators (Oakes & Rogers, 2006; Rogers, 2006). As McAlister and colleagues document (see Chapter 11, this volume), community organizing groups can establish strong and respectful relationships with principals in which power is shared. Such relationships embody what Auerbach (2010) describes as authentic partnerships.

Our effort to model which factors predict high numbers of parents involved in decision-making is meant as an exploratory exercise. There are at least two important cautions that should be heeded when assessing our findings. First, our model was based on principals' self-reports of how many parents were involved in decision-making at their schools. We have no way of knowing the accuracy of these self-reports. Second, the number of parents involved in decision-making tells us nothing about the quality of participation. It fails to differentiate between how parents participate (as "rubber-stamps" for principal requests or as equal participants in decision-making) or what substantive issues they decide (choosing what food to serve at the Halloween festival or how to distribute resources from the school site budget).

Nevertheless, the findings from our model are suggestive and point toward areas where further research is merited. For example, our findings indicate that parent participation in school sanctioned events does not necessarily lead to more parent participation in decision-making. We need more research that differentiates between different forms of parent participation and considers the relationship among these different types of participation.[12] Additional research might also explore how school context shapes the quantity and quality of parent participation in decision-making. How can principals who are serving low-income communities promote parent participation in decision-making and how can community-based organizations and community organizing groups contribute to such participation? Similarly, it will be valuable to explore how principals' gender shapes principal practice relative to school decision-making.

Finally, the fact the principals in our study reported such dramatic differences in the number of parents participating in decision-making suggests that not everyone takes seriously the rhetoric of policymakers and professional groups about the importance of empowered parent engagement. In a policy environment where what is counted is what ends up counting, there is little or no public information about how many parents participate in decision-making across different public schools. If we want more principals to embrace Angelo Patri's vision, we need polices that support, encourage, and monitor principals' efforts to enlist parents' democratic potential.

Notes

1. See,for example, the professional standards for California administrators (http://www.acsa.org/MainMenuCategories/ProfessionalLearning/PromisingPractices/CPSELs.aspx) or the "Standards for School Leaders" adopted by the Interstate School Leaders Licensure Consortium (http://www.e-lead.org/principles/standards1.asp).
2. See, for example, the Talent Development High Schools Program (http://web.jhu.edu/CSOS/tdhs/index.html); the Accelerated Schools Model (http://www.acceleratedschools.net/); and the Comer School Development Program (http://medicine.yale.edu/childstudy/comer/index.aspx).
3. It is important to note that federally and state mandated district and school Title I and bilingual advisory councils provide other contexts for Los Angeles parent participation. Auerbach (2007) provides evidence that many administrators in Los Angeles do not hold the work of these school-level parent councils in high estimation.
4. We exclude principals of middle schools, high schools, continuation schools, adult schools, and span schools (which include students across a broad range of grades). The primary reason why we exclude these other principals is that we wish to draw meaningful comparisons among principals with similar roles and serving schools of similar size.

5. Throughout this chapter, we will refer to schools where more than half of the students receive free or reduced price meals as "high-poverty schools" and schools where less than half of students receive free or reduced price meals as "low-poverty schools."
6 Tables 4.2–4.5 report 128 cases as a result of missing data for some principals.
7. Although five of the independent variables in our model are categorical, in the interest of parsimony, we treated them as continuous. We tested the categorical properties of the variables by creating indicator variables in separate analyses. The results of these separate analyses were not substantially different from the final model presented here.
8. Table 4.8 is based on data for 123 cases due to missing data for some variables included in the model.
9. There is a dearth of inferential models exploring the relationship between principal, parent, and school characteristics and democratic shared governance in schools. Our analysis represents an exploratory exercise to hone in on some of these relationships in a large urban school district. As a result, we chose the more generous p-value of 0.10 to detect interesting and theoretically sound relationships that might explain the likelihood of increasing the number of parents involved in decision-making at an elementary school.
10. It is important to note that elementary schools in the Los Angeles Unified School District are far larger, on average, than elementary schools across the country. In our sample, roughly one third of elementary schools enrolled fewer than 500 students and 15% enrolled more than 1,000 students. Across the nation, 60% of elementary schools enroll fewer than 500 students and 4% enroll more than 1,000 students (U.S. Department of Education, National Center for Education Statistics, 2009).
11. Whether principals encourage parent volunteers to participate in decision-making may be related to what principals count as participation in decision-making—for example, if they consider participation in PTA as decision-making (see Gordon, Chapter 8, this volume).
12. One interesting example of such research is the work of Paru Shah (2009) who finds that Latino participation in Local Site Council Governance in Chicago correlated with more participation by Latino parents in other public school activities.

References

Anderson, G. L. (1998). Toward authentic participation: Deconstructing the discourses of participatory reforms in education. *American Educational Research Journal, 35*(4), 571 –603.

Auerbach, S. (2007). Visioning parent engagement in urban schools. *Journal of School Leadership, 17*(6), 699–734.

Auerbach, S. (2010). Beyond coffee with the principal: Toward leadership for authentic school-family partnerships. *Journal of School Leadership, 20*(6), 730–759.

Barton, A. C., Drake, C., Perez, J., St. Louis, K., & George, M. (2004). Ecologies of parental engagement in urban education. *Educational Researcher, 33*(4), 3–12.

Cook, C., Heath, F., & Thompson, R. L. (2000). A meta-analysis of response rates in web- or internet-based surveys. *Educational and Psychological Measurement, 60*(6), 821–836.

Eagly, A. H., Karau, S. J., & Johnson, B. T. (1992). Gender and leadership style among school principals: A meta-analysis. *Educational Administration Quarterly, 28*(1), 76–102.

Epstein, J. L. (1990). School and family connections: Theory, research and implications for integrating sociologies of education and family. In D. G. Unger & M. B. Sussman (Eds.), *Families in community settings: Interdisciplinary perspectives* (pp. 99–126). New York: Haworth Press.

Epstein, J. L. (1995). School/family/community partnerships: Caring for the children we share. *Phi Delta Kappan, 76*, 701–712.

Epstein, J. L., Galindo, C. L., & Sheldon, S. B. (2010). *Levels of leadership: Effect of district and school leaders on the quality of school programs of family and community involvement.* Paper presented at 15th International Roundtable on School, Family, and Community Partnerships, Denver, CO.

Galston, W. (2007). Civic knowledge, civic education, and civic engagement: A summary of recent research. *International Journal of Public Administration, 30*(6), 623–642.

García Bedolla, L. (2006). Rethinking citizenship: Noncitizen voting and immigrant political engagement in the United States, In T. Lee, K. Ramakrishnan, & R. Ramírez (Eds.), *Transforming politics, transforming America: The political and civic incorporation of immigrants in the United States* (pp. 51–70). Charlottesville: University of Virginia Press.

Giles, C. (2006). Transformational leadership in challenging urban elementary schools: A role for parent involvement? *Leadership and Policy in Schools, 5*(3), 257–282.

Griffith, J. (2001). Principal leadership of parent involvement. *Journal of Educational Administration, 39*(2),162–186.

Hamilton, C. (1968). Race and education: A search for legitimacy. *Harvard Educational Review, 38*(4), 669–684.

Harwell, M., & LeBeau, B. (2010). Student eligibility for a free lunch as an SES measure in education research. *Educational Researcher, 39*(2), 120–131.

Hein, N. P. (2003). Mexican American parent participation and administrative leadership. *Journal of Latinos and Education, 2*(2), 109–115.

Hoover-Dempsey, K. V., & Sandler, H. M. (1997). Why do parents become involved in their children's education? *Review of Educational Research, 67*(1), 3–42.

Horvat, E. M., Weininger, E. B., & Lareau, A. (2003). From social ties to social capital: Class differences in the relations between schools and parent networks. *American Educational Research Journal, 40*(2), 319–351.

Kaplowitz, M. D., Hadlock, T. D., & Levine, R. (2004). A comparison of web and mail survey response rates. *Public Opinion Quarterly, 68*(1), 94–101.

Lareau, A. (2003). *Unequal childhoods: Class, race, and family life.* Berkeley: University of California Press.

Long, J. S. (1997). *Regression models for categorical and limited dependent variables.* Thousand Oaks, CA: Sage.

Lopez, G. R., Scribner, J. D., & Mahitivanichcha, K. (2001). Redefining parental involvement: Lessons from high-performing migrant-impacted schools. *American Educational Research Journal, 38*(2), 253–288.

Lott, B. (2001). Low-income parents and the public schools. *Journal of Social Issues, 57*(2), 247–259.

Malen, B. (1999). The promises and perils of participation on site-based councils. *Theory into Practice, 38*(4), 209–216.

Marschall, M. (2006). Parent involvement and educational outcomes for Latino students. *Review of Policy Research, 23*(5), 1053–1076.

Nakagawa, K. (2000). Unthreading the ties that bind: Questioning the discourse of parent involvement. *Educational Policy, 14*(4), 443–472.

National Center for Education Statistics (NCES). (2008). *2007 national household education surveys program, parent and family involvement file* [Data file]. Retrieved from http://nces.ed.gov/nhes/dataproducts.asp#2007dp.

No Child Left Behind (NCLB) Act of 2001, § 1118 (4).

Oakes, J., & Rogers, J. (2006). *Learning power: organizing for education and justice.* New York: Teachers College Press.

Oplatka, I. (2003). School change and self-renewal: Some reflections from life stories of women principals. *Journal of Educational Change, 4*(1), 25–43.

Osterman, K. F., Crow, G. M., & Rosen, J. L. (1997). New urban principals: Role conceptions at the entry level. Urban Education, *32*(3), 373–393.

Patri, A. (1917). *A schoolmaster of the great city.* New York: Macmillan.

Puriefoy, W. (2005, June 8). Why the public is losing faith in the "No Child" law. *Education Week,* pp. 34–35.

Putnam, R. (2000). *Bowling alone: The collapse and revival of American community.* New York: Simon & Schuster.

Rogers, J. (2004). Creating a public accountability for California schools. *Teachers College Record, 106*(11), 2171–2192.

Rogers, J. (2006). Forces of accountability? The power of poor parents in No Child Left Behind. *Harvard Educational Review, 76*(4), 611–641.

Rogers, J., Sanders, M., Terriquez, V., & Velez, V. (2008). Civic lessons: Public schools and the civic development of undocumented students and parents. *Northwestern Journal of Law and Social Policy, 3*(2), 201–218.

Shah, P. (2009). Motivating participation: The symbolic effects of Latino representation on parent school involvement. *Social Science Quarterly, 90*(1), 212–230.

Sheldon, S. B., & Van Voorhis, F. L. (2004). Partnership programs in U.S. schools: Their development and relationship to family involvement outcomes. *School Effectiveness and School Improvement, 15*(2), 125–148.

Shirley, D. (2010). A brief history of public engagement in American education. In M. Orr & J. Rogers (Eds.), *Public engagement for public education: Joining forces to revitalize democracy and equalize schools* (pp. 27–51). Stanford, CA: Stanford University Press.

Terriquez, V., & Rogers, J. (Forthcoming). Becoming civic: The active engagement of immigrant parents in public schools. In E. Olivos, O. Jiménez-Castellanos & A. Ochoa (Eds.), *Bicultural parent engagement: Advocacy and empowerment.* New York: Teachers College Press.

U.S. Department of Education. (2004). *Parental involvement: Title I, part A, non-regulatory guidance.* Washington, DC: Author.

Van Voorhis, F., & Sheldon, S. (2004). Principals' roles in the development of US programs of school, family, and community partnerships. *International Journal of Educational Research, 41*, 55–70.

Warren, M. (2005). Communities and schools: A new view of urban education reform. *Harvard Educational Review, 75*(2), 133–173.

Weiss, H. B., Kreider, H. M., Lopez, D. M. E., & Chatman-Nelson, D. C. M. (2009). *Preparing educators to engage families: Case studies using an ecological systems framework* (2nd ed.). Thousand Oaks, CA: Sage.

Winship, C., & Mare, R. D. (1984). Regression models with ordinal variables. *American Sociological Review, 49*(4), 512–525.

5

ADVOCACY-BASED PARTNERSHIPS, SPECIAL EDUCATION, AND AFRICAN AMERICAN FAMILIES

Resisting the Politics of Containment

April Ruffin-Adams and Camille M. Wilson[1]

The provision of special education services is an essential area of schooling that determines the educational quality and outcomes of some of the most vulnerable student populations. Still, the role that principals and other educational leaders should play in employing equitable special education practices receives too little attention in educational leadership preparation programs and scholarship (Burrello, Lashley, & Beatty, 2001; DiPaola & Walther-Thomas, 2003; Frattura & Capper, 2007). An increased understanding of how educational leaders can best interact with parents and families in special education is particularly needed given that families look to these leaders to monitor and influence the educational placement of their children within general or special education programs—acts that can have lifelong consequences for children's social and professional trajectories (Blanchett, 2006; Donovan & Cross, 2002; Harry & Klingner, 2006).

Educational leaders' ability to help build partnerships among teachers, staff, themselves, and African American families is especially critical given the large percentage of African American children—specifically boys—who are enrolled in special education programs and academically struggling in schools (Kearns, Ford, & Linney, 2005; Smiley, 2009). According to the U.S. Commission on Civil Rights (2009), 33% of the students diagnosed as mildly mentally retarded were African American, and the Children's Defense Fund (2007) reported that "Black students are more likely than any other students to be in special education programs for mental retardation or emotional disturbance" (p. 13) A special education referral may be the first step to permanent social and educational disenfranchisement for African American boys. According to Harry and Anderson (1994), the special education placement of African American boys can mean "relegation to a stigmatized land of no return, in which a watered-down curriculum and overly structured social experiences have little parallel in either regular education or real life" (p. 615). According to the National Assessment for Educational Progress (NAEP; 2009), African American high school students drop out of school at a rate two times higher than their White male peers.

Although there is an abundance of research on the disproportionate representation of African American boys in special education (Blanchett, 2006; Donovan & Cross, 2002; Duncan, 2002; Harry & Klingner, 2006; Kunjufu, 2005;West-Olatunji & Baker, 2006), little is known about how African American parents make decisions regarding their sons' placement. In most cases, mothers are the primary caregivers and decision-makers regarding their children's education (Cooper, 2007, 2009); however, African American mothers have historically been disenfranchised participants in schooling (Cooper, 2007, 2009) and, as will be illustrated, they have had strained relationships with educators. For these reasons, it is necessary that educational leaders form authentic partnerships with these mothers, meaning partnerships that value the families' involvement, support advocacy, and ultimately create more democratic spaces for them to contribute to the quality and equity of their children's education (Auerbach, 2010).

In this chapter, we draw upon our collective experiences as educators and as a school social worker and a researcher of school-family partnerships to (a) examine the educational referral process that serves a pivotal gatekeeping function in special education; (b) describe the involvement of African American families, particularly mothers, in that process; and (c) propose how educational leaders can better partner with African American families to ensure students' proper educational referral and placement. To adequately build partnerships with African American families, it is critical that educational leaders understand how such partnerships encompass a distinct and complex web of cultural, social, and political contexts that affect families' knowledge, power, and ability to advocate for their children.

To help ground our discussion and analysis, we will offer a fictionalized case that conveys a realistic account of the problematic ways many African American mothers experience the special education process and interface with educational leaders. The case, which is a composite of the first author's professional experiences, will help us contextualize the special education process and analyze the educational and racial politics that often lead to biased special education practices and educational leaders' ineffective relationships with African American families. Such relationships are typically grounded in the politics of containment—political dynamics that can segregate, oppress, and disempower students and families (Collins, 1998; Cooper & McCoy, 2009). We will draw from an integrated conceptual framework that incorporates key concepts from Black feminist thought, critical race theory, and Foucault's theories of power (Collins, 1998; Foucault, 1979; Ladson-Billings & Tate, 1995) to situate the politics of containment within contemporary special education contexts and recommend how educational leaders can help build partnerships to disrupt such politics.

The Special Education Referral Process and African American Families

The Individuals with Disabilities Education Act (IDEA; 1990) was enacted to ensure that all students receive a free and appropriate public education (FAPE) in the least restrictive environment possible, in addition to protecting the rights of parents and their children with disabilities. Exceptional children are often considered those with disabilities such as autism, hearing impairments, visual impairments, mental disabilities, speech-language impairment, orthopedic impairments, or traumatic brain injury (North Carolina Board of Education, 2008). Low incidence disabilities, such as cerebral palsy, are typically described as the developmental disabilities children have that impact their education and are usually identified before the children begin school. High incidence disabilities can be explained as the subjectively defined disabilities not usually identified prior to students entering school. According to Reschly (1993), disabilities such as learning disabled, mildly mentally retarded, and behaviorally and emotionally disabled can be explained by a social system model because they are not directly linked to biological or developmental factors.

The special education referral process begins when teachers become aware of students with academic achievement and behavioral problems (Hosp & Reschly, 2003). After a teacher refers a student for evaluation for a specific disability requiring special education services, IDEA requires a group of qualified individuals, often called a child study team, to determine whether or not an evaluation should be conducted. If an evaluation is necessary, several tests are given to the student to determine if he or she qualifies for special education services. Referrals to special education must meet specific qualifications to demonstrate that students meet the criteria for a disability category (Donovan & Cross, 2002; Harry & Klingner, 2006). The disability categories where African American boys are disproportionately represented are learning disabled (LD), which is described as a discrepancy between IQ and achievement; educable or mildly mentally retarded (EMR or MMR), which describes a student whose scores fall below the standard age norms; and behaviorally/emotionally disturbed (B/ED), which occurs when academic achievement is impacted by behavioral and emotional difficulties in classroom settings (Harry & Klingner, 2006). Although teachers must ensure that students meet the qualifications for a category, referrals for special education assessment must be academic and not behavioral in nature. The distinction between behavioral and academic referrals was implemented through the IDEA reauthorization in an attempt to reduce the number of minority referrals to special education based on behavioral problems alone (Donovan & Cross, 2002; Harry & Klingner, 2006).

Examining the referral process is critical for educational researchers interested in equity because referral is an important predictor of special education placement, and most students who are referred by their teachers are placed in special education (Donovan & Cross, 2002; Hilliard, 1992; Hosp & Reschly, 1993). In many cases the risk of referral is dependent upon how referred students compare to their classmates' academic achievement and behavior (Harry & Klingner, 2006). Local norms of acceptable and unacceptable student behavior influence the referral process, causing variability in the characteristics and composition of special education classrooms (Donovan & Cross, 2002).

Cultural Bias in the Referral Process

Without equity-oriented leadership, educators' biases (or benign neglect) can easily jeopardize the integrity of special education referral and placement processes—biases that significantly harm African Americans. Obiakor and Ford (2002) note how many African American children whom educators suspect need special education placement have been negatively affected not by disability but by poor instruction, deficit-based teachers who are culturally disconnected from them, and by educators as a whole who fail to see African American children through a lens of "goodness."

Research and the first-hand accounts of parents and critical educators, such as Ford (2002), Prater (2002), and Williams and colleagues (Williams, Frederick-Stanley, & Fair, 2002), have conveyed that the true educational needs of African American children can be conflated with or misdiagnosed as unfounded pathologies. In addition, educators often stereotype Black boys as being unintelligent and disruptive in school (Duncan, 2000; Ferguson, 2000; Howard, 2008; Monroe, 2005), and Black families as being dysfunctional or uncaring (Cooper, 2009; Edwards, 2004; Fields-Smith, 2006; Hale, 2001; Loder-Jackson, McKnight, Brooks, McGrew, & Voltz, 2007; Prater, 2002). Such students and families can be stigmatized by class and ability status, too. Children living in poverty typically come to school lacking basic resources and social exposure to aid them in excelling academically; yet their underperformance can be misconstrued as a learning deficiency, which causes educators to mistake the poverty-related effects on achievement for disability (Ford, 2002; Prater, 2002; Williams et al., 2002).

Frattura and Capper (2007), researchers and former special education teachers and administrators, state:

> Frankly we are shocked by the pervasiveness of this deficit view of families that persists even among well-meaning teachers and school leaders, among educators who have received some training in White privilege or

> poverty, and among educators who consider themselves leaders or advocates of social justice. We are also amazed by the unwillingness of these educators to engage with families of poverty, families of color, or families with same-gender parents, on these families' terms.
>
> *(p. 95)*

Given such observations, African American families with children who are suspected of having learning-related disabilities are more apt to face a destructive mix of educators' deficit-based thinking and educational practices that forever limit their educational pathways and life options. Many of the children come from families that lack economic resources, a fact that is too often overlooked by the assessors. In response, many African American mothers are left struggling to protect their children's interest in an educational system that has historically been unresponsive to their families' needs.

African American Mothers' Educational Participation

Parent involvement is essential for the successful academic outcomes of students (Hurd & Edwards, 1996; Hurd, Moore, & Rogers, 1995). K-12 educators indicate a desire to have parents participate in their children's educational decisions; however, many educators fail to involve parents and then blame parents for their lack of interest and desire to collaborate with schools (Cooper, 2009; Henry, 1996; Trotman, 2001). Further, some educators expect parents to participate in ways that align with the school's prescribed agenda. There is an expectation that parents will be visible on the school site, accessible to teachers, and provide students with the necessary materials needed for academic success (Cooper, Riehl & Hasan, 2010; Delgado-Gaitan, 1991; Lareau, 1996). Indeed, parents participate in their children's education in ways that reflect class and culture differences (Lareau, 1996). Low-income African American parents often feel isolated and marginalized in school settings (Cooper, 2005; Delgado-Gaitán, 1991; Harry, 1992; Hurd & Edwards, 1996; Lareau, 1996; Trotman, 2001). These feelings may contribute to their low visibility in schools.

Although some parents may not be physically present in schools, their absence does not mean they are not actively involved in their children's education. In fact, several researchers of parent involvement and African American families have found that African American parents engage in their children's schooling at home, including helping with homework, providing culturally relevant information to supplement the school curriculum, making their children practice reading and math skills, and promoting college (Cooper, 2009; Hurd & Edwards, 1995; Thompson, 2003). These activities illustrate a conscious decision by parents to be involved in their children's education.

Nevertheless, African American parents' participation in decisions regarding their children's special education placement is relatively low (Boyd & Correa, 2005; Harry, 1992; Rao, 2000). This low participation may be attributed to parents' views of the special education system. According to Boyd and Correa (2005), African American families' opinions of the special education system are shaped by several interrelated factors including: "(1) the socio-cultural experiences of African Americans in American society, (2) the development of biases toward educators working within the system, and (3) their level of acculturation" (p. 3). Although African American parents initially attempt to participate in the special education process, their efforts are often undermined by the structure of the system (Rao, 2000).

According to Harry (1992), the structure of the special education system reflects two professional thought traditions:

> (1) a deficit view of African American parents on which compensatory education practices have been based, and (2) the medical model on which special education is based and the resulting deficit view of African American children that has been promulgated by continued misassessment and miseducation.
>
> *(pp. 123–124)*

This belief structure posits African American families as socially and culturally deficient and constructs African American children as intellectually inferior or socially deviant compared to White students; as a result, it deters African American parents' advocacy and involvement. Indeed, African American parents and families often perceive special educators who uphold deficit-based beliefs as unfairly labeling them and their children as "at-risk," being disrespectful and discounting of cultural differences in parenting styles, and being overly focused on legal compliance and documents (Boyd & Correa, 2005; Rao, 2000). Because many African American parents feel disenfranchised, some withdraw their participation from the entire process while others struggle to advocate for their children.

Advocating to Assert and Reclaim Power

Educational advocacy is an essential act of both activism and care that parents and other caregivers demonstrate to protect children, secure equal educational opportunities for them, and hold educators accountable for both excellence and equity (Cooper, 2009). Advocacy displayed by marginalized individuals and groups is a courageous act often undervalued or unrecognized by educators (Cooper, 2007, 2009; Fields-Smith, 2006; Prater, 2002). Advocacy entails families not accepting a victim position or an apathetic role in education whereby they give up their power or wholly defer to the decisions, preferences, and expectations of educators and special education placement policies that do not always have all children's best needs in mind. Educators can feel threatened at times by families' advocacy, leading them to underestimate its importance because the culturally relevant forms of advocacy that many African mothers practice typically differs from the types of parent involvement activities educators welcome (Cooper, 2009). African American mothers' efforts to advocate for their children who are disproportionately labeled as "at-risk" or having special needs can vastly differ from other parent behaviors at schools that derive from White, middle-class norms (Cooper, 2009; Cooper, Riehl, & Hasan, 2010).

As Cooper (2009) explains, African American mothers' advocacy efforts include "advocating for the interests and needs of children before inequity arises; confronting educators to speak out against perceived inequities;...engaging in organized protests to bring about educational reform; and choosing alternative schools when traditional public schools lack satisfactory teachers, resources, and fair policies" (p. 390). Such practices involve "using culturally relevant strategies to negotiate predominantly White educational systems [to] be resilient in the face of educational racism, and to motivate their children to achieve" (Cooper, 2009, p. 382). Often these types of advocacy also involve families displaying anger or aggression that educators are quick to judge as bullying, irrational, and counterproductive; instead, these behaviors can be a meaningful, nonthreatening, and rational reaction to families' repeated experience of being devalued, dismissed, discriminated against, and excluded (Cooper, 2007, 2009).

African American mothers' angry reactions to these schooling experiences can particularly occur within special education contexts (Prater, 2002). Still, many mothers lack awareness of how to be effective advocates and end up assuming more passive roles in the special education referral process. The exclusionary and marginalizing dynamics of special education beg for educational leaders' intervention to help make the referral and placement process more equitable and family-friendly.

Conceptual Framework: The Politics of Containment

To understand the difficulty of forming effective school-family partnerships and parent involvement in special education, a conceptual framework is needed that considers the impact of power relations on the complicated, embedded, and intersecting nature of race, gender, and class in American public schools. Indeed, understanding the pervasiveness of the politics of containment within the special education system will help educators, researchers, and parents to recognize possibilities for collaboration beyond those that currently exist.

The term *politics of containment* refers to the power structures and dynamics that keep members of society in the particular socioeconomic and political spaces of either empowerment or disempowerment based on race, class, gender, sexual orientation, ability, and other identity factors (Collins, 1998; Giroux, 2005). As described below, two prominent containment strategies used to uphold hierarchical power relations in the United States are racial segregation and surveillance (Collins, 1998). Racial segregation leads to the "the division of racial groups into physical and symbolic spaces based on the belief that proximity to the group deemed inferior will harm the allegedly superior group" (Collins, 1998, p. 280). The second strategy of control is surveillance, "whereby people's words and actions are constantly watched and recorded" (Collins, 1998, p. 281). Surveillance in the new politics of containment is used to control, observe, and examine the lives of the poor and underprivileged. In special education, surveillance is evident in the heightened ways that African American males' behavior and achievement are monitored, scrutinized, and disciplined more harshly than those of other student groups in large part because of educators' presumptions that these males are predestined to academic failure or socially disruptive behavior (Children's Defense Fund [CDF], 2007; Ferguson, 2000; Monroe, 2005)

Three complementary bodies of theory inform our conceptual framework of the politics of containment in relation to special education, including Black feminist thought, critical race theory, and Foucault's philosophies of institutional power.

Links to Black Feminist Thought

Black feminist thought is an epistemological framework that addresses Black women's distinct ways of knowing, experiences, and understanding of the world (Collins, 1990, 2000). The framework considers both the oppression that Black women endure that relates to race, class, and gender, as well as their ability to resist such oppression and enact agency to improve their lives and the lives of their families. Collins's (1990) explication of Black feminist thought validates Black women's self-defined views and experiences while countering others' attempts to define, theorize, and tell the stories of Black women based on stereotypical assumptions, images, and narratives that maintain their subordination in society. She specifically situates Black women's life experiences and knowledge construction within the politics of containment (Collins, 1998).

In her discussion of the "new" politics of containment, Collins (1998) questions its effects on African American women and asks how and why, in spite of the significant gains and advancements made in the civil rights and the women's movements, African American women's position in modern society does not reflect these triumphs. In the past, African American women's oppression was evident in the legal policies of racial segregation and discrimination; however, within the new politics of containment, it relies on sophisticated and less obvious forms of racism. Indeed, the "changing patterns of the global economy, the wholesale denial of deeply entrenched racial practices in the United States," along with the "the emergence of a rhetoric of color blindness arguing that institutionalized racism has disappeared" challenge the reality that racial barriers still exist (Collins, 1998, pp. 30–31). Long gone are the legally sanctioned methods of control, segregation, and surveillance characterized by slavery and the Jim

Crow era. In the post-Civil Rights age African American women must live in the complicated reality of institutionalized racism and legalized desegregation.

For African American mothers involved in the special education referral process, the politics of containment can be seen in the multiple ways many educators view these mothers and their children as ignorant, deficient, or unworthy. Such biased attitudes, based on hierarchical power relations, lead to the oppression, marginalization, and segregation of African American students and their mothers. It is through these attitudes that educators can become deliberately or unknowingly complicit in excluding African American families from a high quality general education by enacting inequitable policies and practices; indeed many special education programs have segregating effects given that exceptional children are often placed and educated in classrooms and spaces apart from the majority of students in general classes (Burrello et al., 2001; Frattura & Capper, 2007). Moreover, educators often assume that African American mothers have limited knowledge while educators and other professionals have valuable knowledge and expertise; thus, exclusionary decisions like inappropriate special education placements are made.

The Institutional Power of Schools

To better understand the meaning of surveillance and racial segregation in the politics of containment, critical race theory (Ladson-Billings & Tate, 1995) and Foucault's (1979) theory of power are used to highlight the impact of normalization, the institutionalization of power structures, racism, and the connection between knowledge and power.

Critical race theory is valuable in illustrating the institutionalization of racial segregation and discrimination in the special education referral process. Using a critical race theoretical lens, it becomes evident that social and educational inequities "are logical and predictable results of a racialized society in which discussions of race and racism continue to be muted and marginalized" (Ladson-Billings & Tate, 1995, p. 47). Critical race theorists believe viewing race as a factor in inequity is critical; failing to do so denies the experiences of raced people and the problematic aspects of classification (Ladson- Billings & Tate, 1995). In the special education context, classification occurs once students are diagnosed with (or "classified" as) having a disability and referred to specialized services, they are then typically segregated and schooled in enclosed classrooms rather than thoroughly integrated into the academic and social spaces that nonexceptional children share (Burrello et al., 2001). Given the disproportionate placement of African Americans in special education, many special education programs end up being racially segregated and "contained" spaces as well (Kunjufu, 2005; Obiakor & Ford, 2002)

Foucault's theory of power is useful in understanding how surveillance operates within the special education referral process. In his work, Foucault sought to explain how through power, people are regimented, contained, and regulated. There are several institutions designed to enforce order, namely schools, the military, asylums, and prisons. Simply stated, schools are social institutions that teach people to respond in predictable ways (Cheshier, 1999). According to Foucault, education is a form of discipline used to maintain social order. Foucault theorized that power is a way to objectify human beings through their interactions with each other. In special education, disciplinary power and surveillance based on norms defined by White, middle-class cultural standards are the mechanisms of control used to perpetuate the politics of containment for African American women and their children. Thus, special education highlights the already entrenched notion of "otherness" that African American families feel when they encounter many educational leaders and teachers.

To illustrate our conceptual framework, we share the first author's first-person reflections on inequities in the special education process and then explore the politics of containment by analyzing a case example based on a realistic account of her experiences with mothers, teachers, and educational leaders in special education.

Reflections of a School Social Worker: April Ruffin-Adams

The child study team that decides whether students should be evaluated for special education services usually involves teachers, school administrators, psychologists, speech-language pathologists, special education teachers, a school social worker, and the parents of referred students. School social workers involved in the special education referral process are in a unique position to advocate for early intervention for behavioral and educational problems; inform parents of their rights (Allen-Meares, 2007); and counter deficit-based assumptions of African American families that erroneously lead some educators to underestimate African American families' educational involvement and care (Cooper, 2007, 2009). Drawing on their relationships with students and families in multiple contexts, social workers can consult with teachers as they make decisions to refer students for educational assessments that may potentially lead to special education placement. By asserting their role effectively, school social workers can contribute to the reduction of inappropriate special education referrals.

As a parent involvement school social worker in an urban elementary school, I was responsible for cultivating relationships with parents and school staff to help ensure student success. In my role I was often struck by the different ideas of involvement, participation, and knowledge held by educators and parents. My perspective was unique. I understood and saw firsthand the teachers and educational leaders who worked to make the best decisions for students based on their educational knowledge and experience. Unfortunately, too often these decisions were not informed by a broader understanding of the child that parents held, and they led to African American students, especially boys, being misplaced in special education "to get some extra help." However, as research on African American boys in special education reveals, a special education referral can negatively and permanently affect students' educational pathways (Harry & Anderson, 1994).

During my visits to students' homes, it was mothers who most often expressed concern and resignation about the possibility of their children being placed in special education. In many cases, the mothers viewed the impending placement as negative yet they felt compelled to follow the school's recommendations for their children. During my conversations with many of the mothers I visited, they cited the ways they were involved in their children's education. I listened as they detailed their trips to the local library, moments spent reading with their children, and nightly homework reviews. The majority of the involvement described by these women was not visible to the school staff. The apparent invisibility of mothers at school meetings and events impacted their ability to create effective partnerships with their children's teachers and school leaders. Such partnerships could have opened up lines of communication and trust to prevent misinformed special education referrals or facilitate proper placement, thereby minimizing the oppressive impact of the politics of containment.

The Role of Educational Leaders

In my experience as a school social worker, the role that principals and other educational leaders play in the referral and subsequent special education placement process greatly varies. For instance, I've witnessed some leaders participate in the initial child study meetings, where parents are not present, by observing and listening to team members share greater context about the student, their classroom setting, instruction, and performance. These leaders then serve as sources of information for parents or sources of teacher support at the referral meeting. As Frattura and Capper (2007) observe, however, such meetings are often filled with technical jargon and legalities that the average parent is challenged to understand. Some principals are hands-on in the process by actively offering opinions and clarification, while others are hands-off, do not attend special education-related meetings, and wait to receive reports from other administrators who attend.

At worst, however, I have seen principals work in concert with general education teachers to ensure that certain students with known discipline problems are placed in special education to alleviate classroom disruption and lower suspension rates, even when those students do not possess a true disability. The referral and placement decisions were made based on a belief as to what was best for classrooms or schools overall, yet the interests and rights of individual students were jeopardized as a result. Moreover, since students referred to special education are usually among the lowest performing students in their schools (Farkas, 2003), their removal from general education classes—and sometimes the school—also ensures that they do not decrease a school's test scores. Such restrictive responses by educational leaders and other staff are clearly inequitable yet they occur too often as leaders with inadequate preparation in special education respond to accountability pressures to produce high testing outcomes (DiPaola & Walther-Thomas, 2003).

Unfortunately, the literature that addresses both special education and leadership is scant. In line with my experiences, DiPaola and Walther-Thomas (2003) explain that "principals lack the course work and field experience needed to lead local efforts to create learning environments that emphasize academic success for students with disabilities" (p. 12) and often fall short of applying their role as instructional leaders to special education issues. Hence, leaders typically attend to procedural and legal compliance with IDEA rather than ensuring appropriate instruction for student progress.

The following case is based on actual parent-teacher interactions and events that occurred while I was a school social worker in a southeastern metropolitan school district. The names of all participants have been changed.

Illustrative Case Example: Ms. Chavis

Hansberry Elementary School is located in a small metropolitan area in the southeastern United States in a lower income, predominantly African American community. Hansberry was a new school with a new principal, Ms. Honeydew, a middle-aged White woman new to the Hansberry area. She boasted a proud record of test score improvement in her previous positions as principal. The stress of moving into the new school over the holiday break and the impending end-of-year testing had created an intense working, teaching, and learning environment for Ms. Honeydew, teachers, and students.

Aaron, a 12-year-old in the fourth grade at Hansberry, was becoming increasingly hostile and disruptive in class and had been referred for placement in an emotional-behavioral disorder classroom (EBD). A week before a scheduled meeting to discuss his assessment and special education placement, Aaron's mother, Ms. Chavis, a 25-year-old single, African American woman, called to say she was unable to come to the school to attend the meeting because she had to go to work. This was one of several rescheduled meetings for Ms. Chavis. Upon hearing about another postponed meeting, Ms. Honeydew became upset and decided to call Ms. Chavis's supervisor at the local taxicab company to inform him of the gravity of her son's situation. Together the principal and supervisor developed a plan to have Ms. Chavis released from work anytime she had a meeting at Aaron's school. Upon hearing about this development from her supervisor, Ms. Chavis came to the school a couple of days later enraged to confront Ms. Honeydew because she would lose money if she was unable to work. Ms. Chavis's supervisor would not allow Ms. Chavis to come back to work without notification from Ms. Honeydew. Confronted by the angry

Ms. Chavis, Ms. Honeydew remarked that if Ms. Chavis cared about her son's education, she would place it before her job.

This type of interaction had become typical for this mother and principal because most of their communication revolved around Aaron's discipline problems. In addition, Ms. Chavis had a functioning relationship with Aaron's teacher, Ms. Johnson, a veteran African American teacher who was the second teacher he had that year. He was placed in Ms. Johnson's class when he became too much of a distraction in his prior class, which was led by his first teacher, a White middle-aged woman who had returned to teaching after staying at home with her daughters for 10 years and who had made the original referral.

When the day of the original, scheduled meeting came, Ms. Chavis arrived at the school in time for the special education meeting after all, and she asked to "just sign" whatever paperwork was needed. Hurriedly, the team members consisting of the principal, me (the social worker), Aaron's teacher, and the school psychologist attempted to explain each form to Ms. Chavis. After the meeting several members of the team remarked that this was the first time they had seen Ms. Chavis in the school. I, at the time a young African American school social worker, interjected that I had worked with Ms. Chavis on several occasions and she seemed very engaged. I added that Ms. Chavis was a hard worker struggling to take care of her family, including three children, with limited education; the midmorning scheduled meeting was when Ms. Chavis made most of her cab fares. The team members responded in frustration that Ms. Chavis's effort and care were not apparent given her hostile attitude, her hurriedness at such an important meeting, and the fact that she had not participated in any other school event such as open houses, parent-teacher meetings, or the recent spring concert. Team members also stressed that no other time of day was convenient for a meeting given their class schedules.

After this meeting, team members agreed that all communication from the school to Ms. Chavis would be made through me, the school social worker, since I had established a good rapport with the mother, unlike Ms. Chavis's tense rapport with the principal or teachers. I began to work with Ms. Chavis to keep her informed of Aaron's progress in school and to schedule meetings during Ms. Chavis's off days. In return, Ms. Chavis shared how the experience in the meeting with Ms. Honeydew made her feel "useless and insulted." She said she was relieved that she could now just communicate with me.

Case Analysis

Several issues emerge from the case example that warrant further analysis using a politics of containment conceptual lens. Children and their parents involved in the special education system become a part of a complex legal system that has evolved because of a history of problems associated with special education service delivery and the ambiguity involved in conceptualizations of disability

(Ong-Dean, 2009). Smiley (2009) urges educators and researchers "to push ourselves to not just name the inequity but to also dissect the process within which it happens and interrupt that practice" (p. 18). Examining Ms. Chavis' experiences can help educators explore the ways in which the politics of containment operates in the special education referral process and how power relations, institutionalized racism, and surveillance influence the system.

Ms. Honeydew's phone call to and arrangements with Ms. Chavis's supervisor show how institutionalized power relations can impede collaborative school-family partnerships. Even if the principal's actions were well-intentioned, the mother perceived them as an attempt to control her life and interfere with her livelihood in ways that were unwelcome. The principal's treatment of the situation, by asserting unsolicited control over Ms. Chavis' decision-making, was an inappropriate use of power. Ms. Honeydew's actions perpetuated the politics of containment through the use of surveillance tactics which attempted to monitor and control Ms. Chavis's participation in Aaron's education (Collins, 1998). Though Ms. Chavis's involvement was needed, Ms. Honeydew's response reflected a belief that African American women are incapable of rational decision-making and adult behavior. This view effectively infantilizes poor Black women and further alienates them from active participation in the special education referral process (Collins, 1998).

Ms. Chavis's relationship with educational leaders at Aaron's school was impacted by her feelings of inadequacy when advocating for her son's education. Ms. Chavis did not feel equipped with the power, clout, or influence to effectively engage in dialogue with some of the educators. Although parents have had the ability to be involved in their children's special education decision making since the 1970s, parents who take advantage of this policy are typically affluent, educated, and comfortable making claims regarding their children's education (Ong-Dean, 2009). To further complicate matters, Ms. Chavis's visibility in Aaron's school was limited by her need to work to provide for her family. From a Black feminist perspective, the lack of dialogue between Ms. Chavis and the school made her invisible to the educators working with her son. Indeed, her lack of presence in the school left Aaron's teachers to form their own image of her as a parent and to draw their own conclusions about her involvement in his education. Ms. Chavis's advocacy efforts for her son were best known by his teacher, Ms. Johnson, and by myself as the social worker, with whom Ms. Chavis felt comfortable communicating. While I saw this mother as an involved parent and tried to convey her situation to other staff, my efforts were not enough to bring about an effective school-family partnership. Ms. Chavis's attempts to advocate against oppressive educational practices and the ways she demonstrated care for her child were viewed by the school as aggressive and angry rather than understood as acts of political and social resistance to the politics of containment she and her son experienced at Hansberry School.

Aaron's behavior issues in his first classroom with the White teacher prompted the special education referral. However, Aaron's behavior problems improved significantly after he was moved to Ms. Johnson's class in the middle of the school year. Ms. Johnson was able to work collaboratively with Ms. Chavis, Aaron, and me (the school social worker) to create a more positive and productive learning environment for Aaron. Ms. Johnson's understanding of African American students may have helped facilitate the successful relationship building. Because some African American students, particularly those coming from low-income families, are reported to display behaviors that are less compatible with the school environment than those of their White and Asian American peers (Farkas, 2003), it is imperative to have teachers and school administrators who understand those behaviors and are willing to work collaboratively with families to assist struggling African American students.

Leadership Recommendations and Conclusions

The exclusionary and marginalizing dynamics that can emerge as part of the special education referral and placement process with African American families beg for educational leaders' guidance and intervention so that such processes will become more equitable and family-friendly. Given the critical role that educational leaders play in shaping school climate, instructional quality, student expectations, and home-school relations, we assert it is essential that partnering with families who are referred to special education services be integrated into the core of leaders' work (Burrello et al., 2001; DiPaola & Walther-Thomas, 2003; Frattura & Capper, 2007). As Frattura and Capper (2007) explain, it is not uncommon for a social worker to be the only person who seeks the personal history of families and establishes a significant rapport with them, as opposed to teachers and school leaders doing so as well. Hence, just as in our case example of Ms. Chavis, the responsibilities of developing family-based knowledge of students and strong home-school relationships can get relegated to one person versus being a shared practice that educational leaders model for teachers and staff.

To better partner with families, we affirm the need for leaders to work with teachers and staff to ensure that parents and other adult caregivers be more informed about their children's academic or behavior challenges as soon as educators detect them; that families and other caregivers be engaged in dialogue at the first consideration of a special education referral so educators and staff can learn from their perspectives and consider alternative options and preventative measures (Ford, 2002); that families be fully informed of their rights and options in layperson's language (Frattura & Capper, 2007); and consulted about convenient times (and sometimes locations) for meetings. Such practices align with Auerbach's (2010) recommendations that leaders coconstruct authentic partnerships with families by sharing power, supporting their advocacy, and collaborating with them in a way that makes them feel valued and engages them in democratic participation. Auerbach (2007) further suggests that leaders can be most effective when they collaborate with families from a place of moral imperative, instead of approaching partnership work as an add-on duty, a top-down process, or as a mere strategy to increase achievement.

The hardest and most important part of creating authentic school-family partnerships involves making ideological shifts; building trust with those families perceived as different; rejecting deficit-based thinking and practices; and exiting one's comfort zone in order to learn and lead with others (Cooper, Riehl, & Hasan, 2010). Theories regarding the politics of containment help reveal that all stakeholders lose when families are judged or "surveilled" through deficit-based lenses and when they are pressured to "normalize" to educators' expectations without educators also being sensitive to families' cultures, lifestyles, and needs. Students can end up segregated into inappropriate programs and settings, families can become more isolated from and repelled by schooling, and educators can lose the chance to help students achieve and fully contribute to schools and communities. For African Americans and other families of color, the politics of containment also perpetuate racism.

Of course, the responsibility of integrating special education, leadership, and family partnership work should not fall on just one person. Educational leaders must receive assistance at multiple levels to improve partnerships. This entails university leadership preparation programs developing curriculum and internship experiences that groom leaders who not only know the special education law, but who learn to provide instructional leadership in this area. Leaders must also confront stereotypes of disability and develop inclusive approaches to serving students and families in the special education process (Dooley & Dooley, 2002; Prater, 2002). Furthermore, school districts should provide professional development to leaders that assists them in their growth and enables them to increase the knowledge and team-building skills of others. For instance, it is imperative that both general and special education teachers improve their ability to fairly assess students' exceptionalities based on appropriate criteria and legitimate impairments rather than stereotypic assumptions related to race, class, gender, or ability (Dooley & Dooley, 2002; Frattura & Capper, 2007).

Finally, it would greatly help to develop professional learning communities that incorporate collaborative inquiry activities, engage general and special educators in dialogue and resource sharing, and prompt educators and staff to critically reflect on their views about culture, family, diversity, and disabilities (Ford, 2002; Shepherd & Hasazi, 2007). Ideally, families would also participate in such groups, even on an occasional basis, so that all school community members could develop shared vision and goals. Partnership success rests on the actions of families, too. Once educators reach out to families, then families must marshal the courage to collaborate and take risks to increase their trust in educators' efforts and care.

Overall, there are many ways to resist the politics of containment that hinder the partnerships between educators and African American families in special education. Resistance requires effort, cooperation, and ultimately, transformative leadership from all parties to encourage greater student advocacy, nurture alliances, and improve children's educational experiences and outcomes.

Note

1. Camille M. Wilson previously published under Camille Wilson Cooper, including the works listed in our references as Cooper, C. W.

References

Allen-Meares, P. (2007). *Social work services in schools* (5th ed). New York: Pearson.

Auerbach, S. (2007). Visioning parent engagement in urban schools: Role constructions of Los Angeles administrators. *Journal of School Leadership, 17*(6), 699–735.

Auerbach, S. (2010). Beyond coffee with the principal: Toward leadership for authentic school-family partnerships. *Journal of School Leadership, 20*(6), 730–759.

Blanchett, W. J. (2006). Disproportionate representation of African American students in special education: Acknowledging the role of White privilege and racism. *Educational Researcher, 35*, 24–28.

Boyd, B. A., & Correa, V. I. (2005). Developing a framework for reducing the cultural clash between African American parents and the special education system. *Multicultural Perspectives,* 7(2), 3–11.

Burrello, L. C., Lashley, C., & Beatty, E. E. (2001). *Educating all students together: How school leaders create unified systems*. Thousand Oaks, CA: Corwin Press.

Cheshier, D. (1999, December). Foucault & Educational Reform, *The Rostrum - National Forensic League's magazine*. Retrieved from http://www.nflonline.org/uploads/Rostrum/debate1299_cheshier.pdf

Children's Defense Fund (CDF). (2007). *America's cradle to prison pipeline: Summary report*. Washington, DC: Author.

Collins, P. H. (1998). *Fighting words: Black women and the search for justice*. Minneapolis: University of Minnesota Press.

Collins. P. H. (1990). *Black Feminist Thought: Knowledge, Consciousness, and the Politics of Empowerment*. Boston: Unwin Hyman.

Collins, P. H. (2000). *Black feminist thought: Knowledge, consciousness, and the politics of empowerment* (2nd ed.). New York: Routledge.

Cooper, C. W. (2005). School choice and the standpoint of African American mothers: Considering the power of positionality. *Journal of Negro Education, 74*(2), 174–189.

Cooper, C. W. (2007). School choice as "motherwork": Valuing African American women's educational advocacy and resistance. *International Journal of Qualitative Studies in Education, 20*(5), 491–512.

Cooper, C. W. (2009). Parent involvement, African American mothers, and the politics of educational care. *Equity and Excellence in Education, 42*(4), 379–394.

Cooper, C. W., & McCoy, S. Z. (2009). Poverty and African American mothers: Countering biased ideologies, representations, and the politics of containment. *Journal of the Association for Research on Mothering, 11*(2), 47–57.

Cooper, C. W., Riehl, C. J., & Hasan, L. (2010). Leading and learning with diverse families in schools: Critical epistemology amid communities of practice. *Journal of School Leadership, 20* (6), 760–790.

Decuir, J. T., & Dixson, A. D. (2004). "So when it comes out, they aren't that surprised that it is there": Using critical race theory as a tool of analysis of race and racism in education. *Educational Researcher, 33*(5), 26–31.

Delgado-Gaitán, C. (1991). Involving parents in the schools: A process of empowerment. *American Journal of Education, 91,* 20–46.

DiPaola, M. F., & Walther-Thomas, C. (2003). Principals and special education: The critical role school leaders. Gainesville, FL: The Center for Personnel Studies in Special Education, University of Florida.

Donovan, S. Z., & Cross, C. T. (2002). *Minority students in special and gifted education.* Washington, DC: National Academy Press.

Dooley, E. A., & Dooley, K. L. (2002). Legal foundations of special education for African American learners. In F. E. Obiakor & B. A. Ford (Eds.), *Creating successful learning environments for African American learners with exceptionalities* (pp. 17–25). Thousand Oaks, CA: Corwin Press.

Duncan, G. (2000). Urban pedagogies and the celling of adolescents of color. *Social Justice, 27*(3), 29–42.

Duncan, G. (2002). Beyond love: A critical race ethnography of the schooling of adolescent Black males. *Equity & Excellence in Education, 35*(2), 131–143.

Edwards, P. A. (1993). Before and after school desegregation: African-American parents' involvement in schools. *Educational Policy,* 7(3), 340–369.

Farkas, G. (2003). Racial disparities and discrimination in education: What do we know, how do we know it, and what do we need to know? *Teachers College Record, 105*(6), 1119–1146.

Ferguson, A. A. (2000). *Bad boys: Public schools in the making of Black masculinity.* Ann Arbor: University of Michigan.

Fields-Smith, C. (2006). Motivation for participation: Why highly involved African American parents participate in their children's education. *Journal of School Public Relations, 27*(3), 234–257.

Ford, B. A. (2002). African American community resources: Essential education enhancers for African American children and youth. In F. E. Obiakor & B. A. Ford (Eds.), *Creating successful learning environments for African American learners with exceptionalities* (pp. 159–173). Thousand Oaks, CA: Corwin Press.

Foucault, M. (1979). *Discipline and punish: The birth of the prison.* New York: Vintage Books.

Frattura, E. M., & Capper, C. A. (2007). *Leading for social justice: Transforming schools for all learners.* Thousand Oaks, CA: Corwin Press.

Giroux, H. A. (2005). *Border crossings.* (2nd ed.). New York: Routledge.

Hale, J. (2001). *Learning while Black: Creating educational excellence for African American children.* Baltimore, MD: Johns Hopkins University Press.

Harry, B. (1992). Restructuring the participation of African American parents in special education. *Exceptional Children, 59*(2), 123–131.

Harry, B., & Anderson, M. G. (1994). The disproportionate placement of African American males in special education programs: A critique of the process. *Journal of Negro Education, 63*(4), 602–620.

Harry, B., & Klingner, J. (2006). *Why are so many minority students in special education? Understanding race and disability in schools.* New York: Teachers College Press.

Henry, M. E. (1996). *Parent-school collaboration: Feminist organizational structures and school leadership.* Albany: State University of New York Press.

Hilliard, A. G. (1992). The *pitfalls* and *promises* of special education practice. *Exceptional Children,* 59(2), 168–172.

Hosp, J. L., & Reschly, D. J. (2003). Referral rates for intervention or assessment: A meta-analysis of racial differences. *Journal of Special Education, 37,* 67–80.

Howard, T. C. (2008). Who really cares? The disenfranchisement of African American males in PreK-12 Schools: A critical race theory perspective. *Teachers College Record, 110*(5), 954–985.

Hurd, E. P., & Edwards, M. J. (1996). A long time in this world: Parental involvement among African American families. *School Social Work Journal, 20,* 13–24.

Hurd, E. P., Moore, C., & Rogers, R. (1995). Quiet success: Parenting strengths among African Americans. *Families in Society, 76*, 434–444.

Individuals with Disabilities Education Act (IDEA PL 101-476, 101st Cong., 104 Stat. 1142 (1990).

Kearns, T., Ford, L., & Linney, J. A. (2005). African American student representation in special education programs. *The Journal of Negro Education, 74*(4), 297–310.

Kunjufu, J. (2005). *Keeping Black boys out of special education.* Chicago, IL: African American Images.

Ladson-Billings, G., & Tate IV, W. (1995). Toward a critical race theory of education. *Teachers College Record, 97*, 47–67.

Lareau, A. (1996). *Unequal childhoods: Class, race, and family life.* Los Angeles, CA: University of California Press.

Loder-Jackson, T. L., McKnight, A. N., Brooks, M., McGrew, K., & Voltz, D. (2007). Unmasking subtle and concealed aspects of parent involvement: Perspectives from African-American parents in the urban south. *Journal of School Public Relations, 28*(4), 350–379.

Monroe, C. R. (2005). Understanding the discipline gap through a cultural lens: Implications for the education of African American students. *Intercultural Education 16*(4), 317–330.

North Carolina State Board of Education. (2008). *Procedural safeguards: Handbook on parents' rights.* Retrieved from http://www.ncpublicschools.org/docs/ec/policy/resources/2008/parent-handbook.pdf

Obiakor, F. E., & Ford, B. A. (2002). School accountability and reform: Implications for African Americans with exceptionalities. In F. E. Obiakor & B. A. Ford (Eds.), *Creating successful learning environments for African American learners with exceptionalities* (pp. 3–15). Thousand Oaks, CA: Corwin Press.

Ong-Dean, C. (2009). *Distinguishing disability: Parents, privilege, and special education.* Chicago, IL: University of Chicago Press.

Prater, L. P. (2002). African American families: Equal partners in general and special education. In F. E. Obiakor & B. A. Ford (Eds.), *Creating successful learning environments for African American learners with exceptionalities* (pp. 145–157). Thousand Oaks, CA: Corwin Press.

Rao, S. (2000). Perspectives of an African American mother on parent-professional relationships in special education. *Mental Retardation, 38*, 475–488.

Reschly, D. J. (1993). Consequences and incentives: Implications for inclusion/exclusion decisions regarding students with disabilities in state and national assessment programs. In J. E. Ysseldyke & M. L. Thurlow (Eds.), *Views on inclusion and testing accommodations for students with disabilities* (pp. 35–46). Minneapolis: University of Minnesota, National Center on Educational Outcomes.

Shepherd, K., & Hasazi, S. B. (2007). Leadership for social justice and inclusion. In L. Florian (Ed.), *The Sage handbook of special education* (pp. 475–485). London: Sage.

Smiley, A. D. (2009, Winter). Consenting adults: Conducting case conferences with confidence. *Connections: The Journal of the National School Reform Faculty.* Retrieved from http://www.harmonyschool.org/www/pdf/connections/2009.win.consenting_adults.pdf

Thompson, G. L. (2003). *What African American parents want educators to know.* Westport, CT: Praeger.

Trotman, M. F. (2001). Involving the African American parent: Recommendations to increase the level of parent involvement within African American families. *Journal of Negro Education, 70*, 275–285. Retrieved from http://search.proquest.com/docview/222068520?accountid=14604

U.S. Commission on Civil Rights. (2009, April). *Minorities in special education: A briefing before the United States Commission on Civil Rights.* Retrieved from http://www.usccr.gov/pubs/MinoritiesinSpecialEducation.pdf

U.S. Department of Education. (2009, July). *Achievement Gaps How Black and White Students in Public Schools Perform in Mathematics and Reading on the National Assessment of Educational Progress Statistical Analysis Report.* Washington, DC: U.S. Printing Office.

West-Olatunji, C. A., & Baker, J. C. (2006). African American adolescent males: Giving voice to their educational experiences. *Multicultural Perspectives, 8*(4), 3–9.

Williams, D. L., Frederick-Stanley, C., & Fair, A. (2002). Culturally responsive leadership for African Americans with exceptionalities. In F. E. Obiakor & B. A. Ford (Eds.), *Creating successful learning environments for African American learners with exceptionalities* (pp. 205–216). Thousand Oaks, CA: Corwin Press.

6

AUTHENTIC ENGAGEMENT WITH BICULTURAL PARENTS AND COMMUNITIES

The Role of School Leaders

Edward M. Olivos

It has become an almost unquestionable truth in education research, policy, and practice that school-home-community collaboration is an important ingredient for academically successful schools and students (Henderson & Mapp, 2002). Few researchers, teachers, or school officials would openly doubt that there appears to be some form of positive return for students when their parents are involved and when educators make efforts to reach out to parents and community members (Epstein, 2001; Henderson & Berla, 1994). In fact, Henderson and Mapp (2002) concluded in their synthesis of family and community involvement literature that "the evidence is consistent, positive, and convincing: families have a major influence on their children's achievement in school and through life" (p. 7).

Despite the research supporting the benefits of active parent participation, some assumptions about this practice are problematic, especially when referencing bicultural (i.e., "minority") parents and communities (Boethel, 2003; Jordan, Orozco, & Averett, 2001). The first issue concerns the definition of parent involvement and who has the authority to define it. Whose definition of parent involvement is legitimized and whose values does this definition represent? This leads us to the second issue, which is identifying the "appropriate roles of family and community members in connections with the schools" (Jordan et al., 2001, p. viii); that is, those actions that are accepted by school authorities as desirable and legitimate forms of parent participation. And, finally, the third issue concerns understanding how commonly accepted definitions of parent involvement and appropriate roles are applied to bicultural parents and communities. Specifically, what are the additional expectations and limitations educators place on parents from nondominant bicultural communities?

Darder (1991) identifies as bicultural those individuals and groups who "learn to function in two distinct sociocultural environments: their primary culture, and that of the dominant mainstream culture of the society in which they live" (p. 48). Biculturalism is thus a form of mediation that individuals and groups participate in as they negotiate dominant discourses about their existence while also facing their own distinct lived realities as members of subordinate cultures. Darder further argues that the term *bicultural* represents a more accurate picture of contemporary public school populations than the commonly used adjective *minority*. The latter is not only a misnomer in many school contexts but it is also "a term that linguistically, and hence politically, reflects and perpetuates a view of subordinate cultures as deficient and disempowered" (p. xvi).

This chapter deals critically with the concept known as "parent involvement" in schools by first problematizing current practices as they relate to bicultural parents. Next it highlights what I argue are embedded tensions in the relationship between bicultural parents and school authorities (administrators and teachers) that often preclude and hinder genuine relationships between them (Olivos, 2004, 2006). The chapter concludes by presenting a framework for engaging bicultural communities in working through these tensions by advocating for a paradigm shift toward greater parent engagement rather than mere involvement. The goal here is to move the idea of bicultural parent participation in schools away from an "accommodationist" perspective toward a more "transformational" perspective (Shirley, 1997). Parent involvement refers here to traditional practices of parent participation in education while parent engagement,[1] as defined by Shirley (1997) "designates parents as citizens in the fullest sense—change agents who can transform urban schools and neighborhoods" (p. 73). This broader educational and political goal expands the concept of involvement to include school reform and increased civic engagement, leadership capacity development, and community development.

Sanctioning Parent Involvement

In general, in the research literature, "involved" parents are those who participate in traditional and recognizable parent involvement activities or demonstrate supportive behaviors that educators believe benefit their students' academic and social endeavors (Henderson & Mapp, 2002; Jordan et al., 2001). Involved parents may, for example, attend school-sponsored functions, get to know other parents, or talk more frequently to teachers or administrators. Moreover, involved parents may be privy to information about their children's school experiences or their rights as parents; they therefore may be in a better position to intervene on their children's behalf when school-centered problems arise. By contrast, "uninvolved" parents are often identified as those who fail or refuse to participate in school-sanctioned activities or who demonstrate disobliging attitudes or behaviors in the eyes of school authorities (Shannon, 1996). These are the parents who educators believe are oblivious to the goings-on at the school and their children's education. They may not know who their children's teachers are, they do not fill out school paperwork in a timely or correct manner, or they do not know how to get answers for school-related questions. They and their children are therefore in a disadvantaged position to reap all the benefits that schools have to offer.

The traditional body of research on parent involvement attempts to show a direct relationship between parent involvement in schools and student achievement. Low levels of parent involvement are often linked to low academic achievement, while higher levels of parent involvement apparently influence higher student achievement (Henderson & Mapp, 2002). However, a simple correlation between parent involvement and academic achievement is problematic for bicultural parents on several fronts (Jordan et al., 2001). For example, existing conceptual and methodological approaches to parent involvement often center around an archetypal middle-class White family, which tends to either ignore or negate bicultural parents' realities, what they have to offer their children, and what they can achieve in the school context (Brantlinger, 2003; Olivos, 2006).

A Narrow Band of Accepted Parent Behavior

There is an overemphasis on school-centered definitions of parent involvement in the research literature and in practice. Educators generally define and operationalize it using a narrow band of accepted, deferential behaviors and outcomes (Jordan et al., 2001; McCaleb, 1997; Olivos, 2006). In practice, this is played out when "family and school involvement frequently means helping reach goals defined by schools (administrators and teachers) that reflect only school values and priorities" (Jordan et al., 2001, p. viii). Relying exclusively on school- and institution-centered definitions of parent involvement is problematic for bicultural working-class parents and communities, however, since school authorities often provide them with very few decision-making opportunities as it is.

The band of acceptable parent involvement behaviors constricts as the social and cultural capital of the parents declines in social prestige (Lareau & Horvat, 1999). For example, upper- and middle-class parents may be expected and encouraged to choose from a broader array of involvement activities (participating on hiring committees, budget committees, and district-level advising), while bicultural, working-class, and low-income parents may be encouraged to follow more closely regimented and restricted activities (helping their children with homework, signing permission slips, and volunteering with paper cutting or making copies).

Educators' Attitudes

Educators' attempts to sanction the roles and influence of parents in the school context, particularly bicultural parents, have led some researchers to conclude that despite "official rhetoric in its favor, parent involvement is not always regarded favorably by school personnel" (Henderson, Marburger, & Ooms, 1986, p. 2). For some educators, this may be a bold or even unfair statement—an indictment against school personnel or their well-intentioned actions. It has been my experience, however, that this statement is often quite accurate (Olivos, 2006, 2008). There are indeed those in our schools who just do not want to deal with another set of prying eyes or ears. And while the number of educators who actually feel this way may be small, the impact it has on parents' and communities' feeling of being welcomed in schools is noticeable and damaging (Allen, 2007; Olivos, 2006).

This is a delicate scenario for educational leaders who strive to make parents feel welcome and who promote opening doors to communities that have often felt neglected. Educators have an occupational responsibility to help all students do well. However, neither teachers nor school administrators have impenetrable boundaries that protect them from the biases, tensions, or inequalities of the surrounding community or broader society (Darder, 1994; Olivos, 2006). Educators' view of those who deserve deference often depends on the social standing of the individuals or groups in the broader society (Brantlinger, 2003; Lareau, 1989; Lareau & Horvat, 1999). As Lawrence-Lightfoot (1978) accurately stated over 30 years ago, "Sociopolitical and ideological visions are brought to the classroom [and the school] through the values, attitudes, and behaviors of teachers" (p. 5). These biases are operationalized in the interpersonal relationships between educators, students, and parents, and in the expectations and tolerance educators have of nondominant parents and communities (Núñez, 1994; Olivos, 2004, 2006)

Educator discomfort with parental "intrusion" in professional educational matters amplifies when it is intertwined with preconceived beliefs and biases about certain bicultural children or communities (Allen, 2007; Brantlinger, 2003; Lareau & Horvat, 1999; Lawrence-Lightfoot, 1978). These perceptions about families and communities are not static, however. They range along a continuum from seeing parents from a deficit perspective to seeing them from an additive one (Gonzalez, Moll, & Amanti, 2005; Valencia & Black, 2002). Where educators' perceptions eventually lie are more often than not contingent on their personal views about parents' social position in the racial and economic hierarchy (Allen, 2007; Lightfoot, 1978).

Contradictory Expectations

Researchers have documented contradictions between educators' expectations of bicultural parents, who do not share the cultural and linguistic capital of the school, and what they are actually allowed to do (Auerbach, Chapter 3, this volume). Lareau (2003), for example, concluded that educators often held contradictory expectations of parents, expecting them to be unquestionably supportive of and deferential to school decisions but also wanting parents to "take leadership roles in solving their children's educational problems" (p. 27 as cited in Allen, 2007, p. 5). Shannon (1996) put forth a similar argument when she aptly stated that:

> Parent involvement for minority language parents can be paradoxical. Traditionally, they are not involved and teachers complain. However, teachers also complain about the aggressive parent involvement of majority, middle-class Anglo parents. If minority language parents choose to become involved, they may be perceived ... to be aggressive. Unfortunately, the majority parents' aggressiveness is tolerated, whereas the minority parent's [*sic*] action may be not only ignored and dismissed but also attacked as irrational.
>
> (*p. 83*)

The above noted paradox must be acknowledged for what it is: contradictory and disingenuous. Educators cannot have it both ways. They must be sincere in their beliefs of what they want and expect from parents (*all* parents) and identify those contradictory messages that are sent to families. School leaders can help in this process by having school personnel problematize the concept of parent involvement under the guiding premise that not all forms of parent involvement are the same (Olivos, 2006). That is, not all parents are truly treated equally in our schools, nor are their endeavors equally valued (Fine, 1993; Ramirez, 2003; Shannon, 1996). After acknowledging this contradiction, school leaders can help move school personnel forward by identifying mindsets, policies, and practices that either explicitly or implicitly devalue the contributions of bicultural parents and communities. This is done with the goal of helping schools verify if their practices are inclusive or restrictive of bicultural parents' and communities' input and contributions.

Bicultural Parent Engagement

A significant portion of the current body of literature about parent involvement assumes that the experiences and expectations of bicultural parents fit within a one-size-fits-all European American middle-class paradigm. For example, critics of Joyce Epstein's (2001) often cited and used framework point out that it puts forward members of middle- and upper-class White communities "as models to emulate" (Brantlinger, 2003). This one-sided definition of involvement often results in educators being at odds with bicultural families who may have different ideas of how they wish to be involved in their children's education (Cline & Necochea, 2001; Hughes, Valle-Riestra, & Arguelles, 2002

Núñez, 1994; Olivos, 2006, 2008; Ramirez, 2003). Thus, whereas educators frequently tend to "view a parent's role solely as a support for academic achievement," parents may see their role as "supporting the total well-being of the child" (Jordan et al., 2001, p. 13). This may mean then, for example, that some bicultural parents feel uncomfortable engaging in long honored school traditions like Open House or parent-teacher conferences, or in meeting the time commitment expectations for volunteering and homework assistance (Ramirez, 2003).

As Henderson et al. (1986) noted 25 years ago, parent participation in schools can assume many different forms. More recently, Allen's (2007) work on partnerships with culturally, linguistically, and economically diverse families emphatically rejected many conventional indicators of parent involvement for their lack of authenticity. She argued that "counting the number of parents who come to PTA meetings, bring cookies to parties, or sign reading logs is not the kind of parent involvement that leads to increased academic development" (p. 8). She called instead for a parent involvement framework that has a "transforming vision," one that will forge authentic relationships and partnerships between schools and culturally and linguistically diverse communities. Other researchers have similarly argued for a transformative framework of parent involvement (McCaleb, 1997; Olivos, 2006; Olivos & Ochoa, 2006a, 2006b), as outlined later in this chapter.

The experience of bicultural parents challenges implications of the Epstein typology that parent involvement is an apolitical affair, that the school system functions equitably for all students, and that bicultural parents' reception and treatment at schools are equal to those of their middle- and upper-class White counterparts. Henderson and Mapp (2002) aptly acknowledged that "while engaging families can help improve student achievement, it is not enough to overcome the deficits of low-quality schools" (p. 76)—a factor that is often ignored in parent involvement research.

Bicultural parent engagement in public schools is by nature an inherently political endeavor (de Carhalho, 2001; Oakes & Rogers, 2006; Shirley, 1997). That is, the need to make failing schools more responsive to bicultural communities by questioning and acting against dominant institutional and personal bias is a political project (Fine, 1993). So, too, is the belief that parent engagement should include as a goal the development of bicultural parents as community change agents (Olivos & Ochoa, 2006a, 2006b; Shirley, 1997). This development can include tapping into community skills, knowledge, beliefs, and assets (González et al., 2005), as well as organizing for community change and increased political and civic engagement (Evans, 2009; Oakes & Rogers, 2006; Shirley, 1997).

Organizing and working for educational and social transformation is empowering for all involved. Bicultural parents begin to see themselves as change agents and self-interest evolves to include a broader array of social and community concerns (Evans, 2009). Similarly, as educators begin to understand the sociopolitical and economic conditions that create inequities in schools and communities, they can take action alongside parents to develop a transformational reform effort (Olivos, 2006). It is not until school authorities become aware of the social inequalities in bicultural school communities and their role in perpetuating those conditions, however, that they will be able to visualize a path of action.

Listening to the Voices of Bicultural Parents: Tensions between Families and Schools

As the public schools become more ethnically, racially, linguistically, and economically diverse, educators are turning more toward the parents and the community for support of their work in educating children. Yet, how sincere is the outreach to parents? How involved do educators actually want the parents to be? Parent participation in schools will always involve some sort of tension, particularly if there are differing views about what should be happening in the schools or if parents begin raising concerns. Furthermore, as Shannon (1996) pointed out above, educators only seem to accept critiques from parents who they perceive as knowledgeable in school affairs or whose middle- or upper-class socioeconomic status requires some level of acquiescence on the part of school personnel.

In over 15 years of working with bicultural parents, many have expressed to me feelings of being unwanted or intimidated at their children's schools. Even those parents who have experienced empowerment as school activists have expressed frustration in trying to deal with schools that are unfriendly and unkind, and school authorities who are unreceptive or openly hostile (Cline & Necochea, 2001; Olivos, 2004, 2006; Ramirez, 2003). This has always been a difficult situation for me as I've tried to understand how school personnel can claim to want to involve parents but also by the same token create climates or display attitudes that make some parents feel unwelcome. In my research, I have documented the following issues as prevalent themes in the concerns of bicultural parents, primarily Latino families: insincere outreach for partnerships, devaluing native culture and language, low academic quality or academic rigor, and institutional and personal biases against bicultural students and parents (Olivos, 2004, 2006, 2009; Olivos & Ochoa, 2008). Below I provide some examples that have implications for school leaders who aspire to more authentic engagement with bicultural families.

Insincere Outreach Efforts

Parents I have worked[2] with over the past two decades have often said that one of the greatest barriers to their involvement in their children's schools was the lack of sincerity in outreach for partnerships on the part of the school authorities (teachers and administrators). The parents understood the strong association between productive home-school relations and student school performance and well-being. But they felt that many school authorities did not communicate with them in an open, welcoming manner. As a result, these bicultural parents felt disrespected by or alienated from the school, and relationships with school authorities were weak or nonexistent.

An example of this pattern can be seen in a Latina mother's interpretation of a principal's letter sent home to all parents:

> We received a letter at the beginning of the week, during the first days of the school year, where it stated very nicely, "We'd like to have the children get to know their teachers. We want there to be a bond between the teacher and the child. We need the parents to please maintain a distance until we call for them." In other words, "We don't want you here." So this affected the parents who, instead of helping the teachers with their work, left. So, we had a group of [Latino] parents [who were interested in being involved at my child's school], but with so many prerequisites [scheduling visits, signing logs, confirming visits with the administrator, etc.] she [the principal] got rid of us. No. There is a big problem at [my child's school]. The principal doesn't accept any visitors. No. She can't. She's too busy to see anybody.

While the interpretation of the letter by this parent can certainly be questioned, the impact it had on her perception of the school's relationship with the Latino parents cannot. That is, only the principal knows the actual intent of her letter just as only the parent knows how this letter affected her motivation and desire to be present at her child's school. According to the above quote, it is apparent that the letter merely served to distance the school administrator from a group of parents that may have already been hesitant to be involved at the school.

Other parents I've worked with have found the insincerity of school officials via more subtle interactions. In the example below, another Latina mother, who was a member of the School Site Council and Governance Team, reflects on her "conforming" relationship with the school principal. Conformity in this context refers to the parent's belief that she would not question the authenticity of the principal's overtures, despite concerns raised by other parents about the principal's receptivity to their input in school matters. The parent attributed this conformity not to a lack of effort on the part of the principal but to a lack of sincerity in her overtures to the parents:

> I was very conformist so long as the principal had after school activities, carnivals, parent meetings; if she would bring us bread or coffee. She goes out to greet the kids, speaks very nicely to the [Latino] parents. With that

> she keeps the [Latino] parents very happy and submissive. As long as she keeps doing that, we're not going to say anything. Because I'm going to say, "Well, the principal always comes out. She comes out to greet the children. She brings us coffee, she has meetings." That's conformity.

While the principal's attempts to greet parents and offer refreshments may seem like a very positive step toward bicultural parent engagement, this parent was questioning the sincerity of their initial interactions during a period of disagreement with the principal about decision-making matters at the school (Olivos, 2003). Again, the principal's actual intent is only known by her. Yet, the parent's interpretation is noteworthy in that it demonstrates a lack of trust in and respect for the principal's actions. This perceived insincerity is particularly problematic in that both examples above come from a school context in which bicultural (mostly Latino) families constituted over 85% of the population. This distrust, of course, is also problematic if school leaders are indeed determined to improve relationships with bicultural parents.

A similar disconnect in the perceptions of school leaders and Latino parents about outreach became apparent at an educational summit that I helped organize in Eugene, Oregon, in 2010. The school and district authorities in attendance proudly shared their efforts to better reach out to bicultural parents and community members. These administrators saw themselves as having engaging and welcoming environments at their schools for all parents, but this was often contradicted by the words and experiences of the Latino parents in attendance. The parents consistently voiced concerns about distant or cold relationships between teachers and parents, lack of communication and sincerity in the schools' outreach efforts, and underrepresentation in school decision-making.

For school leaders, the challenge is clear. If more authentic home-school partnerships are sought, then outreach and relationships matter. Insincere overtures by school officials are difficult to mask and easy to recognize. This insincerity is not only apparent in the tone of communications and the restrictive band of acceptable behaviors educators allot to bicultural parents. It is also exemplified when bicultural parents are periodically invited to participate in school discussions, but poorly represented in actual decision-making at the school.

School leaders must therefore promote in their buildings a reexamination of existing relationships between schools, families, and communities, as Allen (2007) and many authors in this volume recommend. This reexamination must not only be focused on those teachers or staff members who display blatantly hostile attitudes toward bicultural parents but on the entire school culture and its practices. These practices may be perceived by school personnel as being inclusive or open, but for bicultural parents, many of these same practices may in fact be viewed as distancing, disrespectful, or insincere.

Devaluing Native Culture and Language

Parents I've worked with throughout the years (most notably in California and more recently in Oregon) have often complained that districts, schools, and educators do not capitalize on the communities' cultural and linguistic capital. Many of these parents want their children to know two languages or have access to their native/heritage language. This is both an important life skill for the children and a way to facilitate parent participation in their learning, as one parent observed in discussing a bilingual program:

> The instruction that the schools provide our children in their native language helps them to form values and ideologies that are comprehensible to them. And we as parents can participate more actively in their education as well as contribute with all our history to our children.

This message regarding bicultural children's home language is lost on many educators. Parents have often felt that the educators at their children's schools viewed and treated non-English-speaking or non-White parents as lacking in useful skills and their native language as deficient (Olivos, 2006). For parents in California, this dynamic was most evident in their struggle to have their children either placed in, or be allowed to remain in bilingual education classes after Proposition 227, the 1997 ballot measure that severely limited bilingual education access in California. This was demonstrated poignantly in the words of a Latina mother I knew in San Diego who objected to the district's attempt to dismantle the existing bilingual education programs: "The district puts out a very flashy sign saying that it supports bilingualism and the Latino students' native language, but it's a deception. They manipulate us politically, socially, and economically so that they can take away our language."

Bicultural and bilingual parents also believed that schools did not make efforts to reach out to non-English speaking communities, even if they constituted the majority of the school population. They pointed to the lack of translators, school personnel who represented the community's racial or linguistic composition, and accessible materials in languages other than English (Zehr, 2011).

My experience in working with Spanish-dominant Latino parents has led me to conclude that often bicultural parents are merely looking for positive affirmations of their native cultures and languages in their children's schools. This affirmation can take various forms from having bilingual and bicultural school personnel to having a school curriculum or outreach effort that acknowledges the diversity of the school community. The efforts called for, in my opinion, are minimal in terms of personnel and resources, yet the outcomes and results could be meaningful. School leaders who take steps to affirm bicultural families' language and culture, backed up by sincerity in outreach to parents who do not speak English as their primary language, could see greatly improved relations with bicultural communities.

Low Academic Quality and Rigor

In addition to concerns about outreach and language, the parents I've worked with have also raised concerns about the quality of education their children were receiving. They expressed dismay that their children were being provided with what they perceived to be an education that was lower in rigor, with less accountability and fewer resources than schools in more affluent areas. As one parent commented on the contrasts between schools in low- versus high-income communities:

> One begins to notice the difference right away, "We don't have this. They do. This we don't have either, but they do." One notices that the differences begin all the way from the streets. I notice and I wonder: "Why do they have so many schools and we don't?" Our children have to get up early, at five o'clock in the morning, in order to be ready at 6 a.m. at the bus stop. Why all this? It's affecting our children.

This particular parent was upset about the fact that many parents had to send their children to schools in more affluent areas of her city in order to get a "good" education. She expressed dismay at there not being strong academic opportunities for community children in the local schools. She and other parents I worked with also felt that although poor academic programs and low teacher and administrator accountability for results affected their children's opportunities to learn, the blame for low achievement was often placed on the parents (Olivos, 2003, 2006). As she stated, "The school wants to dodge all of its responsibility and instead blames us, the parents" (Olivos, 2003, p. 155).

In my work in Oregon, bicultural parents raised similar issues about the quality of education their children were receiving. They voiced concerns about large class sizes, lack of academic advising, low teacher and school expectations for their children, and poor oversight of poor teachers.

Concerns about low academic quality are often uncomfortable for educators to address since they typically feel they know best about "professional" educational matters and are therefore hesitant to admit deficiencies in their programs. Yet, this is an area that must be appropriately scrutinized if school officials sincerely value the voice and opinions of their constituents. Indeed, as Henderson and Mapp (2002) noted, parent involvement should not be used as a supplement to poor academic instruction or school shortcomings.

Institutional and Personal Bias

In my research I frequently have come across bicultural parents who reported bias against them and their children in schools. They highlighted what they felt were factors that contributed to mistreatment and negative attitudes, and they named these biases racism or elitism (Cline & Necochea, 2001; Olivos, 2006).

Numerous researchers have also documented either the presence of overt racism or classism in schools against bicultural or low-income parents, or the perception parents have about the existence of racism and classism at their children's schools (Bratlinger, 2003; Cline & Necochea, 2001; Lareau & Horvat, 1999; Olivos, 2006; Ramirez, 2003). These parents often express that they feel looked down upon or infantilized by school authorities. To illustrate, I present an incident involving a Latina mother, which she interpreted as being racist.

This mother was an active member of her school's governance committee as well as an often outspoken critic of the principal. After one incident in which the mother had repeatedly requested to meet with the principal, this mother relayed her concern to another neighborhood parent who also had a child at the same school. The other parent was a White, English-speaking woman whose husband was a teacher at a local high school. Upon hearing the Latina mother's complaint, the White parent became concerned as well as she viewed herself as an ally to the Latino parents, and she made a request to speak to the principal. She was granted this meeting immediately despite the fact that the principal had ignored repeated requests by the Latina mother to meet about the same issue. The Latina mother commented:

> One notices the difference. If one has a problem and they send a note to the principal asking for a meeting, they never get a response, the principal doesn't reply. They don't give you a response. And that's what we noticed when we were in a particular struggle. When we would send complaints, we'd never get a response. Then one day, one of the ladies that was with us, not completely but she supported us, sent the principal a letter asking for a meeting. She's American [White]. That very same day she got a meeting. That very same day!

The extent to which acts of racism or classism are verifiable from the perspective of educators is definitely a different story. Just because parents view a practice as racist does not necessarily make it so. But why would school authorities allow their school's policies or practices to even be perceived in that light? Indeed, allowing negative perceptions about schools to go unaddressed only leads to further community disengagement. These are difficult conversations about diversity, equity, and social justice that school leaders should be engaged in with not only their staff but also the community at large.

School Leaders Can Make the Difference

The data examples in this chapter are interpreted using conceptual frameworks I have developed individually (Olivos, 2004, 2006) and with colleagues over the last 10 years (Olivos & Ochoa, 2006a, 2006b; Olivos, Jiménez-Castellanos, & Ochoa, in press). The frameworks I draw from have two independent but interrelated goals in mind. The first is to identify those tensions around equity and diversity (e.g., race, class, immigration status, gender, language) that create mindsets and assumptions that then lead to deficit-based parent engagement policies and practices (Valencia & Black, 2002). The second goal of the frameworks is to move the idea of parent participation in schools for bicultural parents from an accommodationist perspective to a more "transformational" perspective that advocates for the democratization of schools. It is my belief that only through sincere, purposeful, and authentic engagement with bicultural parents and communities around these goals, will schools be able to properly serve their children. When parents are engaged as critical partners, parent and community engagement is linked to learning (Henderson & Mapp, 2002); when families are engaged as advocates for student progress, their children perform better and have higher school retention (Parent Institute for Quality Education [PIQE], 2010; Ritblatt, Beatty, Cronon, & Ochoa, 2002); and when schools work with community organizers they get results (Henig, Hula, Orr, & Pedescleaux, 1999; McAlister et al., this volume; Oakes & Rogers, 2006; Shirley, 1997).

In my book, *The Power of Parents* (2006), I include several sections that address the role of administrators in home-school-community relations. Many of the scenarios described, taken from the voices and experiences of bicultural parents, unfortunately paint administrators as barriers who resist change. Many bicultural parents recognized that the principal is the person with the most relative power in the school and that nothing positive can really happen without the sincere support of school administrators. Yet, many of these parents "have indicated to me that these individuals are the persons that most impede their relationship with the school" (Olivos, 2006, p. 95).

For politically active parents and teachers, school administrators have been characterized as resistant to community efforts to disrupt inequitable schooling practices (Olivos, 2006). They are seen as individuals who are more loyal to their careers and the existing school system, despite its embedded inequities, than to the communities and students they serve (Olivos & Ochoa, 2008). For administrators, this critique is a hard pill to swallow. Much like coaches of professional sports teams, principals are often given too much credit and equally too much blame for the conditions at local schools. Notwithstanding, clearly, principals are the individuals onto whom responsibility falls for poor performance or poor home-school relations. Thus, it is school leaders who must lead the charge in working toward creating an authentic collaboration between schools, bicultural parents, and bicultural communities.

Working toward Authentic Collaboration with Bicultural Parents and Communities

This chapter calls on school leaders and other educators to have a transformative vision for bicultural parent engagement that also acknowledges the importance of tensions and inequalities inherent in social and cultural politics. It asks school leaders to be cognizant of the fact that as human beings, we all walk through the "ideological fog" of our social training, which often has not done enough to help us understand our biases so we can make an effort to control them. Our goal as educators, however, is to begin to observe the school community and to realize there are many social and institutional inequities that we ideologically oppose and that we must act upon. Schools and society are engaged in a constant interplay of influence, in which outside society affects what goes on in the school and what takes place in the school influences the outside society (Lawrence-Lightfoot, 1978; Olivos, 2006). When school leaders ignore the dynamic interaction between society and the school, they are resisting the natural phenomenon of human interaction. It takes more effort and energy to resist the social and cultural politics within the school than to move with the fluid changes and shifts of the needs of school communities. Schools currently represent the status quo that is not working for bicultural parents, and bicultural communities represent the flow necessary to democratize schools. School leaders would do better if they tried to understand the flow of the needs of the communities rather than contain it.

I have argued elsewhere for a "socio-constructivist approach" to parent engagement that values bicultural parents' perspectives and contributions (Olivos & Ochoa, 2006a, 2006b). The actualization of this model calls for bicultural parents and community members to stop seeing themselves as docile "objects" driven by the dominant monocultural values and practices of the school culture. Rather, they should see themselves as "subjects" who create spaces to promote activities and practices that reduce inequality of access and oppressive practices. The model calls for them to be critical coinvestigators involved in dialogue, reflection, and action with each other in the micro and macro spaces of their community. Participants as subjects are involved in community work that creates democratic schooling and social awareness for actualizing cultural and economic democracy (Shirley, 1997). Such a guiding framework must be provided if educators are to understand the transformational potential for involving bicultural parents in the public schools.

Most existing approaches to parent involvement do not seek to create the conditions necessary to examine power relations and educational access and equity (Olivos, 2006; Olivos & Ochoa, 2006a, 2006b). The empowerment of parents requires both individual consciousness and social action. Through empowerment, students and parents learn to critically appropriate the knowledge that exists outside of their immediate lived experiences so as to broaden their understanding of themselves, the world, and the possibilities for transforming their lives (McLaren, 2007). School leaders should engage bicultural parents in education with this transformation in mind.

As I conclude this chapter, I reflect on my short period as an interim principal at a small urban charter school in San Diego, which had a very diverse population. Viewing home-school relations from this transformational perspective allowed me to understand the complex experiences school leaders encounter in trying to balance personnel, academic, and community issues. Pressures to increase test scores, manage dwindling budgets, and follow school regulations are indeed real challenges. Notwithstanding these challenges, during my short time in this position, I tried to implement what I believed were engaging practices for bicultural parents and community members. This included inviting them into budget meetings, hiring committees, and curriculum discussions. Their contributions were powerful and these were meaningful opportunities to make their views known to educators.

It is impossible to avoid tensions in schools. Tensions and conflict are ever present, particularly when diverse groups share close quarters and have divergent (or what may appear divergent) outcomes and outlooks. It is therefore up to school leaders to model authentic relationships with bicultural communities and to create conditions at their schools that will allow for difficult and necessary conversations about equity, diversity, and school democratization to take place. It will be through this partnership that urgently needed systemic change will happen.

Notes

1. I use the term *parent involvement* when referring to most existing practices or conceptualizations of parent and community participation in schools and the term *parent engagement* when referring to what I consider "transformational" practices and conceptualizations (Olivos & Ochoa, 2006a, 2006b).
2. The quotes in this section come from various studies I have done over the last 15 years. They are also translated from Spanish. In some cases they are summarized rather than verbatim.

References

Allen, J. (2007). *Creating welcoming schools.* New York: Teachers College Press.

Boethel, M. (2003). *Diversity: School, family, and community connections.* Austin, TX: National Center for Family & Community Connections with Schools.

Brantlinger, E. (2003). *Dividing classes: How the middle class negotiates and rationalizes school advantage.* New York: RoutledgeFalmer.

Cline, Z., & Necochea, J. (2001). ¡Basta ya! Latino parents fighting entrenched racism. *Bilingual Research Journal, 25*(1&2), 1–26.

Darder, A. (1991). *Culture and power in the classroom: A critical foundation for bicultural education.* Westport, CT: Bergin & Garvey.

de Carvalho, M.E.P. (2001). *Rethinking family-school relations: A critique of parental involvement in schooling.* Mahwah, NJ: Erlbaum.

Epstein, J. L. (2001). *School, family, and community partnerships: Preparing educators and improving schools.* Boulder, CO: Westview Press.

Evans, M. P. (2009). *Inside education organizing: Learning to work for educational change* (Unpublished doctoral dissertation). Boston College, Chestnut Hill, MA.

Fine, M. (1993). [Ap]parent involvement: Reflections on parents, power, and urban public schools. *Teachers College Record, 94*(4), 682–710.

González, N., Moll, L. C., & Amanti, C. (Eds). (2005). *Funds of knowledge: Theorizing practices in households, communities, and classrooms.* Mahwah, NJ: Erlbaum.

Henderson, A. T., & Berla, N. (Eds). (1994). *A new generation of evidence: The family is critical to student achievement.* Washington, DC: National Committee for Citizens in Education.

Henderson, A. T., & Mapp, K. L. (2002). *A new wave of evidence: The impact of school, family and community connections on student achievement.* Austin, TX: Southwest Educational Development Laboratory.

Henderson, A. T., Marburger, C. L., & Ooms, T. (1986). *Beyond the bake sale: An educator's guide to working with parents.* Columbia, MD: The National Committee for Citizens in Education.

Henig, J., Hula, R., Orr, M., & Pedescleaux, D. (1999). *The color of school reform: Race, politics, and the challenge of urban education.* Princeton, NJ: Princeton University Press.

Hughes, M. T., Valle-Riestra, D. M., & Arguelles, M. A. (2002). Experiences of Latino families with their children's special education program. *Multicultural Perspectives, 4*(1), 11–17.

Jordan, C., Orozco, E., & Averett, A. (2001). *Emerging issues in school, family, and community connections.* Austin, TX: National Center for Family & Community Connections with Schools.

Lareau, A. (2003). *Unequal childhoods: Class, race, and family life.* Berkeley, CA: University of California Press.

Lareau, A., & Horvat, E. M. (1999). Moments of social inclusion and exclusion: Race, class, and cultural capital in family-school relationships. *Sociology of Education, 72*(1), 37–53.

Lawrence-Lightfoot, S. (1978). *Worlds apart: Relationships between families and schools.* New York: Basic Books.

McCaleb, S. P. (1997). *Building communities of learners: A collaboration among teachers, students, families, and community.* Mahwah, NJ: Erlbaum.

McLaren, P. (2007). *Life in schools: An introduction to critical pedagogy in the foundations of education* (5th ed.). Boston, MA: Pearson.

Núñez, R. (1994). *Schools, parents, and empowerment: An ethnographic study of Mexican-origin parents' participation in their children's schools.* Unpublished Doctoral Dissertation. Claremont, CA/San Diego, CA: Claremont Graduate School & San Diego State University.

Oakes, J., & Rogers, J. (2006). *Learning power: Organizing for education and justice.* New York: Teachers College Press.

Olivos, E. M. (2003). *Dialectical tensions, contradictions, and resistance: A study of the relationship between Latino parents and the public school system within a socioeconomic "structure of dominance."* Claremont, CA/San Diego, CA: Claremont Graduate University & San Diego State University.

Olivos, E. M. (2004). Tensions, contradictions, and resistance: An activist's reflection of the struggles of Latino parents in the public school system. *The High School Journal: Chicana/o Activism in Education: Theories and Pedagogies of Trans/formation, 87*(4), 25–35.

Olivos, E. M. (2006). *The power of parents: A critical perspective of bicultural parent involvement in public schools.* New York: Lang.

Olivos, E. M. (2009). Collaboration with Latino families: A critical perspective of home-school interactions. *Intervention in School and Clinic, 45*(2), 109–115.

Olivos, E. M., Jiménez-Castellanos, O., & Ochoa, A. M. (Eds.). (in press). *Bicultural parent engagement: Advocacy and empowerment.* New York: Teachers College Press.

Olivos, E. M., & Ochoa, A. M. (2006a). Toward a transformational paradigm of parent involvement in urban education. In J. Kincheloe, P. Anderson, K. Rose, D. Griffith, & K. Hayes (Eds.), *Urban education: An encyclopedia* (pp. 196–208). Westport, CT: Greenwood.

Olivos, E. M., & Ochoa, A. M. (2006b). Operationalizing a transformational paradigm of parent involvement: Parent voice and participation. In K. Cadiero-Kaplan, A. M. Ochoa, N. Kuhlman, E. M. Olivos, & J. Rodriguez (Eds.), *The living work of teachers: Ideology and practice* (pp. 199–217). Covina, CA: California Association for Bilingual Education (CABE).

Olivos, E. M., & Ochoa, A. M. (2008). Reframing due process and institutional inertia: A case study of an urban school district. *Equity and Excellence in Education, 41*(3), 1–14.

Parent Institute for Quality Education (PIQE). (2009). *Parent Institute annual report.* Retrieved from http://piqe.org/Assets/Corporate/AnnualReports.htm

Ramirez, A. Y. F. (2003). Dismay and disappointment: Parent involvement of Latino immigrant parents. *The Urban Review, 35*(2), 93–110.

Ritblatt, S. N., Beatty, J. R., Cronon, T. A., & Ochoa A. M. (2002). Relationship among perceptions of parent involvement, time allocation, and demographic characteristics: Implications for policy formation. *Journal of Community Psychology,* 7(5), 519–549.

Shannon, S. (1996). Minority parent involvement: A Mexican mother's experience and a teacher's interpretation. *Education and Urban Society, 29*(1), 71–84.

Shirley, D. (1997). *Community organizing for urban school reform.* Austin, TX: University of Texas Press.

Valencia, R. R., & Black, M. S. (2002) Mexican Americans don't value education!—On the basis of the myth, mythmaking, and debunking. *Journal of Latinos and Education, 1*(2), 81–103.

Zehr, M. A. (2011). *Civil rights deal signals federal push for translation services: Expanded services for parents part of Phila. accord..* Retrieved from http://www.edweek.org/ew/articles/2011/03/03/23language.h30.html?tkn=UXYFGmB2VSzSVZyFlxQ0hq9F83%2FzLDBhyVrO&cmp=clp-edweek

PART III

Leading Partnerships through Policy and Program Development

7

POLICY ASPIRATIONS AND DILEMMAS OF IMPLEMENTATION

Leadership for Partnerships in Ontario, Canada

Joseph Flessa and Hélène Grégoire[1]

The current educational policy environment in North America focuses on leadership, particularly principal leadership, as a powerful lever for school change. "School leadership sits in the first position," according to one study of school reform (Bryk, Sebring, Allensworth, Luppescu, & Easton, 2010, p. 197). In fact, a review of the literature on the impact of leadership concludes that "leadership is second only to classroom instruction among all school-related factors that contribute to what students learn at school" (Leithwood, Louis, Anderson, & Walhstrom, 2004, p. 3). Reform advocates from the political right and political left, applying lessons from effective schools research, argue that the right person in the principal's office makes much, if not all of the difference in organizing adults' work effectively within the school to raise academic standards and reduce achievement gaps. To state this another way, "The school principal … orchestrates the collaborative process of school transformation" (Bryk et al., 2010, p. 203).

Research on parent engagement and community partnerships often tells a similar story. Case studies of dedicated educators resisting prevailing deficit-based perspectives about communities, making important connections beyond the walls of the school, have contributed to our understanding of what kinds of partnerships are possible under the right conditions and with the right supports and people (e.g., Auerbach, 2007; Cooper, Riehl, & Hasan, 2010; Pushor & Murphy, 2004).

Nevertheless, such illustrations are by definition exceptional, worthy of examination precisely because the portrait they provide of school-community connections is unusual. Under what conditions would positive connections between home and school become typical rather than exceptional? To answer such a question requires a look at policy because policy can be understood as an instrument to promote broader system change and to bring local, idiosyncratic efforts to scale. In this chapter we are interested in the ways that Ontario provincial policies relevant to community engagement and partnership articulate aspirations for bringing schools and communities into closer collaboration. We are aware of work like that of Schutz (2006), which has examined the ways that parent and community engagement policies have failed to live up to their lofty goals. Our reflective chapter differs in approach. Rather than evaluating effectiveness, we have chosen to describe the programs and initiatives that make up the policy landscape and the assumptions that drive them. In part, our decision is shaped by the fact that the policies we examine are quite new; little systematically gathered, publicly available data exist to support evaluatory conclusions. We believe that a description like ours, by highlighting prevailing trends, can point out ways that gaps or blind spots might affect results.

We begin the chapter by briefly describing the public education system in Ontario and then describe the educational policies and various programs that support a range of school-family-community partnerships. After drawing attention to some of the assumptions and tensions that undergird the policies and programs, we identify the dilemmas of assessing engagement policies. We conclude by reflecting on the ways the Ontario experience confirms or complicates other researchers' observations about school reform and parent-community engagement and by suggesting implications for leaders.

The Ontario Policy Context

With a few notable exceptions (e.g., Hands, 2008; Malatest & Company, 2002; Pushor, 2010), most of the North American literature on parent engagement describes the experience of U.S. schools. By focusing on the experience of Ontario, Canada, this chapter contributes to readers' understanding of different approaches available to policymakers outside a U.S. accountability framework shaped by No Child Left Behind (2002).

Ontario is Canada's most populous province and home to its largest city, Toronto. There are slightly more than 2 million students in elementary and secondary education in the province. About 95% of these students are enrolled in English language schools while 5% attend French language schools (Canadian Education Association, 2010, p. 24).

In Canada, public education falls under provincial jurisdiction, with the exception of federally funded elementary and secondary schools in First Nations communities. Although the past decade has shown a growing role for federal policy in shaping what happens in U.S. schools, there is little political interest, regardless of ideology, in increasing the federal role in Canadian education (Nagy & Lupart, 1994). Organizationally, Ontario also differs notably from U.S. jurisdictions in that it publicly funds Catholic schools. Overall, the system is made up of 72 district school boards led by the Ministry of Education, including 31 English Public, 29 English Catholic, four French Public, and eight French Catholic boards (Anderson & Ben Jaafar, 2006).

For most of the past decade, Ontario has been the site of a high profile and well-documented systemwide school reform movement (see Campbell & Fullan, 2006; Levin 2007, 2008). Given its strong emphasis on centralized policy levers, we have chosen to focus this chapter on provincial policy rather than district or school-based policy. Although districts and schools clearly will differ in their approaches to and success in forming authentic partnerships, the overriding policy framework at this time in Ontario emphasizes centralized policies originating in government ministries. In some instances school districts are given flexibility in the application of policy frameworks and expectations. Nevertheless, the goals are set centrally and the policies we describe set parameters for thinking about partnerships in school contexts. We are not suggesting here that school-family-community connections originated in Ontario with these policies. Indeed, all local communities and schools have histories of involvement and a range of experiences and relationships. Our point is that the current policy environment sends certain signals about what counts as engagement and partnership, what kinds of partnerships are valuable and warrant additional coordination or funding support, and what resources and incentives are required to support stated goals. Noticing what is included in policy conversations about partnerships as well as what is left out can assist us in understanding the emphases and, potentially, outcomes of various approaches.

Ontario school reform has three stated core priorities: "high levels of student achievement … reduced gaps in student achievement … [and] increased public confidence in publicly funded education" (Ontario Ministry of Education, 2008, p. 4). To support these three goals, the government has founded an English-style secretariat focused on numeracy and literacy, aligned curriculum and testing, funded class size reduction in grades 1 through 3, and established a strategy to increase high school completion rates (see Canadian Education Association, 2010). Simultaneously, alongside these reforms are several initiatives designed to increase, improve, or create a range of forms of participation and partnership between schools and communities, as we describe below.

Educational Policies that Support Partnerships

According to Auerbach (2010), *authentic partnerships* are defined as "respectful alliances among educators, families, and community groups that value relationship building, dialog, and power-sharing as part of socially just, democratic schools" (p. 731). Such partnerships require new mental models that are no longer based on deficit thinking but rather on a strength-based perspective. Reciprocal, two-way relationships cannot develop without a strong belief that each partner has something of value to contribute (Auerbach, Chapter 3, this volume). What is the role of policy in cultivating these sorts of beliefs and in fostering relational trust and power sharing? Our analysis here is based on a systematic examination of provincial policies that either explicitly address parent-community engagement with schools or, from our perspective, serve potentially to support such goals. One of our purposes is to provide a descriptive basis for understanding the current policy environment in Ontario relevant to community engagement.

Policy Tenets and Assumptions

In our scan of the Ontario policy context, we identified 12 specific policies pertinent to partnerships. Given the significance of changes in government to Ontario education policy, we limited our examination to 2005 to 2010, years when a Liberal government implemented its education agenda. The policies we examined lay out specific guidelines for schools on topics ranging from the mundane (school facilities use, contracting external partners) to issues with greater historical and political import (equity, inclusive education, French language schools, and First Nation, Métis, and Inuit education). One policy directly addresses leadership (Ontario Leadership Strategy and the Leadership Framework) and one policy explicitly names parent engagement (Parent Engagement Policy). Table 7.1 provides a brief summary of the 12 initiatives.

TABLE 7.1 Provincial Policies Related to School-Family-Community Partnerships

Policy	*Description*
Parent Engagement	
Parents in Partnership: A Parent Engagement Policy for Ontario Schools (2010)	Lays out goals for collaboration and connection between systems and parents.
Regulation 330/10 (2010)	Amends Ontario Regulation 612/00, which required schools to have school councils, to also require school boards to establish Parent Involvement Committees (PIC) at the district level.
Equity and Inclusion	
First Nation, Métis and Inuit Education Policy Framework (2007)	Calls for Ministry of Education, school boards, and schools to work together to improve the academic achievement of the Aboriginal students who attend provincially funded schools in Ontario. Strong school-community partnerships are essential to achieving the goals set out in the framework.
Ontario Equity and Inclusive Education Strategy (2009)	Outlines "a series of annual action items that provide a clear direction for the Ontario education community to identify and remove discriminatory biases and systemic barriers to student achievement and celebrate diversity and respect for all in our schools."

Policy	*Description*
Policy/Program Memorandum 119 (2009)	States that "All publicly funded school boards will review and/or develop, implement, and monitor an equity and inclusive education policy."
Policy Statement and Guidelines on the Admission, Welcoming and Support of Students in French-Language Schools in Ontario (2009)	Asks French-language school boards to clarify and streamline their admission policies, and to develop or update a protocol to make French-language schools more welcoming of students and parents.
Politique d'aménagement linguistique (PAL) (2005)	Policy intended to help educational institutions increase their capacity to create teaching and learning conditions that foster the development of the French language and culture to ensure the academic achievement of every student.
Leadership	
Ontario Leadership Strategy (2006)	Three-year action plan with goals for recruitment, selection, and professional development of school site leaders.
Ontario Leadership Framework (2006)	Describes a set of core leadership competencies and effective practices for principals, vice-principals and supervisory officers, including skills in actively engaging the diverse community, building collaborative cultures, and engaging in dialog which builds community partnerships.
Infrastructure	
Facility Partnerships Guideline (2010)	Directs all school boards to develop policies regarding the facility partnership process, including the notification of potential community partners about available space and co-building opportunities.
Partnerships with Community and Social Services Agencies	
Policy/Program Memorandum 149 (2009)	Protocol for partnerships with external agencies for the provision of services in Ontario schools by regulated health professionals, regulated social service professionals, and paraprofessionals.
Safe School Strategy (2008)	Aimed at ensuring that students feel safe at schools and on school grounds and at more effectively combining discipline with opportunities for students to keep learning. Alternative to suspensions and expulsions, as well as services offered to students who have been expelled or are on a long-term suspension may involve referrals to a community agency.

A look across these policies suggests that the role of Ministry policy is first to identify particular topics warranting action by districts and schools; to identify aspired-to goals; and finally to lay out the governance or organizational mechanisms through which actions should proceed. Given our focus on leadership for partnerships, four of the policies warrant special attention here. First and most obvious is the Parent Engagement Policy, which lays out goals for collaboration and connection between systems and parents. The policy recognizes, encourages, and supports many forms of parent engagement; identifies strategies to remove barriers to involvement (e.g., communications and language); supports parents in acquiring the skills and knowledge they need to be involved in their child's learning; and provides for parent voice at the local level. In addition, the policy statement, Ontario Regulation 612/00, which required schools to have school councils, was amended by Regulation 330/10 in 2010 to require school boards to also establish a Parent Involvement Committee (PIC) at the district level. The government currently provides boards with base funding of $5,000 and 17 cents per student for a PIC and an additional $500 per school council to support parent engagement activities.

These policies assume that statements of policy goals have important symbolic importance. It operates with the logic that mandated structures will encourage formalization of relationships between parent-community groups and schools-districts, and that parents will benefit from these connections just as schools do. Finally, the policy acknowledges that funding is necessary to support the work of parent committees within schools and districts.

A third policy relevant for discussions of partnerships, particularly in schooling contexts where they have been least likely to have been sustained or, in times of changing demographics, have been most challenging to establish, is the Ontario Equity and Inclusive Education Strategy. The strategy provides direction to "identify and remove discriminatory biases and systemic barriers to student achievement and celebrate diversity and respect for all in our schools" (Ontario Ministry of Education, 2009a, p. 2). One of its guiding principles is that "effective and meaningful school–community partnerships are an essential component of an equitable and inclusive education system" (Ontario Ministry of Education, 2009b, p. 13). Specific expectations for school boards and schools include implementing strategies to review existing community partnerships so that they reflect the diversity of the broader community and working toward representation of diverse groups on school committees. Policy/Program Memorandum No. 119 states, "All publicly funded school boards will review and/or develop, implement, and monitor an equity and inclusive education policy."

Implicit in this policy is the idea that data collection instruments designed to identify equity barriers related to racism, sexism, homophobia, and other forms of discrimination are key in closing achievement gaps. Furthermore, this policy suggests that achievement goals and school-community goals are not in conflict. The policy also assumes that equitable partnerships require relationships with a diverse range of communities and that school committee structures are an important aspect of partnership work; therefore, committee membership matters.

Finally, the Safe School Strategy shows an interesting connection between partnerships and explicit outcomes like reduced bullying and improved school climate. School boards are required to provide programs to students who have been expelled or are on a long-term suspension that allow them to continue their education and access services such as anger management or career counseling. The policy instructs schools to respond to all inappropriate behaviors in the most appropriate way instead of using automatic suspensions and expulsions; this could include a range of consequences, such as meetings with parents and referrals to community agencies. As a result of this policy, school boards are encouraged to work more closely with local community agencies, such as mental health providers and child and family services, and are given funding to provide at-risk students with access to additional community-based supports. Every school is also required to have a safe school team, which must include parent representatives and a community partner. An assumption here is that negative behaviors inside schools require outside supports to be addressed effectively. The committee structure institutionalizes one form of connection between home and school; the policy's encouragement to connect youth with mental health or other social supports outside school creates an incentive for school leaders to scan the environment for partners with whom to collaborate.

These policy frameworks are interesting to us because of the ways in which they seek to address both elementary and secondary schools at once. Much of the parent involvement literature focuses on the elementary sector, whereas much of the community partnerships literature focuses on the secondary sector (e.g., Hands, 2005, 2008, Chapter 10, this volume). These provincial policies straddle both. Interestingly, the Leadership Strategy, while asserting the importance of partnerships, strikes us as one step away from direct partnerships work and support. It is undeniably important to establish expectations for the selection and evaluation of school administrators, and include in the list of competencies some skill at making connections with families and community. But their results are also less immediately observable than those of other policy instruments listed in Table 7.1.

Dilemmas of Implementation

Several implementation dilemmas apply across the policies we examined. What are the inducements or drivers within policy that might be expected to change behavior? Although we acknowledge the symbolic weight and importance of Ministry statements on equity or First Nations education, we are unclear as to what incentives exist to move potentially reluctant schools or districts toward operationalizing Ministry goals. To put it colloquially, we wonder if the carrots attached to some of these policies (e.g., money for parent committees at the district and school levels) are sufficiently appetizing to make districts take on the hard work of establishing positive relationships where previously there may have been, at best, mistrust. And this may not even be the right question. If school leaders are engaging parents and community members solely because they expect a carrot (in the form of money or some other reward), then they are not doing it out of a genuine belief that parents have something important to contribute.

Consistent with an observation one of us made elsewhere, few of these policies deal "directly with educators' attitudes or beliefs about parents" (Flessa, 2008, p. 20). We see some evidence in the Equity and Inclusive Education Strategy and the First Nation, Métis, and Inuit Education Policy Framework of the importance placed on cultural awareness. Given the leadership imperative to resist deficit-based attitudes about parents as a prerequisite for establishing true partnerships, as noted by Flessa (2009) and many authors in this volume, the absence of explicit attention to deficit thinking in other policy documents is noteworthy. We are left wondering how policies, whether centralized or decentralized, can influence the dispositions of educators to take different approaches to school-family-community partnerships if they do not explicitly describe strategies for identifying and resisting deficit frameworks.

Auerbach (2010) identified dialogue, parent advocacy, and community revitalization as important components of authentic partnerships. Several of the policies that we examined address these aspects. The stated goals of the First Nations policy framework takes as its starting point the importance of community dialogue and collaboration; the nuts-and-bolts facilities planning document is seen as instrumental to utilizing schools as community hubs. The equity and inclusive schools policy framework explicitly states that schools have a responsibility to include members of underrepresented communities in important school committees. Committee membership and dialogue are not synonymous, but it seems like a reasonable first step toward dialogue to require schools to be more intentional about including different voices and perspectives in school-based groups where parents have influence (cf. Gordon, Chapter 8, this volume).

We note a final tension here relevant to conversations about school leadership and partnerships. When principals alone are held accountable for showing results (e.g., Have school improvement goals been identified and pursued effectively? Has the graduation rate increased?),there may be time pressures that require principals (perhaps understandably) to limit community participation. What does "strong leadership" look like in a participatory context? Policymakers' timeframes may not align comfortably with school leaders' knowledge that relationships with families and communities require investments of resources and time and may not show immediate results in the most traditional ways.

Educational Programs that Support Partnerships

If policy is at least in part a statement of aspirations, particular educational programs are attempts to make those aspirations real. For this reason, we move now to a description of specific educational programs pertinent to partnerships (see Table 7.2). The list in Table 7.2 is not exhaustive and does not include school-community partnerships that do not stem from provincial government initiatives; brief descriptions are based upon publicly available materials. Though some programs support a number of policies, we have classified them based on the major emphasis of the programs. For example, many of the programs listed under Partnerships with Community Groups and Service Providers stem from the Ministry's commitment to reducing the achievement gap and could therefore have also been identified as being equity-related.

TABLE 7.2 Provincial Initiatives that Support School-Family-Community Partnerships

Program	*Description*
Parent Engagement	
Parents Reaching Out (PRO) Grants	PRO Grants fund local, regional and provincial initiatives designed to break down the barriers to parent engagement faced by many parents in Ontario.
Parenting and Family Literacy Centres (PFLCs)	PFLCs provide parents/caregivers and their young children the opportunity to participate in play-based learning activities that help them get a head start on development and learning.
Infrastructure	
Community Use of Schools (CUS)	Funding is provided to all school boards to make both indoor and outdoor school space more affordable for use after hours.
Priority Schools	Not-for-profit groups have free after-school access at 175 "priority schools," making programs either free or at greatly reduced price.
Partnerships with Community Groups and Service Providers	
Student Support Leadership Initiative (SSLI)	Encourages partnerships between school boards and community agencies in order to increase capacity to make appropriate and effective referrals to children's mental health services for students and their families through collaborative planning and coordination.
Connections for Students	Provides more coordinated transitions for students with Autism Spectrum Disorders in collaboration with autism service providers and parents/guardians.
Settlement Workers in Schools (SWIS)	The SWIS program places settlement workers from community agencies in elementary and secondary schools that have high numbers of newcomer students. One of the functions of the settlement worker is to outreach and assist newcomer parents.

(*Continued*)

TABLE 7.2 Continued

Program	*Description*
Full-Day Kindergarten	Full-day learning for four- and five-year-olds was launched in 2010 to give Ontario's youngest students a stronger start as they benefit from an integrated day at school. Four- and five-year-olds learn under the guidance of a teacher and an early childhood educator. Parents may also enroll their child for extended hours, for a reasonable fee, before and after regular school hours.
Focus on Youth (FOY)	The FOY program allows community partners to provide opportunities for young people to be engaged in positive summer activities in safe and supportive environments.
Specialist High Skills Major Program	Specialist High Skills Majors allows students to focus on a future career through a bundle of classroom courses, workplace experiences and sector certifications. It is part of a strategy to bring back students who have left school without finishing their diploma.
Student Nutrition Program	This program provides healthy breakfasts, snacks, and lunches at many schools. The programs are developed by schools and community agencies and are run by volunteers.
Urban Priority High Schools (UPHS)	The UPHS initiative targets high schools in urban priority areas to reach youth in need. The goal is to help these secondary schools develop the necessary supports and resources to meet the needs of their students and communities.

We identified 13 provincial programs that have implications for school-family-community partnerships in Ontario. Most are funded though the Ontario Ministry of Education. Other agencies funding pertinent programs are the Ministry of Health Promotion and Sport, Citizenship and Immigration Canada, and the Ministry of Children and Youth Services. The jurisdictional issues here are interesting and relevant for educational reformers concerned with increasing connections between communities and schools. In what ways can the range of policy actors be brought to the table to address issues of common concern? In any school or district, to whom should the responsibility for coordination of partnerships fall?

Five programs have a coordination mandate central to their emphasis. Community Use of Schools and Priority Schools (providing community groups with access to school space); Connections for Students (connecting students with autism service providers); full day kindergarten program (connecting school programming with child care programming); Student Support Leadership Initiative (coordinating the provision of mental health services to students); and settlement workers (bridging immigration issues and schooling issues) are the clearest examples.

Two programs—Urban and Priority High Schools and Specialist High Skills Major Program—are essentially school-based and focus on directing new resources to meet the needs of struggling learners. According to materials describing the Urban and Priority High Schools (UPHS) program, "Schools are reaching out to students and their families, working to develop a safe and positive school climate. A safe school and engaged parents are critical to creating an environment where students can succeed" (Ontario Ministry of Education, n.d.). An underlying assumption here is that a central and often neglected aspect of school improvement is to improve connections between home and school.

Implementation of UPHS requires school leaders to manage some interesting dilemmas. Leadership for new partnerships in a school would direct a principal or leadership team toward collaborations and process-oriented approaches to encourage new voices to participate in school decisions. At the same time, though, by virtue of being identified for additional resources because of their academic needs, these schools are under scrutiny to improve outcomes on traditional academic measures. This might pull a leadership team's attention toward higher visibility academic or curricular decisions and away from the inherently ambiguous work of collaborating with families and agencies. We do not mean to suggest that this is an intractable dilemma. Indeed, we began this chapter with a quote from Bryk and colleagues indicating that school-family-community partnerships can serve as an important lever of school reform. But given a high school leader's limited time and ever-expanding, sometimes contradictory mandate (instructional leadership and leadership for partnerships), the best path to take is not self-evident.

The Specialist High Skills Major Program offers high school students the opportunity to work toward a potential career that matches their skills and interests, including in community agencies. The leadership work here is to look outside the walls of the school and to coordinate, publicize, and implement this initiative with students who have been unsuccessful in secondary school. There is an interesting tension here facing school leaders. Potentially, the conditions that may have created the problems that face some youth in the first place—the absence of good classroom instruction, relevant curriculum, encouraging personal relationships, and school climate—are not addressed head-on. Instead, the emphasis is on making connections between the secondary school and other institutions. This observation is not intended to belittle the potential contribution of this program; there are several complementary initiatives in the program that attend to instructional issues. Nevertheless, paying attention to the ways that different initiatives shape and direct school leaders' attention is central to any accurate examination of implementation.

Two program initiatives, the Parents Reaching Out (PRO) grants and the Parenting and Family Literacy Centres, directly relate to parent involvement. PRO grants fund local, regional, and provincial initiatives designed to break down the barriers to parent engagement faced by many parents in Ontario. For example, PRO grants have been used to develop programs that provide multilanguage services, help parents work with their children at home, and build connections across diverse cultures in the school. The grants also provide funding for parent organizing activities and are not restricted to school-based organizations. The provincial government changed its funding approach after the first year of the program to direct more grants to communities affected by poverty (People for Education, 2010). There were concerns that the initial roll out of the grants seemed to reward those parent groups and schools already best positioned to garner resources in a grant application adjudication process. However, by directing resources to high poverty settings, the Ministry was able to address this potential pitfall while simultaneously providing the provincial government with a synergy in its overall poverty reduction policies.

Parenting and Family Literacy Centres (PFLCs) are intended to provide parents with both a location and, where necessary, the skills to engage their young children, from birth to age 6, in play-based literacy building activities that will assist with school readiness. As described on government Web sites, the focus is on development and learning. As such, there are libraries at PFLCs to lend materials to encourage caregivers to read to children in their home language. The PFLCs serve as a hub where families can meet with one another and find links to community resources pertinent to health, special learning needs, and other complementary services. An assumption here is that partnerships are mutually beneficial to both educational institutions and to children and families. A policy aspiration associated with PFLCs is that by creating places where families can build skills to support their young children, teaching and learning in children's earliest years will improve.

Dilemmas of Assessment

Parent involvement and community partnerships are commonly assessed informally at the local level. Did more people attend this year's literacy night than last year's? Is the relationship with the community group utilizing school space after school a friendly one? How much money did the parent council raise this year? More systematic approaches to assessment and evaluation are less common in both the research literature and in professional practice. Also atypical are evaluation approaches that attend to the kind of authenticity that Auerbach (2010, Chapter 3, this volume) calls for. How would community redevelopment, parent empowerment, or collaboration be measured comprehensively? What would count as evidence?

Our scan of the policy and program landscape for partnerships in Ontario suggests that where assessments exist at all, they typically take the form of formative program evaluations. Program evaluations of this sort make sense and we have no doubt that it is in a government's interest to demonstrate the effectiveness of various program expenditures, particularly in these times of tightening resources. However, we are aware of no overarching evaluation or assessment plan that would place all of the different partnership options into a framework and provide a deeper understanding of whether, in what ways, or by what means collaborative partnerships have been improved compared both to previous arrangements and to aspired-to goals. For example, one stated goal of government policy in Ontario is to improve public support for public education. By what measure has support improved?

Part of the problem with assessing parent and community engagement is that there are a range of "goods" to be examined, and not all of them lend themselves to the kind of counting that evaluators generally do. For example, in a low-income school where leaders are working hard to establish new partnerships with parents and community groups, conflict might arise where it did not previously exist. Parents who previously did not feel entitled to voice their concerns might see themselves for the first time as influential in decision-making and they might have strenuous disagreements with school officials—or with each other. Encouraging involvement and connections does not necessarily mean everyone will agree all the time. But precisely this kind of engagement—serious connections between two institutions, the school and the family, charged with responsibility for children—has the potential to form the foundation of a more democratic community with increased social and political capital among parents (cf. Chrispeels, Chapter 9, this volume). How would an evaluator of the Urban Priority High Schools initiative, for example, know if these kinds of relationships are growing? And are they even central to the vision policymakers had when they started this program?

Leadership for Partnerships: Reflections on the Ontario Experience

Educators and researchers alike lament the gap between theory and practice or between policymakers' intentions and the realities of work in schools. We are reminded that although often the purpose of policy is to change what schools do, the reality of implementation and the complexity of educational organizations mean that schools also change policy (Cuban, 1998).

Much of the literature on parent and community involvement calls for greater roles for parents in schools and greater sharing of power and authority by schools, as discussed in many chapters of this volume. There are exceptions worth noting, however, from across the ideological spectrum. De Carvalho (2000) argues that the current emphasis on increasing parent involvement in schools is elitist and benefits only the most resourced families with disposable time and income. She also argues that calls for parent involvement increase as school professionals wash their hands of their responsibility to educate all students. Whitman (2008) views parent involvement as little more than a waste of educators' time since a school's role, particularly for marginalized students, should be a paternalistic one of making up for students' home-based deficits and lack of school readiness. From Whitman's perspective, schools should avoid making connections with individuals that make accomplishing the academic mission of schooling more difficult—and from Whitman's perspective, parents of families affected by poverty are difficult.

Our view is that parent and community involvement and connections represent a potential resource that can be brought to bear on issues of school climate, itself a resource for school improvement (Bryk et al., 2010; Grubb, 2009). The link between provincial policy on parent and community engagement and a specific school's academic outcomes is a challenging, but not impossible, one to study (see Bryk et al., 2010). We certainly have accumulated a large body of evidence that adversarial or apathetic relationships between families and schools are impediments to positive school culture and to a sense of collective effort required for schools to improve (Flessa, 2009; Lipman, 2004). But as Cuban (1998) has noted in his reflections on school reform, policy directions set above the school level are always interpreted, shaped, and changed at the school site level. The work of building positive partnerships requires establishing and maintaining relationships. These efforts require commitment on both sides.

No policy can, by fiat, mandate commitment. Policies can require compliance and can direct resources toward certain hoped-for ends. The role of leadership in the current centralized policy environment is full of contradictions. On the one hand, there is increasingly a call for entrepreneurial, autonomous, strong school leaders with the knowledge and skills to work on instruction, management, and politics simultaneously (Cuban, 1988). On the other hand, given the tight coupling between ministry policy and school actions (less visible here but certainly observable in class size reduction policy or literacy policy), principal effectiveness is judged according to how well they are able to implement received mandates and align school goals with those of the Ministry. Assessing the importance of leadership in improving school-family-community partnerships requires careful collection of policy implementation data for evaluation.

Although it will strike some readers as cliché, we therefore conclude our chapter with a call for large scale policy research. We agree with Corter and Pelletier (2005) that there should be "more research examining the processes that link aims, practice and outcomes and more attention to specific outcomes that go beyond client and practitioner satisfaction" (p. 323). In particular, to be most useful to the schools, families, and community partners hoping to establish more positive and productive relationships, studies of implementation will need to attend to the leadership imperatives at the heart of this work. The answer to whether partnership policies have been implemented will be more complicated than a simple yes or no. Studies of implementation need to describe why, how, under what conditions, and with what leadership partnerships have been established and sustained. In Ontario, a wide range of policies has influenced the emergence and development of a wide range of partnerships. To learn more from them requires that researchers follow the policy mandates from the Ministry, through school boards, and into particular schools and communities and note how policy aspirations and goals are changed along the way.

Note

1. The views in this chapter do not necessarily reflect those of the Ontario Ministry of Education.

References

Anderson, S., & Ben Jaafar, S. (2006). *Policy trends in Ontario education: 1996–2006.* Toronto, ON: International Centre for Educational Change, Ontario Institute for Studies in Education, University of Toronto.

Auerbach, S. (2007). Visioning parent engagement in urban schools. *Journal of School Leadership, 17,* 699–734.

Auerbach, S. (2010). Beyond coffee with the principal: Toward leadership for authentic school-family partnerships. *Journal of School Leadership, 20*(6), 730–759.

Bryk. A., Sebring, P. B., Allensworth, E., Luppescu, S., & Easton, J. Q. (2010). *Organizing schools for improvement: Lessons from Chicago.* Chicago, IL: University of Chicago Press.

Campbell, C., & Fullan, M. (2006). *Unlocking the potential for learning: Effective district-wide strategies to raise student achievement in literacy and numeracy.* Retrieved from www.edu.gov.ca/eng/literacynumeracy/inspire/research/ProjectReport_full.pdf.

Canadian Education Association. (2010). *Ontario's primary class size reduction initiative: Report on early implementation.* Toronto: Canadian Education Association.

Cooper, C. W., Riehl, C., & Hasan, A. L. (2010). Leading and learning with diverse families in schools: Critical epistemology amid communities of practice. *Journal of School Leadership, 20*(6), 758–788.

Corter, C. & Pelletier, J. (2005). Parent and community involvement in schools: Policy panacea or pandemic? In N. Bascia, A. Cumming, A. Datnow, K. Leithwood, & D. Livingstone (Eds.), *International handbook of educational policy* (pp. 295–327). Dordrecht, the Netherlands: Springer.

Cuban, L. (1998). How schools change reforms: Redefining reform success and failure. *Teachers College Record, 99*(3), 453–477.

deCarvalho, M. E. (2000). *Rethinking family-school relations: A critique of parent involvement in schooling.* Mahwah, NJ: Erlbaum.

Flessa, J. (2008). Parent involvement: What counts, who counts it, and does it help? *Education Canada, 48*(2), 18–21.

Flessa, J. (2009). Urban school principals, deficit frameworks, and implications for leadership. *Journal of School Leadership, 19*(3), 334–373.

Grubb, W. N. (2009). *The money myth: School resources, outcomes, and equity.* New York: Russell Sage Foundation,

Hands, C. M. (2005). It's who you know *and* what you know: The process of creating partnerships between schools and communities. *The School Community Journal, 15*(2), 63–84.

Hands, C. M. (2008). Circles of influence: The role of school-community partnerships in the character formation and citizenship of secondary school students. *Alberta Journal of Educational Research, 54*(1), 50–64.

Leithwood, K., Louis, K. S., Anderson, S., Wahlstrom, K. (2004). *How leadership influences student learning: Executive Summary.* Minneapolis, MN: University of Minnesota Center for Applied Research and Educational Improvement.

Levin, B. (2007). Sustainable, large-scale education renewal. *Journal of Educational Change, 8*(4), 323–326.

Levin, B. (2008). *How to change 5000 schools: A practical approach for leading change at every level.* Cambridge, MA: Harvard Education Press.

Lipman, P. (2004). *High stakes education: Inequality, globalization, and urban school reform.* New York: RoutledgeFalmer.

R. A. Malatest & Co. (2002). *Parent and education engagement partnership project.* Vancouver: British Columbia Ministry of Education.

Nagy, P., & Lupart, J. (1994). *Is there a national role in education?* Toronto: Canadian Education Association and Ottawa & Canadian Society for the Study of Education.

No Child Left Behind (NCLB) Act of 2001, Pub. L. No. 107-110, § 115, Stat. 1425 (2002).

Ontario Ministry of Education. (2004). *Ontario First Nation, Métis, and Inuit education policy framework.* Toronto: Author.

Ontario Ministry of Education. (2005). *Ontario's aménagement linguistique policy for French-language education.* Toronto: Author.

Ontario Ministry of Education. (2008). *Reach every student: Energizing Ontario education.* Toronto: Author.

Ontario Ministry of Education. (2009a). *Quick facts: Ontario's equity and inclusive education strategy.* Toronto: Author.

Ontario. Ministry of Education. (2009b). *Equity and inclusive education in Ontario schools: Guidelines for policy development and implementation.* Toronto: Author.

Ontario Ministry of Education. (n.d.). *Urban and priority high schools.* Retrieved from http://www.edu.gov.on.ca/eng/safeschools/urbanPriority.html.

People for Education. (2010). *Media release: Poverty reduction strategy falling short on education front.* Toronto: Author.

Pushor, D. (2010). Are schools doing enough to learn about families? In M. M. Marsh & T. Turner-Vorbeck (Eds.), *(Mis)Understanding families: Learning from real families in our schools* (pp. 4–18). New York: Teachers College Press.

Pushor, D., & Murphy, B. (2004). Parent marginalization, marginalized parents: Creating a place for parents on the school landscape. *Alberta Journal of Educational Research, 50*(3), 221–235.

Schutz, A. (2006). Home is a prison in the global city: The tragic failure of school-based community engagement strategies. *Review of Educational Research, 76*(4), 691–743.

Whitman, D. (2008). *Sweating the small stuff: Inner-city schools and the new paternalism.* Washington, DC: Thomas B. Fordham Institute.

8

CREATING ORGANIZATIONAL CULTURES OF FAMILY AND COMMUNITY ENGAGEMENT

The Impact of District Policies and Practices on School Leaders

Molly F. Gordon[1]

The organization of the U.S. school system reflects the underlying democratic assumptions of the public school crusaders and is unique in that the community "owns" the schools. Schools were envisioned to be extensions of their communities and reflect local values (Brunner, 1998; Kaestle, 1983). Over time, however, schools became structured organizationally and politically to exclude rather than include parent and community voices. Today, researchers and policymakers frequently revisit the issue of public school "ownership" and what that means for schools organizationally. How public is public education? There has been increasing consensus that districts and schools have created, through policies and administrative behavior, a more detached relationship with their communities (Crowson, 2003; Driscoll, 1998; Schutz, 2006). As Tyack and Cuban (1995) suggest, many educators have become "too intramural," and because of this, federal, state, and district-level engagement policies have surfaced to try to create greater connections between schools and their communities. For example, the No Child Left Behind Act (2002) required districts to support schools in efforts to be more open and transparent in their operations, to communicate more often with outside stakeholders, and to partner with parents in the learning process.

Although public schools are run by school districts, little research has been done on the role played by district leaders in creating and supporting organizational cultures of family and community engagement. Most studies exploring family and community involvement focus on one or two microlevel strategies at the school level, such as partnering with a local business or implementing a particular parent involvement program. The purpose of this study, on the other hand, was to investigate family and community engagement at the macro or organizational level by looking at district leader engagement policies and practices and their impact on school leader practices. It addresses the following research questions: (a) How do district leaders create an organizational culture of engagement, and (b) how do district engagement policies and practices play out in schools?

Because this study focused on districts and schools organizationally, neo-institutional theory was used as a conceptual tool for analysis. The premise of neo-institutional theory is that the rhetoric, policies, and practices of an institution do not necessarily mirror the behavior of the individuals within that organization (Arum, 2000; Meyer & Rowan 1977; Sarason 1971; Weick 1976). In addition, neo-institutional theory suggests that organizations survive by meeting external demands and by exhibiting a believable myth or façade that legitimates behavior. Furthermore, schools have their own organizational cultures and are only loosely coupled with other organizations, including districts, in their environment (Arum, 2000; Meyer & Rowan, 1977; Sarason, 1971; Weick, 1976). According to Bidwell (2001), there are strong implications in neo-institutional theory for the key role of school and district administrators since they are the main actors who adhere to and perpetuate organizational myths by setting the tone and culture for engagement, adapting to the environment, and creating institutional legitimacy. Meyer and Rowan (1983) argue that schools as organizations may continue certain practices and procedures that have become institutionalized, even if those practices are not useful or do not create the desired outcomes. Institutional theory helped to explain why districts and schools may choose to adopt certain structures for engaging with stakeholders even though these structures may not lead to more authentic partnerships.

Related Literature

Related literature reviewed for this chapter fell into two main categories: (a) studies on the role district and school leaders play in parent and community engagement, and (b) studies on the level of influence of outside stakeholders in schools.

Leaders' Role in Engagement

The research outlined below shows that strong leadership at both the district and the school levels plays a pivotal role in creating and sustaining authentic engagement practices. School leaders play a crucial role in facilitating community involvement without marginalizing stakeholders' democratic voices (Louis, 2003). Principal support is also critical in sustaining effective school partnership programs (Van Voorhis & Sheldon, 2004). In addition, a principal's view of the community strongly influences the quality of school-community connections, including whether or not parents serve on school governance structures (Gordon & Louis, 2009). When principals view parents as equal partners, they are better able to engage families in the ownership of the educational process (Giles, 2006).

Although little research has been done on how district leaders engage with the community and support school engagement efforts, there have been a few studies showing how district support makes a difference in the quality of school partnership programs. For example, Sanders and Harvey's (2002) research illustrated a strong link between a district's focus on partnering and a principal's ability to prioritize school-community relationships. Also, findings from Epstein, Galindo, and Sheldon (2010) showed that both principal support and district assistance had a significant effect on the implementation and quality of basic school partnership programs. These studies are limited, however, in that the sample was drawn from districts already participating in and receiving support from the National Network of Partnership Schools. Other research has shown that a district level boundary spanner could help schools create and maintain successful partnerships with parents and community members and may promote more authentic, democratic relationships (Goldring & Sims, 2005; Honig, 2003, 2006; Miller, 2008). These results contrast with another study that showed that district support did not have a strong impact on the level of principal openness to parent and community engagement (Gordon & Louis, 2009). District mandates, however, can help by getting principals used to interacting with community members, which is the first step in creating more open school cultures for authentic engagement (Gordon & Louis, in press).

Researchers such as Anderson (1998) and Auerbach (2010, Chapter 3, this volume) point to the central role of leaders in promoting authentic partnerships. According to Anderson (1998), principals who were perceived to be honest, communicative, supportive, and collegial provided organizational spaces where authentic engagement and deliberation with teachers and outside stakeholders could be sustained. On the other hand, in schools where principals were more top-down or control-oriented, teachers often responded to this behavior with defensiveness and self-protection, making authentic participation nearly impossible.

The Influence of Outside Stakeholders

Education reformers have argued that schools should not only keep stakeholders informed of what happens at school, but should also involve them in school decision-making. Studies on the effectiveness of school governance structures involving outside stakeholders in decision-making, however, have shown mixed results. For example, research on school site councils revealed that these structures alone did not change the traditional hierarchical power relationships in schools or lead to more shared leadership (Anderson, 1998; Hess, 1999; Malen, 1994, 1999; Malen & Ogawa, 1988; Rogers, Freelon, & Terriquez, Chapter 4, this volume).

On a more positive note, Leithwood, Janzi, and Steinbach (1999) found that in schools where principals are more committed to distributed or shared leadership styles, site councils have more power and influence in helping make critical school decisions. In addition, Louis and colleagues' (2010) national study on leadership found that in high achieving schools, teachers, on average, perceived greater levels of influence of not only school leaders but also of parents and students. Furthermore, more outside stakeholders participate in school governance structures in districts where community engagement is encouraged and supported (see Gordon & Louis, in press; Louis et al., 2010). These studies reinforce the idea that it is beneficial to share leadership and extend the level of influence to the larger school community.

Because little research has been done on district leader practices in this area, this study fills a gap in the literature on the role that school district leaders play in creating organizational cultures of family and community engagement.

Research Design

This study used a comparative case study design, which involved qualitative fieldwork methods. It focused on the bounded system of the educational community in two districts and two schools nested within each of these districts in order to explore how district family and community engagement policies and practices filter down into schools. This study was part of a larger study, *Learning from Leadership: Investigating the Links to Improved Student Learning* by researchers from the University of Minnesota and the University of Toronto, which was funded by the Wallace Foundation (Louis et al., 2010) .

Principal and teacher survey data from this larger study were used to select districts with high scores on engagement related survey items.[2] The sample for this chapter included two mid- to large-sized districts with one elementary and one middle school in each district. One of the districts is located near a military base in a small southern city and the other is located in a suburb of a large city in a western state. The sample was both purposive and intensive in selecting cases where the most information about community and parent engagement could be learned (Merriam, 1998).

The primary data for this chapter come from structured in-person interviews, which were conducted at each sampled site with district and school administrators (once a year from 2005 to 2008), as well as with teachers, parents, school board members, community members, education reporters, and business leaders (in 2005 and 2008). In total, 93 interviews were analyzed for this study. Each site visit lasted approximately 2 days and was an intense examination of leadership policies, practices, behaviors, and relationships. Interview questions addressed the level of influence of outside stakeholders in school improvement efforts, the role of the school in the community and vice versa, school-community interactions, relationships, and engagement practices and policies. All interviews were digitally recorded and transcribed verbatim. As a second source of data, documents such as brochures and school improvement plans, were also collected and analyzed from each site.

Each interview and document was coded using a coding framework based on the theoretical framework and related literature. After identifying recurring themes across each case, two overarching themes emerged: (a) the role of leadership in shaping an organizational culture of engagement, and (b) the use of formal policies and structures for engagement. Both within-case and cross-case analyses were conducted by each of the emergent themes, and patterns were sought that either fit or did not fit with neo-institutional theory. The triangulation of the data helped increase the external validity of the findings.

Before delving into the cases, it is important to mention study limitations. Because it is a case study, findings cannot be generalized to the entire population. Second, these cases were chosen from a pool of randomly selected districts and not chosen from all possible districts within the United States. Lastly, in some of the cases, not all relevant community members or parents (such as parents on site councils) were available or willing to be interviewed at the time the study took place, and therefore some outside stakeholder voices are missing from the analysis.

Glenhurst School District: Heavy Reliance on Mandated Governance Structures

Glenhurst School District[3] was located in a suburb of a large city in a western state. The district had 47 schools with an enrollment of approximately 38,000 students (42% minority and 33% of students qualifying for free or reduced price lunch [FRPL]). Rawls Elementary served about 460 students (52% minority and 63% FRPL) while Heritage Middle School had an enrollment of approximately 980 students (48% minority and 37% FRPL).[4] In Glenhurst, district leaders relied heavily on mandated governance structures to promote family engagement. In addition, they worked hard at keeping open communication lines with the public and being visible in the community. Although district leaders said they valued parent engagement for democratic and student achievement purposes, they acknowledged that engagement practices varied from school to school. The superintendent recognized this problem, but said he hoped his modeling of outreach and visibility set the tone and encouraged principals to engage in the same kinds of activities.

Role of Leadership in Engagement

In Glenhurst, trust in the district improved when Superintendent Cameron came on board in 2003. Community members spoke highly of his hands-on approach and reported he was well respected in the community because of his visibility and accessibility. During the previous administration, staff members were afraid to state their opinions, but with the change in leadership the district became more relaxed and open. Interviewees used such words as *collaborative, open, visible*, and *accessible* to describe Superintendent Cameron.

District leaders valued outside stakeholder feedback and provided spaces for community members and families to give their input on district programs and policies. For example, the superintendent held regular "listening sessions" in the community to listen to the public's concerns and met regularly with a group of business and community leaders to talk about district policies and programs. To gauge community perceptions of the schools, district leaders sent out opinion surveys to parents every other year. In addition, Glenhurst leaders invited the community to weigh in on curricular adoptions, planning, and programs, mainly through a Web site forum for parents or the listening sessions. To help coordinate engagement activities, the district had a Community Involvement Office with a full-time administrator for community involvement who worked with businesses and community agencies, PTOs, and individual parents.

Although the district sought community level input, staff did not always know what to do when they exerted their influence. For example, the assistant superintendent said that more affluent parents often banded together if they did not like something, such as a new math adoption, and overwhelmed the district with phone calls and e-mails. She said that district staff "really have to listen to parents that are unhappy.... They tend to form these e-mail vigilante groups behind the scenes. They will just really bombard you with extremely threatening messages." Even though this kind of community organizing could be intense and narrowly focused, the assistant superintendent said that all community member concerns should be heard and vetted. The school board vice chair likewise said that the democratic process of allowing all voices to be heard was valued by the district, even though it slowed down the process.

Although district leaders invited public input and talked fervently about the value of the democratic process, school level responsibility for engaging with communities and families rested solely on principals. District leaders, therefore, admitted that engagement practices varied school-to-school. When asked if school principals were engaging parents and community members in meaningful ways, the associate superintendent said she did not know for sure.

At the two schools in the sample, each administrator had different philosophies on parent and community involvement and each created very different cultures for engagement. For example, at Rawls Elementary, a critical culture shift occurred when an old principal left and a new one came on board. The previous principal was not skilled in connecting with or reaching out to parents and community members. One teacher said, "He is terrible. He is maybe the worst administrator at making community connections you will ever see in your life." Teachers said that this leader's ineptitude made their work to engage with families harder. The dynamic between the principal and parents created a contentious environment for teachers who felt obligated to defend him for the benefit of the organization as a whole. He was removed from the school after only 2 years.

With the hiring of Principal Quinn at Rawls, relations between parents, community members, and the school improved dramatically. Teachers reported that she was visible and involved in all school family events. During her tenure, membership in the PTO increased and communication improved. Teachers praised Principal Quinn's open and frequent communication style and her efforts to restore trust both within the school and with parents and community members, creating a more inviting school culture. For instance, one teacher described the new culture as "welcoming with plenty of opportunities for continued growth," "free of cliques," and a "risk-taking" environment. In another teacher's words, Principal Quinn "created an open communication line" between the district, school, and families.

At Heritage Middle, on the other hand, when Principal Collard was hired, the school had a reputation of being a "ghetto school" because of discipline issues and its reputation as one of the lowest achieving schools in the district. The principal's primary goals were to change the reputation of the school and increase student achievement. To involve parents, Principal Collard hosted a parent coffee meeting every other month as her way of communicating school issues to them. At first, she was very intimidated by the parents because they put a lot of pressure on her and wanted to know what she was going to do about the discipline and academic problems. She said that "there must have been 60 parents here for this coffee and they were very demanding." Because of the demands, Principal Collard said she had to wear her "PR hat" and "sell the school" to the parents.

Teachers were mixed on this principal's ability to create an inclusive school environment. One teacher said that the decision-making structure in the school was not democratic and called it "secretive." For instance, the principal did a poor job of engaging parents and teachers in decisions about staff cuts, and because of this there was a backlash both within the school and in the community. In general, teachers said Principal Collard tended to only listen to a small group of parents and did not consider the opinions of the whole staff or parents overall. Unlike at the district level or at Rawls Elementary, Principal Collard did not create an open and trusting environment that was conducive to increasing parent and community engagement.

Formal Policies and Structures for Engagement

Glenhurst School District used formal governance structures as the main lever to give parents greater say in school operations. These structures included elected local school committees (LSCs), elected site councils, and parent-teacher organizations (PTOs). According to district policy, LSCs were established by the district "to provide assistance and direction to the individual schools and the Board for the effective operation of the district." The superintendent described the LSCs as "mini-school boards" that "help run the school," but their primary role was to manage district facilities. Although members of the LSCs did not have a formal role in policy formation in areas such as curriculum or instruction, they often banded together to use their power to influence the district in these areas.

In addition to the LSCs, each school had a mandated elected site council involved in setting direction for school improvement with 50% parent and 50% teacher representation. One district interviewee said that both the state and the district put a lot of time and effort into giving the elected site councils credibility and making sure that there was community representation. As one district administrator said, "You have to maintain a democratic public education system; you have to have the public involved." By state law, site councils had the responsibility for staff development as well as school improvement planning, including setting goals for increasing student achievement. Superintendent Cameron met regularly with all members of the site councils and LSCs to listen to their ideas and concerns and to be updated on their activities.

Aside from the formal elected LSCs and site councils, the district mandated that every school have a parent-teacher organization. The influence of the PTOs, however, varied from school to school. The district provided voluntary training for parents on such topics as parent leadership and how to organize and generate more parent involvement at individual school sites. Attendance at the trainings, however, was sporadic. Members of the PTO worked with the principal on school improvement issues, but they did not have the authority to make decisions.

At Rawls, Principal Quinn devised a strategy for increasing involvement by tying Family Night to PTO meetings and by serving dinner to entice more parents to come. The school invited families to dinner and after dinner offered math and literacy classes for parents. After the classes, the PTO met and all parents were invited to stay for the meeting where they served dessert as an incentive to stay. Although more parents came to meetings because of these efforts, Principal Quinn was not satisfied with the numbers. The school continued to struggle with attracting more diverse families to the meetings.

Meanwhile, the small group of parent members on the Rawls Site Council had a little more influence than those who were on the PTO. They worked with the principal to create and revise the school improvement plan and spent a lot of time reading research and working the findings into their plan. In addition, the council focused their efforts on linking curriculum to district and state standards. The job of the Local School Committee at Rawls, on the other hand, was narrowly defined to managing facility use.

At Heritage Middle, on the other hand, PTO members were responsible for raising funds and then awarding minigrants to teachers for projects. In addition, the PTO coordinated parent volunteering in the school. Teachers perceived the PTO as fairly influential because of its power to award grants and because the members kept up with how the school was doing academically. The Heritage PTO president, however, reported that she and other members mainly spoke with the school secretaries, occasionally interacted with teachers for the coordination of volunteers and grants, but that they only interacted with the principal on occasion. Parents on the PTO were used as support for staff in helping with newsletter mailings and calling absent students.

In addition to the PTO, parents on the Site Council at Heritage were in charge of working on the school improvement plan. Teachers, however, reported that the council had very little influence in the school. Once plans were created, they were never revisited and were not consulted on a regular basis. Similar to Rawls, the primary responsibility of the Local School Committee at Heritage Middle was to be in charge of building management only.

Overall, the level of power and influence of these formal governance structures was minimal at the two schools. The LSCs had the greatest amount of influence, but only when they got together as one cohesive group to protest district programs that they did not support, such as a newly adopted math curriculum. At both schools, principals and teachers said that the parents who were involved in governance tended to be White and more affluent. Both principals said they struggled to involve minority and low-income parents either formally or informally.

In sum, Glenhurst District and Rawls Elementary School were organizationally open to greater parent and community involvement. Each leader emphasized accessibility, communication, visibility, and transparency. At Heritage Middle School, on the other hand, the principal was satisfied with the status quo of working with a small group of elite parents and did not prioritize increasing parent and community engagement, except when she needed to wear her "PR hat." Overall, neither the district nor the two corresponding schools put much effort into partnering with businesses or community groups, and all had difficulty engaging larger and more diverse groups of parents.

North White Pine County District: A Focus on Increasing Transparency and Partnering

North White Pine County District was located close to a military base in a small city in a southern state, and was comprised of 35 schools with approximately 24,0000 students (39% minority and 42% FRPL). Maple Island Elementary, a magnet school located within the small city, had an enrollment of 385 students (73% minority and 69% FRPL). Country Grove Middle school, located in a suburb, had about 550 students (42% minority and 48% FRPL). The district had stable leadership and good community relationships. The superintendent was seen as open and approachable, and communicated often with the public. District leaders valued transparency in all district operations and partnered often with community groups. Although the district had policies pertaining to community and parent engagement, these policies were vague and not mandated. Because of this, parent engagement at the school and district levels was sporadic.

Role of Leadership in Engagement

District leaders successfully navigated the demands and challenges of being in a military community with high mobility. Leadership at the district level was stable compared to other districts in the state. Superintendent Wauters was brought up through the ranks and so was already a part of the district when she took office. Because leadership remained stable, the staff was able to work through challenges in a systematic way while maintaining a high level of community trust. One district staff member said that the culture shifted from district-centered to student- and family-centered around 1996, when the district became involved in total quality management. She said that the district began to "look at what the customer wants more than what we [the district] want."

Before district leaders made a final decision as to whether or not to implement new district programs or initiatives, they went "on the road" to various venues such as community centers and businesses to talk to parents and community members. Although going out into the community to talk about controversial topics like redistricting, was, in the words of the district director of community affairs, "not always fun," he said that the community appreciated the chance to give input. The district had "not been afraid to take things on.... We put all our effort into making sure the community was involved and they understand. Whether they show up or not, they were given the opportunity to express their opinions."

In the district office, increasing student achievement was viewed as a community effort. Superintendent Wauters told the community that they had an obligation to make sure that students had every opportunity they needed to be successful. Partnering with local community groups and with other county personnel was a necessity for North White Pine because of its "low-wealth" status and because the central office was understaffed. The stability of district level leadership helped make the vital connections with community groups. According to a member of the Chamber of Commerce, district leaders seemed open to partnerships. District leaders often worked with the county manager and networked and partnered with the local universities and community college faculty and staff to provide teacher training and certification. For example, the district partnered with math and science professors to create a program to help build teacher math and science skills.

Annually, district staff solicited input and feedback in the form of surveys and forums on their Web site from students, parents, colleges, businesses, and community partners, including faith-based groups and the military base, on school and district programs and practices. One district leader summed up the district philosophy about inviting input when he said, "We don't sit on this little island and make the decisions. We seek and value our stakeholder input." When asked what contributed to maintaining positive relationships with the community, he said that it came down to the leadership, both at the district and school levels. He said that reaching out to the community and valuing the input of outside stakeholders was "second nature" and "just the culture that we have."

Although district leaders reached out to and partnered with community groups and solicited feedback from the community on a regular basis, leaders' outreach at the school level varied. At Maple Island Elementary, on the one hand, Principal Bemis said she was "a very transparent leader," and had an open door policy for parents and community members. She often went out to different areas of the community and would go door-to-door to talk to parents. Because of the low-income population, she said it was important for the school to be invested in families and in the community. The principal and teachers, however, were affected by the level of poverty in the community and would sometimes personally pay bills or buy things like groceries for struggling families. To help families, the principal collaborated with community groups, local churches, and the school social worker to find support and services.

One way Principal Bemis tried to involve parents and help the community was by partnering with a local company that bought the school a washer and dryer. If a student came in with dirty clothes, a staff member washed their clothes so that they went home with clean clothes. The principal invited parents in to wash their own clothes free of charge, and teachers often used that time when parents were in the school laundry room to talk to them about their children's academic progress. Although this example shows that Principal Bemis tried to think outside of the box, it also suggests that she thought of the community in deficit terms and focused on what parents lacked in resources rather than how she could empower and engage them in more authentic kinds of partnerships.

Relationships with parents at Country Grove Middle School, on the other hand, were less positive. When Principal Marcelle came on board, she concluded that the community was more focused on athletics than on academics and so she adopted a "no excuses" policy. She reported that one of the first things she said to students and parents was that "we [school staff] will not take excuses from you, your children, our staff or me. If you hear an excuse from me, you need to call me on it. If I hear an excuse from you, I'm going to call you on it." According to several teachers, parents were intimidated by Principal Marcelle and thought that she was a little "crazy." However, teachers said that after a while, parents got used to her style.

One of Principal Marcelle's first goals was to change the culture of the middle school from being sports oriented to being more academically oriented.

The principal and teachers reported that it was difficult to change the mindset of many school staff and parents. In fact, the principal blamed the community for allowing the school to let athletics overshadow academic progress. When she cut some of the athletic programs, she was met with resistance from parents. But she explained that she had

> taken the cussing and the fussing from the parents and whoever because they didn't quite get it or didn't quite like it but I knew it was what was right for those kids at the time. I will not let my teachers take that. I will not let them take that fussing and cussing.

Teachers reported that at times the principal came across as "my way or the highway." The principal reported that she built trust with teachers by buffering them from parents who were angry or distracting to instruction.

Formal Policies and Structures for Engagement

Compared with Glenhurst, North White Pine County relied less heavily on mandated formal governance structures. The only mandate was that school improvement teams had to have 50% parent representation. Instead, the district encouraged, but did not mandate, schools to have PTOs. Each parent organization was required to provide the district with a document describing their purpose and a description of how they planned to operate.

Besides parent representation on school improvement teams, the district also had several weakly worded policies on parent involvement. For example, one policy stated:

> The board recognizes that the public schools are an integral part of the community and that the public has a vested interest in having students develop into productive members of the workforce and society. The board encourages the community to be involved in the schools and to help the schools in attaining board and school goals for student success. (North White Pine County Web site—school policy governing parent organizations)

This policy encouraged the community to be involved, but offered no direction on how to get involved or in what ways (cf. Flessa & Grègoire, Chapter 7, this volume). The policy also stated that it had established its commitment to families and the community through the creation and maintenance of policies around the transparency of public records, open board meetings, allowing community use of school facilities, and allowing visitors to the schools.

Despite having these policies encouraging schools to include parents in school operations, engagement practices played out differently in the two schools. At Maple Island Elementary, for example, the school had a PTA prior to principal Bemis, but she dissolved it after a couple of years because she felt parents who served on it were too "cliquey," did not understand the culture of poverty, and were not making good decisions that were in the best interests of all students. Instead, Principal Bemis created a People Lending Out Their Time (PLOT) team that met monthly. The purpose of the team was not to govern or help with decision-making, but to encourage parents to volunteer at the school level. The kinds of volunteering activities that came out of the PLOT meetings tended to be traditional, such as baking cupcakes or organizing the school carnival. One of the ways that the school tried to involve more parents in the PLOT team meetings was by giving out gift cards to local grocery stores. Teachers also used PLOT meetings to inform parents about what their children were learning in the classrooms and to teach them ways to help their child set goals and learn at home.

Maple Island Elementary also had a strategic planning team that was comprised mostly of school leaders with only a few parents. Despite the principal's efforts to educate teachers and other staff on the issues facing economically disadvantaged families, the school continued to struggle with engaging parents who were representative of the community population. The involved parents tended to be White and more affluent.

In comparison, Country Grove Middle School did not have any parent organization at the time of this research. Instead, the school had a few parents serve on the building leadership team (BLT). The team was made up of a few school staff, the principal, and about seven to eight parents. Those parents who served were White, affluent, and did not have to work during the day. At these meetings, parents sought clarity about school level decisions or processes or about what lessons students were learning in the classroom, but had no decision-making authority themselves.

In an effort to try to increase parent and community involvement, Principal Marcelle decided to start a PTA during the last year of this study. Administrators, teachers, and a few parents spent the year working on strategies for getting more middle school parents involved. Even though the school started the process, one teacher reported that the PTA efforts "did not go" this year. She stated, "I don't know what happened to it. With parents in this area, especially, they work all different hours and times so it's really hard to pick a time of the day that they are going to actually be here." Another reason why the PTA did not get off the ground may have been that the principal said it was "low on my priority list for the first year." In addition, some teachers and the principal said that most of the parents in the community just "didn't get it." This is another instance of deficit thinking in that school members viewed parents as lacking the competency to know what was in the best interest of students.

In sum, North White Pine County District staff worked hard at maintaining strong community relationships. District leaders solicited outside stakeholder input and spent a great deal of time communicating with the public and partnering with community and business organizations. However, the district's several policies on community and parent engagement were unclear and weakly monitored. Because of this, parent engagement at the school and district level was sporadic and both schools struggled with involving low-income and minority parents. Although the district emphasized partnering with community groups and agencies, partnerships at the school level were weak or nonexistent.

Looking across the Cases: Loose Coupling of District Policies and School Practices

In each case, district leadership was vital for opening up the organization and creating an environment favorable to outside stakeholder engagement. District leaders provided spaces, both traditional and virtual, for outside stakeholders to voice their opinions and share ideas on district programs and policies. In addition, district leaders were visible, accessible, and communicated often with the community. Furthermore, each district had a designated administrative boundary spanner whose responsibility it was to work with community members and parents. Although district leaders had mechanisms to involve outside stakeholders, the levers used to get the community involved differed in each case. For example, Glenhurst School District used mandated governance structures to spur public involvement in decision-making while North White Pine partnered with business and community groups and maintained transparency in organizational operations.

Despite district efforts, district-level engagement policies were only loosely coupled with school-level practices. As neo-institutional theorists predict, there was a disconnect between district and school-level policies, practices, and behaviors. District leaders did not make a connection between their own engagement practices and what was happening at the school, and they did not hold their principals accountable for the same kinds of activities practiced at the district level. This calls into question district leaders' rhetoric and stated beliefs about the importance of getting the public involved and creating more democratic systems.

Loose coupling may have occurred because district policies regarding parent and community engagement were unclear. This is consistent with neo-institutional theory in that ambiguous institutional expectations can help to maintain a gap between formal structures and the activities within the organization. North White Pine County, for example, had several vaguely written policies encouraging schools to involve parents and community members, but provided no direction or support for promoting more authentic partnerships. Glenhurst, on the other hand, mandated three separate governance structures for parents and community members to get involved, but policy intentions did not always match practices in schools. Again, this is consistent with neo-institutional theory, which suggests that institutional expectations, including policies, do not always match the behaviors of individuals within the institution. Policies specifying the percentage of community representation on governance structures were clear, but how to authentically engage those who served on them was not. Policies and structures alone did not lead to consistent or meaningful parent and community engagement, a finding consistent with other research (see Malen, 1994, 1999). Although the purpose of having these mandated governance structures was to maintain a democratic school system, the actual school-level practices were more "ritual" than democratic.

In both cases, districts and schools struggled in one way or another to engage parents, community groups, and businesses despite some instances of concerted effort. Most notably, leaders had difficulty involving large groups of parents in meaningful ways, especially parents with diverse backgrounds. School leaders, for the most part, continued to use the same kinds of traditional mechanisms and strategies to engage parents and rarely thought outside the box, despite the fact that these strategies often did not result in increased parent engagement. These findings are also consistent with neo-institutional theory, which asserts that organizations tend to incorporate practices and procedures that have been defined by existing "rationalized" concepts of how organizations ought to work and behave in society, even if they are not effective or do not produce the desired results. Organizations that incorporate policies such as having a PTO or site council and hosting social family dinner nights increase their legitimacy because these are the traditional prevailing practices for how schools "get parents involved" in the educational system.

Discussion and Conclusion

How do district and school leaders create organizational cultures of engagement? Results suggest that organizational conditions such as collaborative and open cultures, shared leadership, and visible and communicative leaders generally fostered greater outside stakeholder involvement at the district and school levels. Organizational conditions that hindered engagement included unapproachable, top-down leadership, and cultures and structures that kept parents and community members focused on tasks unassociated with the educational mission.

How do district engagement policies and practices play out in schools? Results showed that district-level engagement policies, expectations, and modeling did not "trickle down" to the school level. In effect, district-level policies and practices were loosely coupled with school-level policies and practices. Because of this, policy and practice existed at two separate levels, with little connection and no accountability. In most instances, schools and districts continued to use the same kinds of mechanisms and strategies to engage parents even though they did not result in increased parent engagement. According to neo-institutional theorists, schools and districts could be said to maintain legitimacy in the eyes of the public simply because they had these structures.

This study also suggests that principals viewed engagement policies and practices as nonessential, meaning involvement policies and practices were not tied to the overall mission of the school.

Part of the reason why district engagement policies and practices were loosely coupled with schools was because the locus of responsibility for parent, business, and community involvement was unclear in both Glenhurst and North White Pine. District leaders did not hold principals accountable for engaging with outside groups in meaningful ways. Both superintendents took a "hands-off" approach to the schools when it came to making sure that principals were following good engagement practices. In addition, district leaders did not ask principals if they needed help in learning how to engage outside stakeholders or offer other support. These results deviate slightly from Sanders and Harvey's (2002) research that showed a strong link between a district's focus on partnering and a principal's ability to prioritize school-community partnerships.

Implications for practice suggest that if districts want schools to engage with parents and community members in productive and authentic ways, then they may have to not only create clearer policies and strategies for schools to follow, but also monitor engagement practices and hold school leaders accountable. This could be done through regularly scheduled check-ins with a district appointed community involvement liaison where school principals and other staff members report on their progress toward predetermined goals for increasing engagement. In addition, districts could hold an annual meeting where designated school members share with one another the kinds of practices and strategies used to meet engagement goals and any lesson learned from their efforts. Vaguely written policies, encouragement, and even expectations alone will not work. Superintendent modeling of engagement behaviors did not do enough to encourage school leaders to engage the public in the educational process. In addition, even where districts emphasized public engagement, the policies and preferences tended to "trickle down" to schools only in the form of mandated representation on school councils or other formal structures—a necessary, but not sufficient, strategy for engaging stakeholders or creating shared leadership. These structures, instead, perpetuated the status quo and limited opportunities for authentic partnerships in schools.

Also, principals and teachers do not have enough training in how to authentically engage with parents and community members. Without better models, ongoing training, and support principals will likely get bogged down in the daily pressures of running the school and not take the time to create more democratic cultures. District leaders could take a much more active role in teaching principals, teachers, and other school staff how to effectively and authentically engage with parents and community members in the educational process. They could help provide principals and teachers with relevant information on shared leadership, trusting school cultures, and facilitation of meaningful dialogue with parents and community groups. In addition, district leaders could mentor school-level administrators on effective means of outreach. Leaders at both levels may also want to discuss the issue of public school "ownership" and what that means for educators and schools as organizations. With dialogue and support, principals and teachers can expand on and deepen their engagement with families and the larger community and work toward becoming leaders for authentic partnerships.

Notes

1. I would like to thank Karen Seashore Louis for her guidance and support throughout this study.
2. The cases for this chapter were selected from a sample from a larger study, where school districts and schools were stratified and then randomly selected from across the United States to ensure variation in size, student diversity (e.g., race/ethnicity, family income), and district trends in student performance on state accountability measures. See http://www.cehd.umn.edu/CAREI/Leadership/default.html for more information.
3. All names in this chapter are pseudonyms.
4. Demographic data in this chapter come from the 2006–2007 National Center for Education Statistics (NCES) and state department of education Web sites.

References

Anderson, G. (1998). Toward authentic participation: Deconstructing the discourses of participatory reforms in education. *American Educational Research Journal, 35*(4), 571–603.

Arum, R. (2000). Schools and communities: Ecological and institutional dimensions. *Annual Review of Sociology*, 26, 395–418.

Auerbach, S. (2010). Beyond coffee with the principal: Toward leadership for authentic school-family partnerships. *Journal of School Leadership, 20*(6), 728–757.

Bidwell, C. (2001). Analyzing schools as organizations: Long-term permanence and short-term change [Special issue]. *Sociology of Education, 74*, 100–114.

Brunner, C. (1998). The legacy of disconnection between the public schools and their communities: Suggestions for policy. *Educational Policy, 12*(3), 244–266.

Crowson, R. L. (2003). The turbulent policy environment in education: Implications for school administration and accountability. *Peabody Journal of Education, 78*(4), 29–43.

Driscoll, M. E. (1998). Professionalism versus community: Themes from recent school reform literature. *Peabody Journal of Education, 73*(1), 89–127.

Epstein, J. L., Galindo, C. L., & Sheldon, S. B. (2010). *Levels of leadership: Effects of district and school leaders on the quality of school programs of family and community involvement.* Paper presented at the triennial meeting of the International Roundtable on School, Family, and Community Partnerships Network of Scholars (INET), Denver, CO.

Giles, C. (2006). Transformational leadership in challenging urban elementary schools: A role for parent involvement? *Leadership and Policy in Schools, 5*(3), 257–282.

Goldring, E. B., & Sims, P. (2005). Modeling creative and courageous school leadership through district-community-university partnerships. *Educational Policy, 19*(1), 223–249.

Gordon, M. F., & Louis, K. S. (2009). Linking parent and community involvement with student achievement: Comparing principal and teacher perceptions of stakeholder influence, *American Journal of Education, 116*(1), 1–31.

Gordon, M. F., & Louis, K. S. (in press). How districts harness family and community energies for school improvement. In K. Leithwood & K. S. Louis (Eds.), *Linking leadership to learning.* San Francisco, CA: Jossey-Bass.

Hess, A. (1999). Community participation or control? From New York to Chicago. *Theory into Practice, 38*(4), 217–224.

Honig, M. I. (2003). Building policy from practice: District central office administrators' roles and capacity for implementing collaborative education policy. *Educational Administrative Quarterly, 39*(3), 292–338.

Honig, M. I. (2006). Street-level bureaucracy revisited: Frontline district central-office administrators as boundary spanners in education policy implementation. *Educational Evaluation and Policy Analysis, 28*(4), 357–383.

Kaestle, C. F. (1983). *Pillars of the republic: Common schools and American society, 1780–1860.* New York: Hill & Wang.

Leithwood, K., Jantzi, D., & Steinbach, R. (1999). *Changing leadership for changing times.* Buckingham, UK: Open University Press.

Louis, K. S. (2003). Democratic schools, democratic communities: Reflections in an international context. *Leadership and Policy in Schools, 2*(2), 93–107.

Louis, K. S., Leithwood, K. L., Wahlstrom, K., Anderson, S. E., Michlin, M., Mascall, B., … Moore, S. (2010). *Learning from leadership: Investigating the links to improved student learning* (Final Report of Research to the Wallace Foundation). Minneapolis/Toronto: Center for Applied Research and Educational Improvement, University of Minnesota and Ontario Institute for Studies in Education, University of Toronto.

Malen, B. (1994). Enacting site-based management: A political utilities analysis. *Educational Evaluation and Policy Analysis, 16*(3), 249–267.

Malen, B. (1999). The promises and perils of participation on site-based councils. *Theory into Practice, 38*(4), 209–216.

Malen, B., & Ogawa, R. T. (1988). Professional-patron influence on site-based governance councils: A confounding case study. *Educational Evaluation and Policy Analysis, 10,* 251–270.

Merriam, S. B. (1998). Qualitative research and case study applications in education. San Francisco, CA: Jossey-Bass.

Meyer, J. W., & Rowan, B. (1977). Institutionalized organizations: Formal structure as myth and ceremony. *American Journal of Sociology, 83,* 340–363.

Miller, P. M. (2008). Examining the work of boundary spanning leaders in community contexts. *Leadership in Education, 11*(4), 353–377.

Mitchell, C. (2008). *Parent involvement in public education: A literature review.* Retrieved from www.researchforaction.org

Sanders, M. G., & Harvey, A. (2002). Beyond the school walls: A case study of principal leadership for school-community collaboration. *Teachers College Record, 104*(7), 1345–1368.

Sarason, S. (1995). *Parent involvement and the political principle: Why the existing governance structure of schools should be abolished.* San Francisco, CA: Jossey-Bass.

Schutz, A. (2006). Home is a prison in the global city: The tragic failure of school-based community engagement strategies. *Review of Educational Research, 76*(4), 691–743.

Tyack, D., & Cuban, L. (1995). *Tinkering toward utopia: A century of public school reform.* Cambridge, MA: Harvard University Press.

Van Voorhis, F., & Sheldon, S. (2004). Principals' roles in the development of US programs of school, family, and community partnerships. *International Journal of Educational Research, 41,* 55–70.

Weick, K. E. (1979). *The social psychology of organizing* (2nd ed.). Reading, MA: Addison Wesley.

9

PARENTS AS ACTION LEARNERS AND LEADERS

Lessons for Administrators in Working with Families and Intermediary Organizations

Janet H. Chrispeels

> The presumption of equality between parents and schools, and the refusal to address power struggles, has systematically undermined real educational transformation.... [Parents] rarely have the opportunity to work collaboratively with educators inventing what could be a rich, engaging, and democratic system for public education.
>
> *(Fine, 1993, p. 684)*

Over the last 10 years several graduate students[1] and I have had the privilege of studying and evaluating two important parent education and leadership development programs that are trying to address power relationships and enhance the frequency and confidence of parent interactions with schools. The programs are offered by two independent intermediary organizations: the Parent Institute for Quality Education and the Parent School Partnership Program of the Mexican American Legal Defense and Education Fund (MALDEF). Each program is focused primarily on assisting Latino parents[2] to understand how the American educational system works and what roles they could play in supporting children's learning. Although they share similar broad goals, each program also has its own theory of action that has shaped the program design and outcomes. We have learned valuable lessons from both programs that can assist school leaders in forming strong, authentic partnerships with families (Auerbach, 2010, Chapter 3, this volume; Epstein, 2011; Leuder, 2011).

In this chapter, I explore the ways in which these intermediary organizations have empowered parents[3] to be action learners and leaders by enhancing their human, social, and intellectual capital. After outlining these key concepts and presenting a summary of the findings from our studies (Bolívar & Chrispeels, 2011; Chrispeels, 2007; Chrispeels & González, 2002, 2004, 2011; Chrispeels,

González, & Arellano, 2004; Chrispeels, González, Bolívar, & Rodarte, 2007; Chrispeels & Rivero, 2001; González & Chrispeels, 2005), I turn my attention to the kinds of leadership dispositions and actions that are essential if these capital gains are to be fully realized to benefit student learning and community development.

Effects of Limited Social and Cultural Capital on School-Family Partnerships

Numerous studies have documented the mutual benefits of family-school collaboration (Deslandes, 2009; Dornbusch & Ritter, 1988; Epstein, 1991, 2011; Gold, Simon, & Brown, 2002; Henderson & Mapp, 2002; Kellaghan, Sloane, Alvarez, & Bloom, 1993; Sanders, 1998; Sheldon & Epstein, 2005). Nevertheless, not all families have found ways to successfully connect with schools and not all schools have empowered families. One of the roots of inequality is inaccessibility of school and community resources for some families and their failure to participate in ways that teachers expect because they lack the social and cultural capital of middle- and upper middle-class families (Coleman, 1987, 1988; Horvat, Weininger, & Lareau, 2003; Lareau, 1989, 2003; Lareau & Weininger, 2003; Ream & Palardy, 2008; Stanton-Salazar, 1997). In their collective studies these authors found that middle-class families typically had stronger social networks and used the information channels and trusting relationships gained through these networks to secure school advantages for their children. Teachers may resent their advocacy and pressure, but they usually cannot ignore it.

In contrast, these authors also documented that parents from working-class and low-income backgrounds generally did not participate in the ways that teachers expected, such as supervising homework, or attending back-to-school nights or parent-teacher conferences. Parents indicated they felt it was not their role or they lacked information about how to participate. In other words, these families lacked middle-class financial and social capital to effectively engage with schools. More importantly from a leadership perspective, these studies showed that teachers' perceptions of parents' low socioeconomic status shaped the negative or patronizing ways they interacted with families (Valdés, 1996).

A sociocultural lens provides another explanation for fewer productive partnerships between African American and Latino families and schools. Clark (1983, 1993), Delgado-Gaitán (1991) and Valdés (1996) documented that family culture often did not match the school's expectation of home supports or active engagement. Latino families frequently isolated themselves from the school; and because of language barriers the schools frequently did not create welcoming environments or reach out to parents in culturally sensitive ways. In addition, traditional parent-teacher associations or parent advisory committees often failed to facilitate involvement of the majority of low income and non-

English speaking parents (Delgado-Gaitán, 1991; Stelmach, 2004). Underrepresented families on their own, with limited components of middle-class social capital, are challenged to create mechanisms for action that support them as leaders or decision-makers with schools (Henderson, 2004; Lopéz, Kreider, & Coffman, 2005).

The collective work of these scholars has been instrumental in highlighting not only sociocultural barriers and the failure of schools to tap the "funds of knowledge" of the families (Moll & Greenberg, 1990) but also the critical role that schools have to play if greater parent involvement is to be realized. An approach that may offer a solution is partnerships between schools and intermediary organizations such as nonprofits, community organizations, and universities. Recent studies have begun to illustrate pathways these organizations are using to bridge families and schools and foster parent empowerment.

Intermediary Organizations as Cultural Brokers and Facilitators of Partnerships

Intermediary organizations have assumed the task of building the competencies of parents and community groups through education and expanded leadership roles in parent organizing, strategic planning, public conversation, and shared decision-making, among others (McAlister, Mintrop, Chong, and Renée, Chapter 11, this volume; Mediratta, Shah, & McAlister, 2008; Oakes & Rogers, 2007). They have worked to meet community needs independently from official agencies, and at the same time, collaborated with schools and districts. As Henderson (2004) noted, their work ranges from education to advocacy to organizing. Some research has suggested these organizations may challenge the assertions of Vincent (1996) and Stelmach (2004) that most parent involvement efforts only mediate and dilute parent power through co-opting them. Intermediary organizations often serve as *cultural brokers*; that is, they act to mediate or link one cultural group to another (Delgado-Gaitán, 1992). Their role has been particularly important in translating the norms and expectations of middle-class society to immigrant families, providing an opportunity for them to work more effectively with official institutions.

Bronfenbrenner (1978) was one of the first scholars to turn his attention to the process of parent empowerment by recognizing the need to foreground inequalities in power if parents' capacity for change is to be maximized. His work, along with Cochran and Dean's (1991) Cornell University Family Matters Project and Comer's (1980, 1984) school development model represent early efforts, with universities serving as an intermediary, to empower parents to take collective steps to improve their children's education through participation and decision-making. Cochran and Dean in particular countered the dominant deficit model and argued that all families have strengths that need to be respected and cultivated. Similarly, Delgado-Gaitán and Treuba's (1991) extensive work with Latino families also rejected the deficit model and focused on parent involvement power as the ability to effect individual and collective changes.

Several recent studies have examined the role of intermediary organizations in assisting families and communities to effect educational change (Chrispeels & González, 2004; Henderson, 2004; Lopéz et al., 2005; Mediratta et al., 2008). For example, Lopéz et al. (2005) investigated four nonprofit organizations with parent education programs that promoted parent involvement in decision-making, democratic participation, and leadership. This capacity building effort supported individual parents by providing them with knowledge and skills to understand and negotiate with the school system. At the relational level, the program involved parents as leaders and catalysts for change while at the organizational level, the programs developed support systems for school-family relations. Likewise, Mediratta et al.'s (2008) study of community organizing initiatives demonstrated that "successful organizing strategies contributed to increased student attendance, improved standardized-test-score performance, and higher graduation rates and college-going aspirations in several sites" (p. v). They also found that these organizing efforts helped to improve teacher morale. Their evaluations highlighted the inequalities in the educational system, and at the same time, provided evidence of low-income parent communities' influence in the policy arena to address inequities through collective action.

Similarly, the Comité de Padres Latinos (COPLA) in Carpinteria, California, developed by Delgado-Gaitán and Treuba (1991), illustrates a university partnership serving as an intermediary to work with a migrant education program. Through the collaboration, parents were empowered to become more active in their children's education. They pressed for changes in school district policy that they felt discriminated against their children. Over time, the organization created a context where fair and effective negotiations with the school system were possible, as opposed to making the community fit the school.

André-Bechely and Bernstein (1998) reported another collaboration of this kind between Center X at UCLA Graduate School of Education and Information Studies and the parent communities at two Los Angeles high schools. Center X provided parents with the necessary knowledge about changes in curriculum and instruction as well as skills that allowed them to lead for social justice. Their Advanced Curriculum Leadership Project guided parents in taking a leadership role as "policy partners" through a minresearch project with a social justice agenda. The parents' projects facilitated their inquiry and reflection around four main themes that arose from their own interests: the complexity of schooling issues, what is "best" in schools, diversity and equity in the school community, and potential for new leadership roles. These findings point to a useful model of parent education that encourages critical reflection, collaborative inquiry, and action.

As shown through these examples, an important role was played by the intermediary organizations in fostering parent empowerment in ways that were beneficial to schools but which they alone were not able to achieve (Mediratta et al., 2008). Studies of these programs, however, do not provide theoretical explanations of how disenfranchised parents can gain voice and act. In an effort to extend our understanding of the potential for parent leadership development and collective action among low-income families, I turn now to the concepts of human, social, and intellectual capital.

Human, Social, and Intellectual Capital

A perspective held by many administrators and teachers is that families of lower socioeconomic status lack the individual knowledge and skills (human capital) to help their children be successful in American schools. Educators also often perceive the low-income communities in which these families live as powerless (lacking in social capital) to act as a collective to improve their situation. Intermediary organizations' work with diverse communities, however, shows that human, social, and intellectual capital are not fixed entities or quantities but can be affected by education and opportunities for individuals to actively share, exchange, and combine knowledge in ways that lead to improvements in their communities (Bolívar & Chrispeels, 2011; Olsen & Chrispeels, 2009). It is important to explore these concepts and how they may help to explain effective parent leadership development and school-family partnerships.

Human Capital

According to Pil and Leana (2009), human capital is "an individual's cumulative abilities, knowledge, and skills developed through formal and informal education and experiences" (p. 1103). Through these acquired skills and capabilities, an individual is able to act in new ways (Coleman, 1988). Human capital is cumulative, occurs over time in interactions with others, and requires continuous opportunities for learning (Kilburn & Karoly, 2008). Unfortunately, low-income families often have few opportunities to develop human capital that enables them to be effective players in their children's education. They are more likely to lack positive experiences with or knowledge of how the educational system works and what roles they may play. Thus, interactions with schools are often problematic for both families and the school unless efforts are made to foster mutual understanding (i.e., linking the culture of one group with the other).

Understanding that human capital is built through interactions, Coleman (1988) identified the crucial role of social capital in the creation of human capital. He found that high levels of social capital in a family assisted the children in developing their knowledge and skills. In addition, a strong network of parents in the community and working relationships with the institutions also facilitated the growth of students' human capital. As Lareau (1989, 2003) and others have shown, families of low socioeconomic status (SES) are often isolated from each other, and therefore lack opportunities to learn through interaction with other community members—a critical component of human and social capital. Thus, there is a close interaction between human and social capital development.

Social Capital

The concept of social capital refers to the resources (power and information) present in social relationships of a bounded community that can be used to leverage additional resources, which then can be used to maintain or obtain additional advantage for the individual and for the community. Bourdieu (1986) was one of the first to theorize the concept of social capital and to highlight how existing structures and institutions perpetuate the system and minimize change. As a major institution, schools often play a role in serving the dominant group, enabling it to preserve its position and to control "the rules of the game," resulting in unequal access to institutional resources for disadvantaged groups (Bourdieu, 1986; Dika & Singh, 2002).

According to Coleman (1988), social capital development in a community is facilitated by three factors: (a) trust, (b) access to information channels that provide a basis for action, and (c) norms and sanctions that promote common good over self-interest. The absence of one or more of these components provides insights into why certain communities or groups of parents may be at a disadvantage when interacting with the American educational system. Understanding how these factors may represent a pathway to enhance the social capital of disadvantaged parent groups is a central focus of our work.

Intellectual Capital

Although researchers have given considerable attention to social capital, few studies have investigated the relationship between social capital and intellectual capital, which enables a group to act as a collective to bring about change (Bolívar & Chrispeels, 2011). The concept of intellectual capital articulated by Nahapiet and Ghoshal (1998) offers a way to understand this dynamic. Unlike the individual nature of human capital, intellectual capital is understood as the knowledge, experiences, and skills of a collective with potential for collaborative, joint action to create advantage for the group (Nahapiet, 1996). Nahapiet and Ghoshal (1998) identified two main processes: exchange and combination of individual knowledge (human capital) with other community members in a trusting social setting (social capital) that expands access to knowledge for the group and leads to innovation and action. High levels of social capital are essential for intellectual capital to be generated (Moran & Ghoshal, 1996; Nahapiet

& Ghoshal, 1998). In our work, we are interested in understanding how the parent education and leadership classes for Latino parents offered by intermediary organizations may have created conditions for this exchange and combination of knowledge to occur and to identify if this led to actions by the group.

For low-income communities, intermediary organizations play a crucial role in fostering the development of social interactions that build trust, creating channels of information and providing insights into the tacit and explicit community norms needed by the group for it to become social actors (Bolívar & Chrispeels, 2011). If there are ample opportunities for the sharing and exchange of knowledge, intellectual capital will be accrued at the community or organization level and enable the members to take collective action that brings about change and development. It is through the lenses of human, social, and intellectual capital that my colleagues and I have explored the work of the Parent Institute for Quality Education (PIQE; n.d.) and the Parent School Partnership Program (PSP) of MALDEF (2009).

Programs of PIQE and PSP

PIQE and MALDEF's PSP are nonprofit, intermediary organizations that offer parent education and leadership development programs in collaboration with districts, schools, and community-based organizations. The overarching purpose of both programs is to assist Latino families (as well as other immigrant parents in PIQE) in becoming actively involved in the education of their children through (a) increasing parents' knowledge and skills about the school system and how to support their children's education; (b) encouraging home and school involvement; and (c) promoting expectations for their children to attend university. Both programs are guided by the underlying principle that parents, especially Latino immigrants, care deeply about their children's future. To enact that care, PIQE and PSP recognize that parents need access to mainstream information about schools and strategies to facilitate involvement expected by teachers.

Both offer their programs in major cities such as San Diego, Minneapolis, Los Angeles, Chicago, Houston, and Atlanta. PIQE serves many areas of California through 12 regional offices. Schools and PIQE share the cost of the program, with schools typically paying $100 per graduate and PIQE raising the remainder through foundation and other grant support. In contrast, to maintain its independence from government because of the civil rights role of MALDEF, PSP is free to schools and relies entirely on foundation and contribution support. This PSP financial structure translates into fewer classes. Since 1989, about 5,000 parents have graduated from PSP programs compared to the 450,000 from PIQE. However, PSP offers a "training of trainers" program for representatives of other community-based organizations, who, in turn, present the program in diverse communities throughout the United States; thus, its reach is far greater than the 5,000 who have been directly involved in parent classes.

Program Content

The basic 9-week PIQE program encompasses the following content: home-school collaboration, motivation and self-esteem, positive communication and discipline, academic standards and testing, how the school system works, and the road to university. The middle and high school programs cover similar topics but with more emphasis on adolescent development; motivating teenagers to read; obstacles to school success such as drugs, alcohol, and gangs; and college requirements. Both programs have one session with the principal, counselors, and in some cases teachers. To graduate from the program parents must attend the majority of content sessions and engage in activities such as reviewing their child's cumulative folder, establishing a homework center, reading to or listening to their children read, and setting up a conference with the teacher.

The PSP program consists of 12 content sessions and two to four field visits. The content is similar to PIQE's program in some respects but differs in its focus on leadership development. Topics include parent rights and responsibilities, parent-teacher conferences, structure and function of both school and district (with a field trip to a school board meeting), the road to university (with field trip to a campus), the politics of education, accessing the media, and responsible leadership, as well as team building and group processes. There is also an education policy forum with school board members, principals, counselors, and city officials. To graduate from the program, parents must work in a group with other parents to develop an action research project. Parents are also encouraged to act individually on behalf of their children through providing homework support, attending parent-teacher conferences, and reviewing school records.

PIQE and PSP Theories of Action

To understand each organization's theory of action, we reviewed documents, observed classes, and interviewed the founders and instructors (Chrispeels & González, 2011; Chrispeels & Rivero, 2001; Rivero, 2006). Table 9.1 summarizes and compares PIQE's and PSP's theory of action. PIQE's theory of action focuses on reaching many parents and ensuring that most graduate from the program. PIQE assumes that if it reaches many parents, typically a hundred or more during each 9-week program, this will create a critical mass and will begin to change the parent-school dynamic and teachers' perceptions of Latino families while empowering parents to be more forceful voices in the school community. In contrast, PSP has a narrower reach and concentrates on developing a small cadre of parent leaders to be action researchers and leaders in the school to bring about change. Both programs aim to equip parents to be advo-

TABLE 9.1 *Comparison of Theories of Action of PIQE and PSP*

Parent Institute for Quality Education (PIQE)	*Parent School Partnership (PSP)*
1. Train a critical mass of parents (100-200) at each school who become *individual advocates* for their children, thus altering home-school relationships.	1. Changes in the educational system require both legal challenges and the development of parent leaders.
2. Recruit parents through telephone calls made by community aides to ensure attendance of parents; link part of the instructors' stipends to the number of graduates.	2. Recruit parents by distributing flyers at the school. Train a dedicated cadre of 20 parents to be leaders and action researchers.
3. Hire instructors committed to Latinos who have similar backgrounds of poverty and speak parents' language, but have navigated the educational system and can serve as *cultural brokers*.	3. Hire instructors committed to Latinos who speak parents' language, are knowledgeable of the political and educational systems, and can serve as *cultural brokers*.
4. Provide parents with opportunities to learn about the educational system, enhance parenting skills, visit a university, and become advocates for their children.	4. Assist parents to access political and educational systems, to exercise their rights, participate on committees, visit colleges and engage in action research.
5. Schools will respond if sufficient numbers of individual parents make well-informed requests and participate.	5. Change will come through collective action of parents if they know the norms and expectations of the educational system, develop leadership skills, and engage in individual and collective action during and after the PSP Program.

Adapted from Chrispeels & González, 2011.

cates for their own child, but PSP emphasizes being advocates for all children through group action research projects.

Program Impact on Parents' Capital

Through multiple studies of these two programs that tease out the ways that they developed parents' human, social, and intellectual capital, we have begun to understand how the programs empowered parents to be agents of change in their own lives and in the larger school community.

Enhancing Parents' Human Capital

Our quantitative and qualitative studies of PIQE show that the program significantly affected parents' knowledge, beliefs, and actions to support their children's education. Similar effect sizes were found for PIQE using a pre-post test design (Chrispeels & González, 2002) and using a random-assignment controlled experimental design (Chrispeels & González, 2004; Chrispeels, González, & Arellano, 2004). Knowledge gains were highly significant with large effect sizes (Cohen, 1988): 1.06 for elementary school parent participants and 0.85 for parents of secondary students. Knowledge was also shown to be the factor most affected by the PSP program, with post-tests showing significant ($p < .01$) gains in almost all items (Chrispeels et al., 2007).

The knowledge gains showed that both programs provided parents with critical access to channels of information (Coleman, 1988), such as knowing that they could request to see the cumulative record of their child's learning and behavior. Parents were often shocked both positively and negatively about information they found in the file when they requested to see it and realized this information would follow the child throughout their school career (Bolívar & Chrispeels, 2011; Rivero, 2006). Parents reported they were unaware that what happens in early grades can affect their child's placement in higher grades. Perhaps even more disheartening for some was the hostility they faced from school officials when they asked to see the file.

Parents from both programs repeatedly acknowledged that information about attending university and the potential for financial aid had a dramatic effect on their expectations for their children (Chrispeels et al., 2006). Field trips to campuses were major motivators for families. One mother recounted, "[I was] fascinated by the university on our visit. Now I can tell you that my goal in life is that my children go to college and have a career" (Bolívar & Chrispeels, 2011, p. 22). Through these programs, parents had extensive opportunities to expand their individual human capital as well as the collective knowledge of the group as they heard from the instructors and invited guests and shared their own experiences. It was particularly important that the programs provided a knowledge structure through which parents were able to interpret their experiences and come to different decisions about what they should do to support their children in school.

Changing Beliefs, Behaviors, and Home-School Connections

New knowledge is usually needed to change beliefs and bring people to act, with behavior or belief changes often lagging behind (Rivero, 2006). Our data showed that while the PIQE programs had a great effect on knowledge gains, changes in beliefs and behaviors were more modest, such as 0.42 effect on parent self-efficacy to support their children's learning, 0.25 effect on parents engaging in learning activities at home, and 0.32 for changes in parenting practices (Chrispeels & González, 2004, p. 2). Similarly, surveys of PSP participants showed highly significant gains in knowledge and more modest but still significant changes in behaviors and beliefs (Chrispeels et al., 2007). For example, parents may have learned that it was important to conference with their child's teacher, but they may not have taken action during or immediately after the program. Follow-up interviews conducted 4 to 6 months after the conclusion of the programs consistently indicated that parents had visited the school, talked with their child's teacher, or asked to see the cumulative file (Chrispeels et al., 2007; Rivero, 2006).

Pre-post surveys for PIQE and PSP showed positive differences on survey items addressing home-school connections, such as whether parents attended a school meeting, initiated a conference with the child's teacher, met with the counselor, or sought tutoring assistance, but the effect size was not significant. This outcome is somewhat expected since stronger connections with the school may also require a response or invitation from the school (Hoover-Dempsey & Sandler, 1997). These findings suggest that home-school connections require leadership by the school, as we discuss later.

PSP's Unique Focus on Parent Leadership and Action Research

A major difference between the two programs was PSP's commitment to developing parent leaders and engaging them in action research projects (see Table 9.1). Therefore, the pre-post assessments for PSP included questions regarding parent leadership and organizational engagement, which the PIQE survey did not. This factor consisted of six items, all of which showed significant change and five of which were highly significant at the $p < .001$ level (Chrispeels et al., 2007, p. 47). Parents indicated that they had become more active in both school and community, attending school board meetings, joining school committees, pressing policymakers for improvements, and encouraging other parents to get involved.

The interview data regarding parent action research projects at two Los Angeles elementary schools strongly supported the survey data. The projects ranged from working with local police to stop the street and school yard from being used for drag racing to pressing the school board for an additional bungalow to use as a computer center (Bolívar & Chrispeels, 2011). The program structure primarily guided these actions by brainstorming with the parents a list of their concerns and encouraging them to form teams to address an issue of their choosing. Through this process, parents said they learned how to present problems, collect data, and work together as a team (Bolívar & Chrispeels, 2011). Particularly important, the parents reported that they now put their concerns in writing. They also gained an understanding of the power of collective action: "Together we are strong. A group of people...can get things done." They reported that "leadership is not an option, it is an obligation to our community" (Bolívar & Chrispeels, 2011, p. 24).

These statements indicate that parents acquired needed access to important information, developed norms for interaction and learned to trust each other—

all key components of social capital. Parents translated the lessons learned into collective action both during and after the program ended, suggesting they were able to transform their human and social capital into intellectual capital. Our data showed that parents in three neighborhoods where the PSP had been offered previously had formed their own parent groups. In fact, with the support of PSP, they had adapted the program's curriculum and were teaching classes to other parents (Bolívar & Chrispeels, 2011; Chrispeels et al., 2007).

Summary of Program Impact

In summary, a review of these two programs showed that both had significant effects on parents. Operating with somewhat different theories of action, they yielded similar and different outcomes. PIQE established an organizational structure and standard operating procedures that allowed the organization to reach an astounding number of Latino families. The strong effect sizes of the program on knowledge gains also indicate its effectiveness in enhancing parent human capital, creating access to critical channels of information and making explicit the norms and expectations of schools (social capital), thus enabling families that have been traditionally underserved by the educational system to act on their children's behalf. Two evaluations that explore long-term effects documented that high school students whose parents had attended PIQE completed more of the courses required for university admission, persisted through to graduation, and entered 2- or 4-year colleges at higher rates compared to matched groups of Latinos whose parents did not attend PIQE (Chrispeels, Bolívar, & Vaca, 2008; Vidano & Sahafi, 2004). These promising long-term outcomes deserve more study and attention.

Although more limited, the studies of the PSP program also showed that it had a short-term and lasting effect on individual and collective parent knowledge, actions, and beliefs. Similar to PIQE, PSP made explicit middle-class norms and enhanced access to critical information about the system. By developing a small cadre of parents who took concerted collective action, PSP more explicitly developed the social and intellectual capital of participating parents. PSP also created greater access to power brokers, such as board members, police, city council members, and staff.

Both programs developed a sense of trust between participants and the intermediary organization and in some cases trust in the school, which is essential for partnership (Bryk & Schneider, 2004). PSP parents also developed trust with each other as they worked together on projects. This seemed to be an important force for change and a process for ameliorating weak social network ties in low-income and diverse communities noted in the literature (Lareau 1989; Ream & Palardy, 2008). Furthermore, the conditions of the classes created a setting of high trust in which parents exchanged and combined information drawn from their own experiences, from the instructor, and from their collective research to generate new insights, knowledge and ways of acting. With this newly generated intellectual capital they took collective action that benefited parents both individually and the community as a whole (Bolívar & Chrispeels, 2011; Chrispeels et al., 2007).

The theoretical lens of social and intellectual capital highlights the conditions needed to empower parents to be partners in school and community reform. Such parent engagement is unlikely to close the achievement gap unless classroom instruction systematically and in some cases dramatically improves in schools serving low-income families, but assisting parents through culturally sensitive programs is an important support strategy. The central question that remains to be answered is whether school leaders are committed to empowering parents as partners.

Implications for School Leaders and Leadership Development

Forming ongoing partnerships with intermediary organizations to enhance parent access and skills in working with schools could bring strategic advantage to schools in promoting parent engagement and raising student achievement. A productive partnership must go beyond offering a service or complying with a federal or state mandates for parent involvement (Anderson, 1998; Auerbach, 2010). The leadership models offered by Auerbach (2010, Chapter 3, this volume) and others (Chrispeels, 1996; Epstein, 2011; Leuder, 2011) stress the importance of strong two-way, authentic partnerships.

Our studies of the PIQE and PSP programs often revealed strong espousal but weak enactment of parent-school partnerships on the part of educators. For example, teacher surveys indicated they were generally minimally informed about the programs being offered to parents even though both programs asked teachers to distribute flyers about the classes (Chrispeels, 2008; Chrispeels & González, 2002). Parents also told of rebuffs by school office staff and a few teachers' refusal to hold conferences with the parents to discuss students' progress. At the graduation of one PIQE class of 100 parents, the principal commented that he would not allow PIQE to hold another session if parents kept asking for information, especially students' cumulative files. Although middle-class parents might have seen this comment as being in jest, for the Latino parents it appeared to be a threat. Fortunately, most leaders offering the program wanted parents to be involved and welcomed the program, providing needed resources such as space for classes and child care. However, once parents had completed the program and the contract with the organization had ended, there was little follow-up from either the intermediary organization or school leaders to build on what had been started.

Our studies indicate two potential explanations for the lack of follow-through. A critical one is inadequate funding for ongoing partnership work, coupled with a failure to recognize that sustaining partnerships requires advance planning and commitment before engaging with an intermediary agency. It is essential that school leaders pose questions such as: What will be the next steps once the classes are over? What is the level of ongoing collaboration needed to sustain parents' knowledge gains and leadership work? What does the school already have in place that can easily be strengthened to sustain the partnership with families?

Another reason for the lack of follow-through may be the perspectives held by many faculty and staff that immigrant and low-income parents need fixing and are not doing their part to ensure their child's success (Nakagawa, 2000). As a result of this prevalent deficit view, it seemed that many schools felt they had done their part by offering the classes. We observed they often did not maximize the parent-teacher partnership potential that was created by the programs. What implications can school leaders draw from these studies if they want to move beyond the rhetoric of parent involvement to authentic partnerships?

Working with Intermediary Organizations

First, our studies suggest that third-party intermediary organizations can assist principals and serve as cultural brokers to open up channels of communication between school staff and families. To create authentic partnerships with families and communities, however, school leaders and their schools will reap the greatest benefits if they understand the theory of action of the intermediary organization. These two parent education and development programs each had benefits for parents and the schools; nevertheless, as shown, their different theories of action led to some different results. Other programs will have their own theories of action. By exploring a program's goals and the processes used to bring the goals to fruition, school leaders will better understand potential benefits, how they align with school needs and goals, and what actions will be needed by the school to sustain the results.

It is important to recognize that one program is not likely to meet all goals related to parents and partnerships. PIQE's strong recruitment and retention plan, leading to high numbers served, is matched by few intermediary organizations serving families. PSP provided valuable skills to fewer parents, but with these skills parents assumed active roles in addressing school and community problems. Thus, both programs make valuable contributions, and the selection of which intermediary agency to work with should be guided by school needs and parent wishes. Helping parents gain a basic understanding of the system, how they can support their child, how to conference with teachers, and how to raise expectations for school success and college attendance may be an important starting point, as with PIQE. The challenge for most schools is not to stop there but move on to the kinds of action research knowledge and leadership skill building provided by a program such as the PSP.

Examining Beliefs and Practices

Second, school leaders need to recognize that the type of intermediary organization they may choose to partner with is shaped by their own values, beliefs, and skills in working with diverse communities. Current and future leaders must examine their own beliefs regarding parent involvement. Do they want parents to be rule followers who meet school and teacher expectations or partners with knowledge of their children and culture that needs to be counted in decision-making (Yeager & Córdova, 2009)? As leaders, do they want to be buffers and brokers or partners with families?

As Nakagawa (2000) showed, policymakers, educators, and the general public through policies and beliefs have cast parents both as the problem and as the protector or savior. She argued that this dual role has put parents in a double bind that "is most harmful for those whose children are often poorly served by the schools: parents of color and lower income parents" (p. 456). School leaders and staff often blame parents for children's school failures because parents are not involved in ways that match school expectations. At the same time, they assert that the solution must be greater parent involvement. Schools want this involvement without changing their own practices, even in schools and communities that are impoverished by high teacher and leadership turnover, poor facilities, overcrowding, and unsafe neighborhoods. Parent engagement in the poorest communities, as our studies showed, can make a difference for families, their children, and the school community, but it is no panacea for poor instruction, inadequate school and community resources, high unemployment, and family distress (see Olivos, Chapter 6, this volume). Current and future school leaders need opportunities to explore their values, beliefs, and prior experiences with families and to learn from the families they serve. Do leaders see family deficits or do they see family strengths, assets, and funds of knowledge that could be tapped to support student learning (González, Moll, & Amanti, 2005)? When leaders understand how their own values and practices may be contributing to continued school failure and social inequality, they can become empowered to act in new ways in partnerships, just as the parents in our studies did as they gained knowledge and insights.

Third, school leaders need to recognize and value that parents care deeply about their children and their school success, regardless of their race, ethnicity, or socioeconomic status. Leaders need to build a school community focused on creating an ethic of care as a basis for authentic partnerships (Nakagawa, 2001; Noddings, 1992). One of the first places to begin may be the school front office. Leaders need to give special attention to preparing the clerical staff to work with diverse families. As Lightfoot so well articulated in her classic book, *Worlds Apart* (1978), parents and teachers/school staff have different roles. Parents must be advocates for their child and school staff must be attentive to all children's needs. From these different roles, tensions and conflicts are bound to arise. Principals need to explicitly surface these tensions for themselves and with their staff. Acknowledging that families and schools, parents and teachers will not always agree can go a long way toward building mutual respect and trust. Once surfaced, norms can be developed for ways of interacting. In the PSP program, parents repeatedly expressed how valuable it was to learn norms of how to present their concerns with calmness and respect, as well as how to put concerns in writing so as be better heard (Bolívar & Chrispeels, 2011; Chrispeels et al., 2007).

Leaders, faculty, and staff also need to develop their skills in holding meaningful conversations with families and developing norms that promote trustful and respectful interaction. Leadership preparation programs must prepare our future leaders to feel comfortable with ambiguity and tension, to have strategies to engage in constructive conflict, and knowledge of how to promote courageous conversations. Helping parents see the big picture of how the school system works was a critical component of the PSP and PIQE programs. It is equally important for leaders and staff to learn about the strengths and struggles of families and conditions in their communities.

A fourth implication of our work is that examining the strengths and limitations of existing parent involvement structures and activities could help ease potential school-family tensions. For example, are parents, teachers, and students prepared for conferences? Are these conferences just verbal report cards or are they occasions for goal-setting and problem-solving? Do parent-teacher associations and required parent-teacher councils serve as window dressing (Stelmach, 2004) or are these groups engaged in data collection and action research for school improvement, as taught in the PSP program? Strengthening school-family partnerships does not necessarily mean initiating new programs. More importantly, staff and parents need to examine what is, and revise and renew current practices to meet current family and school needs. Making such changes, however, means leaders must know how to collect data, review school programs, build effective teams, and resolve conflicts—skills not always well developed in preparation programs.

Finding Common Ground

A fifth suggestion drawn from the work of H. Giles (1998) for building bridges, constructively engaging families, and reinvigorating family-school partnerships is identifying common concerns. In our study, the PSP program facilitated the process of parents identifying concerns, such as those over teacher punishments for tardiness. Through their action research project, parents and educators dialogued about the issue and developed solutions that better met family, student, and teacher needs and at the same time reduced student tardiness. Thus, the PSP process of parents surfacing and addressing concerns often benefited the schools as well as parents (see McAlister et al., Chapter 11, this volume). The program illustrated a process leaders can use in collaboration with intermediary organizations to address pressing school issues that engage parents and teachers.

Another strategy for building common knowledge and common ground would be to collaboratively engage staff and parents in reviewing school and grade level achievement data. Our study showed that when provided with data about their child's performance as well as tools to collect information, parents in both programs changed their practices and took action. Many schools now assess student progress every 6 weeks and provide professional development for teachers in using data. Leaders could encourage teachers and parents to review grade-level data together to see trends in growth and areas for improvement. Teachers could then explain their next steps and solicit parents' ideas for their involvement. This kind of transparency moves from blaming either teachers or parents for results and creates the opportunity for genuine shared responsibility for student learning.

Drawing on the work of Moll and Greenberg (1990) regarding community funds of knowledge, a sixth step toward authentic partnerships could be implementing instructional designs that utilize problem-based learning (PBL; Lambros, 2004; Lamer, Ross, & Mergendoller, 2009; Ronis, 2008). PBL, which aligns with the action research model of PSP, could collaboratively engage students and their teachers in addressing critical community problems, such as childhood obesity and diabetes, and at the same time motivate students to master core curriculum standards and develop 21st century skills such as problem solving, critical thinking, and teamwork. PBL units offer rich opportunities to involve family and community members as resources and coresearchers. Implementing PBL would require current and future school leaders to better understand how to identify community issues and resources and their potential to enrich the school curriculum. Research has shown that incorporating problem-based learning into leadership preparation programs sharpened future leaders' problem-framing and problem-solving abilities (Bridges & Hallinger, 1997; Chrispeels & Martin, 1998; Martin, Chrispeels, & D'Emidio-Caston, 1998). Expanding the use of PBL in preparation programs and helping current leaders to develop these skills would strengthen their ability to work productively with school committees to solve schoolwide problems.

A final implication drawn from our work suggests that administrators and teachers need knowledge about diverse families and communities as much as families need knowledge about schools. Partnership must be a two-way street (Chrispeels, 1996). In some schools, PIQE staff offered a teacher workshop. Review of the pre-post evaluations of over 300 teachers from 16 schools in the Los Angeles area indicated that most felt it was highly valuable and they gained important insights about how to work with Latino families. They indicated that they saw the need for positive communication with families and creating a welcoming environment. One commented, "We as educators could make the difference in students' and families' lives" (Chrispeels, 2007, p. 10). However, most faculty did not receive this workshop before or during the PIQE parent program. With a strong social norm of framing low-income parents as the problem (C. Giles, 2006), few schools have attended to the knowledge needs of faculty in this area. If school leaders want to foster authentic partnerships with families, they must take the lead in developing their own as well as teachers' knowledge, skills, and sense of efficacy to work with diverse parents and communities (Hoover-Dempsey, Bassler, & Brissie, 1987).

As we have seen, partnering with intermediary agencies enabled low-income parents to be action learners and leaders. Outside facilitators from PIQE and PSP who understood both the school and its families served as a vital cultural bridge between the two worlds. School leaders who welcome and partner with such agencies greatly increase the potential to develop trust, norms for collaboration, and increased access to information for all participants to learn with and from each other. With enhanced social capital, both families and schools will be able to generate the intellectual capital needed to build a strong, democratic community that ensures the success of each child.

Notes

1. It is with deep gratitude and appreciation that I acknowledge the wonderful learning partnerships that I have enjoyed with former graduate students and now Dr. Margarita González, Dr. Jose Bolívar, Dr. Elvia Rivero, Dr. Marisol Rodarte, and Dr. Brenda Arellano. I would also like to thank President David Valladolid and Vice President for Program Development, Patricia Mayer, from the Parent Institute for Quality Education and the many fine instructors I have observed, as well as MALDEF's Thomas A. Saenz, President and General Counsel, and Parent School Partnership Director of National Training, Araceli Simeon-Luna, for their willingness to open their programs for our studies. Their steadfast dedication to ensuring our least well-served students receive the education they need and deserve is always inspiring.
2. PIQE primarily focuses on Latino families, though it also offers classes to several other immigrant groups and has teaching materials translated into English, Russian, Cambodian, Korean, Chinese, and Armenian.
3. The terms *parents* and *families* are used interchangeably in this article, with *parents* referring to the broader concept of any family member who provides care and nurturing for children including grandparents, foster parents, aunts, uncles, and others.

References

Anderson, G. L. (1998). Toward authentic participation: Deconstructing the discourses of participatory reforms in education. *American Educational Research Journal, 35*(4), 571–603.

André-Bechely, L. N., & Bernstein, S. (1998). *Building parent leadership in curriculum reform through school/university collaboration.* Paper presented at the annual meeting of the American Educational Research Association, San Diego, CA.

Auerbach, S. (2010). Beyond coffee with the principal: Toward leadership for authentic school-family partnerships. *Journal of School Leadership, 20*(6), 730–759.

Bolívar, J. M., & Chrispeels, J. H. (2011). Enhancing parent leadership through building social and intellectual capital. *American Educational Research Journal, 48*(1), 4–38.

Bourdieu, P. (1986). The forms of social capital. In J. G. Richardson (Ed.), *Handbook of theory and research for the sociology of education* (pp. 241–258). New York: Greenwood.

Bridges, E., & Hallinger, P. (1991). Problem-based learning: A promising approach for preparing educational administrators. *UCEA Review, 32*(3), 3–7.

Bronfenbrenner, U. (1978). Who needs parent education? *Teachers College Record, 79*, 767–787.

Bryk, A. S., & Schneider, B. L. (2004). *Trust in schools: A core resource for improvement.* Chicago, IL: University of Chicago Press.

Chrispeels, J. H. (1996). Effective schools and home-school community partnership roles: A framework for parent involvement. *School Effectiveness and School Improvement, 7*(3), 7–33.

Chrispeels, J. H. (2007). *Evaluation of the Parent Institute for Quality Education Teacher Workshop.* San Diego: University of California, San Diego.

Chrispeels. J. H., Bolívar, J., & Vaca, R. C. (2008). *Research progress report no. 2.* La Jolla: Education Studies, University of California, San Diego.

Chrispeels, J. H., & González, M. (2002). *The impact of the Parent Institute for Quality Education on families in Los Angeles schools.* Santa Barbara, CA: University of California, Santa Barbara.

Chrispeels, J. H., & González, M. (2004). *Effects of education programs on Latino parents' knowledge, beliefs and practices in middle schools* (FINE Research Digest). Cambridge, MA: School of Education, Harvard University.

Chrispeels, J. H., & González, M. (2011). Mapping family-school partnership programs through theories of action and logic models. In C. Hands & L. Hubbard (Eds.), *Including families and communities in urban education* (pp. 269–301). Charlotte, NC: Information Age Publishing.

Chrispeels, J. H., González, M., & Arellano, B. (2004). *Evaluation of the effectiveness of the Parent Institute for Quality Education in Los Angeles Unified School District: Evaluation report.* Retrieved from http://www.piqe.org/Assets/Home/ChrispeelEvaluation.htm

Chrispeels, J. H., González, M., Bolívar, J., & Rodarte, M. (2007). *MALDEF Parent School Partnership Program: Final evaluation report.* Santa Barbara: Gevirtz Graduate School of Education, University of California, Santa Barbara.

Chrispeels, J. H., & Martin, K. J. (1998). Becoming problem solvers: The case of three future administrators. *Journal of School Leadership, 8*, 303–331.

Chrispeels, J. H., & Rivero, E. (2001). Engaging Latino families for student success: Understanding the process and impact of providing training to parents. *Peabody Journal of Education, 76*(2), 119–169.

Clark, R. M. (1983). *Family life and school achievement: Why poor black children succeed or fail.* Chicago, IL: University of Chicago Press.

Clark, R. M. (1993). Homework-focused parenting practices that positively affect student achievement. In N. F. Chavkin (Ed.), *Families and schools in a pluralistic society* (pp. 85–105). Albany, NY: State University of New York Press.

Cochran, M., & Dean, C. (1991). Home-school relations and the empowerment process. *Elementary School Journal, 91*(3), 261–272.

Cohen, J. (1988). *Statistical power analysis for the behavioral sciences* (2nd ed.). Hillsdale: NJ: Erlbaum.

Coleman, J. S. (1987). Families and schools. *Educational Researcher, 16*(6), 32–38.

Coleman, J. S. (1988). Social capital in the creation of human capital. *American Journal of Sociology, 94*, 95–120.

Comer, J. P. (1980). *School power.* New York: Free Press.

Comer, J. P. (1984). Educating poor minority children. *Scientific American, 259*, 42–48.

Delgado-Gaitán, C. (1991). Involving parents in the schools: A process of empowerment. *American Journal of Education, 100*(1), 20–46.

Delgado-Gaitán, C. (1992). School matters in the Mexican-American home: Socializing children to education. *American Educational Research Journal, 29*, 495–513.

Delgado-Gaitán, C., & Treuba, H. (1991). *Crossing cultural borders: Education for immigrant families in America.* London: Falmer.

Deslandes, R. (Ed.). (2009). *International perspectives on student outcomes and homework: Family-school-community partnerships.* London: Routledge.

Dika, S. L., & Singh, K. (2002). Applications of social capital in educational literature: A critical synthesis. *Review of Educational Research, 72*, 31–60.

Dornbusch, S. M., & Ritter, P. L. (1988, Winter). Parents of high school students: A neglected resource. *Educational Horizons*, 75–77.

Epstein, J. L. (1991). Effects of student achievement on teachers' practices of parent involvement. *Advances in Reading/Language Research, 5*, 261–276.

Epstein, J. L. (2011). *School, family and community partnerships: Preparing educators and improving schools* (2nd ed.). Philadelphia, PA: Westview Press.

Fine, M. (1993). [Ap]parent involvement: Reflections on parents, power and urban public schools. *Teachers College Record, 94*, 682–710.

Giles, C. (2006). Transformational leadership in challenging urban elementary schools: A role for parent involvement. *Leadership and Policy in Schools, 5*(3), 257–282.

Giles, H. (1998, May). *Parent engagement as a school reform strategy.* New York: ERIC Clearinghouse on Urban Education. (ERIC Document Reproduction Service No. ED 419 031). Retrieved from www.ed.gov/databases/ERIC_Digests/ed419031.html

Gold, E., Simon, E., & Brown, C. (2002). *Strong neighborhoods, strong schools: Indicators project on education organizing.* Chicago, IL: Cross City Campaign for Urban School Reform. Retrieved from www.communityschools.org

González, M., & Chrispeels, J. H. (2005). *Effects of parent education programs: Knowledge, beliefs and practices of Latino families in middle schools.* Paper presented at the annual meeting of the American Educational Research Association, Montreal, Canada.

González, N., Moll, L. C., & Amanti, C. (Eds.). (2005). *Funds of knowledge: Theorizing practices in households, communities, and classrooms.* Mahwah, NJ: Erlbaum.

Henderson, A. T. (2004). *The case for parent leadership.* Lexington, KY: Prichard Committee for Academic Excellence.

Henderson, A. T., & Mapp, K. L. (2002). *A new wave of evidence: The impact of family, school, community connections on student achievement.* Austin, TX: National Center for Family & Community Connections with Schools, Southwest Educational Development Laboratory.

Hoover-Dempsey, K. V., Bassler, O. C., & Brissie, J. S. (1987). Parent involvement: Contributions of teacher efficacy, school socioeconomic status and other school characteristics. *American Educational Research Journal, 24*(3), 417–435.

Hoover-Dempsey, K. V., & Sandler, H. M. (1997). Why do parents become involved in their children's education? *Review of Educational Research, 67*, 3–42.

Horvat, E., Weininger, E. B., & Lareau, A. (2003). From social ties to social capital: Class differences in the relations between schools and parent networks. *American Educational Research Journal, 40*, 319–351.

Kellaghan, T., Sloane, K., Alvarez, B., & Bloom, B. S. (1993). *The home environment and school learning.* San Francisco, CA: Jossey-Bass.

Kilburn, M. R., & Karoly, L. A. (2008). *The economics of early childhood policy: What the dismal science has to say about investing in children.* Santa Monica, CA: Rand Corporation. Retrieved from www.rand.org/pubs/occasional_papers/OP227.html.

Lambros, A. (2004). *Problem-based learning in middle and high school classrooms: A teachers' guide to implementation.* Thousand Oaks, CA: Corwin Press.

Lamer, J., Ross, D., & Mergendoller, J.R. (2009). *Project based learning toolkit series: PBL starter kit.* Novato, CA: Buck Institute for Education.

Lareau, A. (1989). *Home advantage: Social class and parental intervention in elementary education.* London: Falmer Press.

Lareau, A. (2003). *Unequal childhoods: Class, race, and family life.* Berkeley, CA: University of California Press.

Lareau, A., & Weininger, E. (2003). Cultural capital in educational research: A critical assessment. *Theory and Society, 32*(5–6), 567–606.

Leuder, D. C. (2011). *Involving hard-to-reach parents: Creating family /school partnerships.* Lanham, MD: Rowman & Littlefield.

Lightfoot, S. L. (1978). *Worlds apart: Relationships between families and schools.* New York: Basic Books.
Lopéz, M. E., Kreider, H., & Coffman, J. (2005). Intermediary organizations as capacity builders in family education involvement. *Urban Education, 40*(1), 78–105.
Martin, K. J., Chrispeels, J. H., & D'Emidio-Caston, M. (1998). Exploring the use of problem-based learning for developing collaborative leadership skills. *Journal of School Leadership, 8,* 423–497.
Mediratta, K., Shah, S., & McAlister, S. (2008). *Organized communities, stronger schools: A preview of research findings.* Providence, RI: Annenberg Institute for School Reform at Brown University.
Mexican American Legal Defense and Educational Fund (MALDEF). (2009). Parent School Partnership (PSP) Program. Retrieved from http://www.maldef.org/leadership/programs/psp/index.html
Moll, L. C., & Greenberg, J. B. (1990). Creating zones of possibilities: Combining social contexts for instruction. In L. C. Moll (Ed.), *Vygotsky and education: Instructional implications and applications of socio-historical psychology* (pp. 319–348). New York: Cambridge University Press.
Moran, P., & Ghoshal, S. (1996). Value creation by firms. In J. B. Keys & I. N. Dosier (Eds.), *Academy of Management best paper proceedings* (pp. 41–45). Cincinnati, OH: Academy of Management.
Nahapiet, J. (1996). *Managing relationships with global clients: Value creation through cross-borders networks.* Paper presented at the 16th annual conference of the Strategic Management Society, Phoenix, AZ.
Nahapiet, J., & Ghoshal, S. (1998). Social capital, intellectual capital, and the organizational advantage. *Academy of Management Review, 23*(2), 242–266.
Nakagawa, K. (2000). Unthreading the ties that bind: Questioning the discourse of parent involvement. *Educational Policy, 14,* 443–472.
Noddings, N. (1992). *The challenge to care: An alternative approach to education.* New York: Teachers College Press.
Oakes, J., & Rogers, J. (2007). Radical change through radical means: Learning power. *Journal of Educational Change, 8,* 193–206.
Olsen, E. M., & Chrispeels, J. H. (2009). A pathway forward to school change: Leading together and achieving goals. *Leadership and Policy in Schools, 8*(4), 38–410.
Parent Institute for Quality Education (PIQE). (n.d.). Parent engagement education program. Retrieved from http://www.piqe.org/prog_parentengage.php
Pil, F. K., & Leana, C. (2009). Applying organizational research to public school reform: The effects of teacher human and social capital on student performance. *Academy of Management Journal, 52*(6), 1101–1124.
Ream, R. K., & Palardy, G. (2008). Reexamining social class differences in the availability and the educational utility of parental social capital. *American Educational Research Journal, 45*(2), 238–273.
Rivero, E. (2006). *A study with an ethnographic perspective: A new perspective on Latino families and their children's schooling* (Unpublished doctoral dissertation). University of California, Santa Barbara.
Ronis, D. L. (2008). *Problem-based learning for math and science: Integrating inquiry and the Internet* (2nd ed.). Thousand Oaks, CA: Corwin Press.
Sanders, M. G. (1998). The effects of school, family and community support on the academic achievement of African-American adolescents. *Urban Education, 33*(3), 385–409.
Sheldon, R. B., & Epstein, J. L. (2005). Involvement counts: Family and community partners and mathematics achievement. *Journal of Educational Research, 98*(4), 196–209.
Stanton-Salazar, R. D. (1997). A social capital framework for understanding the socialization of racial minority children and youths. *Harvard Educational Review, 67*(1), 1–40.
Stelmach, B. L. (2004). Unlocking the schoolhouse doors: Institutional constraints on parent and community involvement in a school improvement initiative. *Canadian Journal of Educational*

Administration and Policy, 31. Retrieved from https://www.umanitoba.ca/publications/cjeap/articles/stelmach.html.

Valdés, G. (1996). *Con respeto: Bridging the distances between culturally diverse families and schools: An ethnographic portrait.* New York: Teachers College Press.

Vidano, G., & Sahafi, M. (2004). *Parent Institute for Quality Education: Special report on PIQE's performance evaluation.* San Diego, CA: San Diego State University, College of Business Administration Marketing Department. Retrieved from http://www.piqe.org/about-researchstudies.php

Vincent, C. (1996). Parent empowerment? Collective action and inaction in education. *Oxford Review of Education, 22*(4), 4656–4682.

Yeager, E., & Córdova, R. A. (2009). How knowledge counts: Talking family knowledge and lived experience into being as resource for academic action. In M. L. Dantas & P. Manyak (Eds.), *Home-school connections in a multicultural society: Learning from and with culturally and linguistically diverse families* (pp. 218–236). New York: Routledge.

10

SUPPORTING TEACHER LEADERSHIP FOR PARTNERSHIPS

A Case Study of the School-Community Partnership Process

Catherine M. Hands

Since the 1980s, researchers have advocated the benefits of partnerships between schools, families, and communities as a means for promoting student achievement (Epstein & Sanders, 1998; Henderson, 1987; Henderson, Mapp, Johnson, & Davies, 2007). With school personnel finding it increasingly difficult to address the diverse needs of students with existing resources (Merz & Furman, 1997), school-community partnerships are a way to garner additional resources, social support, and educational experiences to supplement students' in-school learning opportunities (Hands, 2005).

The onus for the establishment of partnerships falls to the schools (Davies, 2002; Epstein, 1995, 2001; Henderson et al., 2007; Sanders & Harvey, 2002); both principals and teachers need to reach out to parents and community organizations (Epstein, 1995, 2001; Hargreaves & Fullan, 1998; Sheldon, 2005). At large, complex secondary schools, administrators and teachers, either through their departments or acting on their own, are all possible actors when it comes to establishing relationships with community partners. Teacher involvement is considered crucial to partnerships, especially those with parents (Epstein, 2001). Yet the school-community partnership literature typically focuses on the role of the principal and the identification of school-level conditions that promote collaboration; the circumstances and extent of teacher involvement remain unclear (e.g., Sanders, 1999; Sanders & Harvey, 2002). Thus, it is useful to examine the influence of teachers as well as principals on the development of partnerships with businesses and community organizations.

The case study that is the basis of this chapter sought to yield insight into the process of establishing and sustaining school-community partnerships. It addresses the following questions: How do educators in secondary schools develop school-community partnerships? Who is involved in seeking out potential partners and establishing partnerships? What conditions influence a school's capacity for and interest in school-community partnerships? This chapter focuses on teachers' roles in creating these liaisons, principals' roles in facilitating teacher leadership, and contextual influences on partnership cultivation. It is hoped that this work will contribute to the discussion of how teacher leadership can be harnessed to reconnect schools and communities in order to provide a support net for each student and to promote their academic success.

This chapter begins by interweaving a conceptual framework of structure, culture, agency, and distributed leadership with selected empirical literature. It then describes the study methodology and context before presenting findings on principals' facilitation of teacher leadership and the teachers' process of developing partnerships, concluding with implications for research and practice.

Structure, Culture, Agency and Partnerships

Issues of structure, culture, and agency frame the characteristics of schools that facilitate or challenge the implementation of reform initiatives (see Datnow, Hubbard, & Mehan, 2002). In order to understand the complexity of negotiating partnerships, it is helpful to examine the ways in which structure, culture, and agency interact with these initiatives.

Partnerships as Structures

Structure refers to the external forces that impact social action. Relationships are influenced by the structure of schooling and its position within a broader economic system (Anyon, 2005). Thus, the institutional arrangements that schools, families, and communities have traditionally held in relation to each other and to the district, state, and federal government, influence the interactions among constituents (Hubbard & Hands, 2011).

School-community partnerships themselves are a type of school-level structure. They can be described as the "connections between schools and community individuals, organizations, and businesses that are forged to promote students' social, emotional, physical, and intellectual development" (Sanders, 2001, p. 20). These connections provide a vehicle for a bidirectional "flow of information and products across mutual boundaries" (Campbell, Steenbarger, Smith, & Stucky, 1980, p. 2) of the school and the community. They can be categorized as focusing on student support, family support, school improvement, or community development (Sanders, 2001). Wohlstetter, Malloy, Smith, and Hentschke (2003) found partnership activities centered around curriculum, facilities, financial assistance, business and management expertise, and to a lesser degree, liaisons with community, assistance with administrative procedures, and enhancing the schools' legitimacy. Partnership activities have been shown to be influential and beneficial for students and school personnel, as well as their community partners (Hands, 2005; Sanders, 2001).

In the school-community partnership literature, there are school-level structures that impact the development of these relationships. In her survey of the institutions affiliated with the National Network of Partnership Schools (n.d.), Sanders (1999) notes that the key elements of successful partnerships include leadership and guidance, adequate funding and time to develop partnerships, and an action team to actively coordinate and support partnerships. Similar to action teams, steering committees, PTAs, and school councils also have the potential to promote opportunities for family and community involvement in education (Hands, 2010).

Structures such as those resulting from policy or the work of organizations or committees influence social action (Datnow et al., 2002). Beyond the school, some community-based organizations, for example, support family and community members' participation in education by providing information and a vehicle for advocacy (Evans, 2011; Hands, 2005, 2010; Harvard Family Research Project, 2002). The maintenance of the school system's traditional hierarchical structure can also impact social action by preventing the emergence of teacher leaders (Murphy, 2005) for partnerships or other initiatives. This places much of the responsibility on district leaders, and more specifically, principals to cultivate the agency among school personnel that is necessary for school initiative development and implementation of partnerships. At the school level, the structures that principals put in place contribute to or detract from a culture that supports school-community relations and teacher leadership (Hubbard & Hands, 2011). Questions then arise around how principals navigate systemic structures that are seemingly immutable and create new structures to influence a school culture that is compatible with partnership development.

The Role of Culture in Partnering

Understanding the success and failure of school, family, and community partnerships also requires an examination of cultural factors. By looking at the culture of both the school and the community, we gain a better understanding of how the ideologies, beliefs, and values held by constituents shape the nature of collaborative activities (e.g., Bryk & Schneider, 2002).

The culture of an organization has been described as "a pattern of shared basic assumptions that the group learned as it solved its problems…to be taught to new members as the correct way to perceive, think, and feel in relation to those problems" (Schein, 1995 p. 279). Features of organizational culture include patterns of behavior, group norms, espoused values, a formal philosophy, members' skills, members' mental models, and shared meanings (Schein, 1995). The patterns of beliefs, values, social and political relations, as well as expectations that guide behavior and practices distinguish one school culture from another (Gilley, 2000; Steiner, 2002). Principals influence the maintenance and transmission of a culture that is reflected in teachers' activities and goals (Donaldson, 2006; Leonard, 1999) through their support—or lack thereof—for those goals and activities (Muncey & McQuillan, 1996).

Sanders and Harvey's (2002) case study of an elementary school's partnering with the community highlights several features of school culture that are conducive to partnerships. They found that the school's commitment to promoting an academically challenging and supportive learning environment was one of the main factors that influenced community partners to become involved with the school. The school's openness and receptivity to community involvement was also crucial to its success with community and family partnerships (cf. Davies, 2002). The principals determined if collaborative activities were potentially beneficial to students, and ongoing, two-way communication helped partnerships to grow and improve over time (Sanders & Harvey, 2002). Lastly, the principal's support for community partnerships enabled their establishment and assisted in maintaining them; however, the principal's ability to build capacity among school personnel was also deemed important in the maintenance of these relationships.

How is a welcoming environment conducive to collaboration created, and by whom? What role do teachers potentially play in initiating and maintaining partnerships? These are questions that not only address issues of culture, but also relate to agency.

Principal and Teacher Agency: Distributed Leadership

Partnerships are driven by the actions or agency of those involved. A constructivist approach to understanding outcomes assumes that actions—like participation in collaborative activities—occur as the result of face-to-face interactions among constituents over time, during everyday practice, and across contexts (Hubbard, Mehan, & Stein, 2006). While influenced by structural and cultural factors, actions shape and are shaped by the participants involved (Datnow et al., 2002).

Principal leadership is an essential element in the development of strong partnership programs and possibilities for authentic participation (Auerbach, 2010, Chapter 3, this volume; Epstein, 2001; Henderson et al., 2007). Their agency serves to shape the culture and organizational structures that make these collaborations possible. Yet leadership for partnerships moves beyond traditional planning, resource allocation, and organizational management tasks. Kotter (1995) and Blanchard (1996) describe business leaders who promote organizational change as risk takers with little concern for traditional hierarchy who recruit and cultivate new leaders from within—an approach compatible with leadership for partnerships. Similarly, while principals are responsible for establishing a school culture that welcomes partnerships, they alone cannot foster links between schools and communities. Teacher involvement and teacher leadership are necessary for school change as part of distributed leadership (Birky, Shelton, & Headley, 2006; LeBlanc & Shelton, 1997; Murphy, 2005; Neuman & Simmons, 2000; Spillane, Halverson, & Diamond, 2001).

As Spillane and Diamond (2007) note, leading and managing schools is the purview of many individuals who may or may not be in formal leadership positions. Distributed leadership takes into account the interdependence and interaction of individuals and the environment, moving its focus from principals to "the web of leaders, followers, and their situation that give form to leadership practice" (p. 7).

In order to facilitate teacher agency, school culture must encourage teachers to take the initiative to lead (Katzenmeyer & Moller, 2001) and promote positive relationships among school personnel, with principal support for teacher leadership (Murphy, 2005; York-Barr & Duke, 2004). This support can take the form of formal structures legitimizing teachers' leadership roles, such as department headships; informal behaviors that affirm teacher leadership, such as conversations among principals and teachers (Birky et al., 2006); or coaching and feedback (Buckner & McDowelle, 2000; Kahrs, 1996). The principals thus "share power, encourage teacher leadership, and set a tone that validates teachers' views and expertise" (Stone, Horejas, & Lomas, 1997, p. 8).

According to York-Barr and Duke (2004), "Teacher leadership reflects teacher agency through establishing relationships, breaking down barriers, and marshalling resources throughout the organization in an effort to improve students' educational experiences and outcomes" (p. 263). Several scholars extend this definition beyond school-level influence. Teacher leaders can also work across the boundaries of schools and communities to create social networks using, for instance, relationship development advocacy and innovation as vehicles for their agency (Crowther, Kaagen, Ferguson, & Hann, 2002; Paulu & Winters, 1998). Coordinating people and resources as well as encouraging interactions among individuals that support mutual instructional and curricular goals are the core managerial and leadership foci for teacher leadership (Forster, 1997). While most of the literature on teacher leadership focuses on these skills in school reform or instruction, they are the same skills needed to develop school-community partnerships (see Hands, 2005; Sanders, 1999; Sanders & Harvey, 2002).

While occupying different roles, then, both principal and teacher leadership may contribute to the creation of school-level conditions conducive to school-community partnership development. Since both principals and teachers can be actors in the partnership development process, questions arise as to how principals provide opportunities for teacher empowerment in this area and the nature of teachers' work in school-community partnering. With this foundation laid, I briefly describe the study methodology and setting before discussing the central role that teachers were found to play in the partnership process, as well as the support provided by the principals.

Methodology

This chapter draws on data from a qualitative case study of two secondary schools within a southern Ontario school district. The two schools were identified through the district as those with reputations for establishing numerous strong community partnerships. They were Kincaid High School,[1] in a small urban center surrounded by a rural region with a culturally homogeneous community of low socioeconomic status, and Mosdell Secondary School, situated within a multicultural, suburban, low- to middle-income community. Both schools had about 80 school-community partnerships to meet the needs of the students, school, and community partners.

The main data source was 25 semistructured interviews of about 45 minutes each conducted with principals, teachers, school support staff, and representatives of community organizations during three site visits at Mosdell and four site visits at Kincaid. A snowball technique (Merriam, 1998) was used during interviews with school personnel to obtain contacts with community participants. Additionally, I conducted observations of the daily school operations and among school personnel and I reviewed pertinent documents such as school plans and meeting minutes. Multiple sources of data helped to establish validity through triangulation of the data (Merriam, 1998; Yin, 1994). Once interviews were transcribed verbatim, they were sent to the participants for review and clarification. Using the constant comparative method, the data were coded and analyzed within and across cases for emerging categories and themes (Merriam, 1998). In this way, new themes were developed and existing ones were evaluated and modified. For example, the initial theme of "key contact" was revised to "networked contact" when it became evident that most partnerships were created among key contact persons who already knew each other either socially or professionally.

The Social Context for Partnerships

Although associated with the same school district, the secondary schools and communities in this study were very different from one another. Descriptions of these contexts provide a basis for understanding the development of partnerships based on school needs and community characteristics.

Mosdell Secondary School was situated in the suburban, primarily middle-income, multicultural region of Beaconsville in a large urban center. The area was home to a large number of new Canadians, with just under half of the population being foreign-born and half reporting first languages other than English or French. A fifth of the residents were non-European and non-Aboriginal (Statistics Canada, 2001a). Mosdell served 1,560 students and their families from approximately 70 cultural groups.

The guidance department head noted the challenges of providing access to the range of social and academic services needed by Mosdell's diverse students and families. Many families were newcomers so facilitating access to medical and dental care, in addition to demystifying the Canadian school system and expectations for families, were school priorities. This was also a driving force behind Principal John Ferrante's focus on technology and the internationalization of education in an effort to connect with people from other cultures and expand social networks for students, families, and educators alike.

Kincaid High School, located 120 kilometers from a large urban center in the hamlet of Queenstown, drew its population from the surrounding rural community. According to federal census data, Canadian-born residents comprised almost 90% of the population and were mostly of European descent and low-income (Statistics Canada, 2001b). Being situated within a large, sparsely populated rural region, Queenstown was resource-poor with inadequate public transportation, limited public services, and no large industry.

Most of the 900 students at Kincaid were from low-income families. Keenly aware of this, Principal Monica Kenny and her staff tried to provide financial and emotional support. For example, many of the teachers donated to student bursaries for field trips and other expenses, counseled students, and accessed social services on their behalf. As at Mosdell, most Kincaid students were expected to transition from school directly to the workplace instead of to college. By striving to ensure that all students had their needs met, Monica's goal was to cultivate a culture of care at the school, provide academic, social, and occupational skills, and foster students' hope for their future.

Principals' Agency in Facilitating Partnering

While the two schools were situated in very different communities and the needs of the students and communities were varied, both principals identified partnership development as a beneficial strategy for their school. The principals modeled the leadership needed to develop school-community partnerships by creating some of their own partnerships, and they also assisted their teachers in leadership roles through their personal networks (cf. Crowther et al., 2002).

Facilitating Teachers' Partnerships

On occasion, the principals themselves created collaborative relationships with the community. The Mosdell principal, John, had established and maintained a partnership with a media company, which began as a social relationship with the president of the corporation. Through this relationship, John received financial support for the school's radio station. Similarly, as Kincaid's principal, Monica had developed a partnership with a child and youth mental health organization to provide counseling at the school to students in need. She had also recruited a former colleague and Queenstown citizen who was very involved within the community for the school council. This community partner was able to provide the school with access to material and human resources for various partnerships and activities through his personal network of associations with other Queenstown residents.

The principals also instigated partnerships that were subsequently developed by the teachers. As Monica observed, "A lot of times, it's me helping facilitate. I will sometimes start something, and then I get people involved, and then I step back." In her relationship with the local First Nations[2] band council through the school district, Monica and the band's education manager came to an agreement on the parameters of a First Nations student counselor's involvement at Kincaid. Then Monica involved Susan, a Kincaid teacher and First Nations resident, in the partnership. Together, the education manager and Susan monitored the partnership and expanded it to include the band's guidance on creating a First Nations resource center in the school. Thus, Monica made the partnerships possible, and assisted in their growth.

John applied the same approach at Mosdell, observing that "once you start the ball rolling, then [school personnel] start making their own calls, then they start making their own meetings. So before you know it, you've got a network of people doing so much." This view was reflected in the teachers' comments. For example, guidance department head, Gloria, noted that John was highly supportive of her work. When Gloria initiated the partnership with a local college's radio broadcasting department, John was an active participant at meetings where members of the school and college faculties crafted the terms of the partnership.

Teachers at both schools noted that the principal's support was crucial for creating their school-community partnerships, and they considered their principals to be very supportive. Interestingly, the emphasis on partnering at these schools was not a result of an interest in partnering per se. Principals did not create structures such as action teams to establish comprehensive partnership programs, nor did they provide time during the day for faculty to develop these relationships. In particular, time constraints were an ongoing challenge for teachers trying to initiate partnerships. As Gloria observed of partnership development, "It's an add-on. So do I get time? No, it just becomes part and parcel and an addition to my workday." Regardless, both principals and teachers considered school-community partnerships to be an effective strategy for providing the resources needed to promote student achievement and well-being. Partnerships were thus seen as part of effective service delivery at the schools, and cultures supportive of partnering arose organically from the needs of the schools and the students.

Encouraging a Culture Conducive to Partnering

John and Monica had different foci for their schools' cultures; however, the activities in which their staffs were engaged were remarkably similar. To that end, both principals cultivated a supportive atmosphere for partnership-building within the school, even when they were not directly involved in partnership initiation or development. The principals used formal and informal means to promote this culture.

For example, as the formal leaders charged with the responsibility of hiring faculty, both principals took opportunities to articulate the school culture to prospective teachers. In John's words,

> I say to the teachers that come here that are new, "There's a certain amount of capacity that those of us that are here have. If you're hired here at the school, we ask you to help us build our capacity further, take us further. Give ideas, thoughts, approaches that you think will ultimately enhance student achievement. We want to be receptive to you sharing that with us, and we want you to feel that you can try."

Similarly, Monica stated that

> Whenever I interview a new teacher, I tell them that "you will learn you will be involved with kids, probably on a scale in some cases more so than in other schools.... Some of our students are so entirely needy in many areas." And not all are. But the teachers do things innately.

In this way, the principals ensured that new staff were willing and able to proactively address the needs of the students and more broadly, the school.

At both schools, it was formal policy for staff to ask for permission prior to engaging in partnership activities pertaining to the school and the students. Both Monica and John used these opportunities to show support for their staff, sustain the school culture, and facilitate teachers' initiatives. During the interview with John, he asked a teacher who dropped by his office about her experiences taking risks and initiating projects at the school: "I try to make sure opportunities are here.... If you have an idea and you think you want to try it, ... what's the likelihood that you'll get a yes here?" The teacher responded, "always, always." John continued:

> We're really working like crazy to build leadership capacity ... I basically say, "Look, there's 83 of you. You've all got unique talents, you've all got unique abilities, you've all got deficiencies, OK.... But the bottom line is, just go out and do it."

John and Monica were keenly interested in school improvement efforts, and they supported initiatives such as partnerships that had the potential to promote student learning and well-being. They also realized that they could not do it alone; they needed their faculty and staff to look beyond the walls of the school for partners in this endeavor.

Correspondingly, the community partners noted the necessity and presence of the principal's support and a welcoming school environment. The partners considered Mosdell and its principal proactive in seeking out opportunities to interact with the community. At Kincaid, community members noted that Monica and her staff defined their school as a welcoming environment, and in the course of meeting the needs of the students, either sought out community involvement or were receptive to it.

Teachers' Development of Community Partnerships

Study participants agreed that in most cases, community partnerships were initiated by teachers with the support of their principals. The teachers first determined the needs of their students and programs, then used their personal and professional networks to successfully approach potential community partners to address those needs. The teachers negotiated mutually beneficial terms with their partners and worked together to assess the partnership activities' ability to meet each others' needs.

Assessing Student and Program Needs

Before any partnership was initiated, the goals and needs of the school were first assessed. In particular, teacher participants stressed that the academic, social, emotional, and physical needs of the students were the focus and the basis for partnership efforts. For example, Mosdell guidance department head, Gloria, looked at the needs of students from newcomer families in the school community. They often did not know how to access services such as medical and dental care, and they had not yet had opportunities to learn about and to participate in Canadian youth culture. Consequently, she established connections with numerous social service agencies, including a child and youth mental health organization, as well as a partnership between a local college's broadcasting department and Mosdell's communications department.

Other teachers likewise established links on their own to address programming gaps. Mosdell physical education department head, Marie, stated, "You have to go with a strong sense of what it is you want to do. And how it's going to meet the needs of your kids." The initial goal-setting prior to partnership development is consistent with literature on the need for partnership programs to respond to the needs, interests, talents, and grade levels of students and their families (Epstein, 1995, 2001). Marie established a collaboration with a martial arts academy to provide the self-defense instruction that was part of the curriculum but could not be effectively taught by the school's physical education staff. Similarly, Marie and Gloria initiated a partnership with the region's public health department to provide teachers, students, and their families with up-to-date health sciences resources, which were particularly useful for the many students who were newcomers to the country.

At Kincaid, family studies department head, Frances, was responsible for linking several of her classes with two local theater companies and the community child care center. In this economically challenged community, Frances was keenly aware of the need to provide students with skills for personal and professional development, and experience that would aid a successful transition into the workplace or a college setting. Students in the sewing classes received hands-on training making costumes and accessories for theater productions. They developed marketable skills while providing the financially strained theater companies with necessary production support. The students in parenting and child development classes interacted with a variety of children ranging in age from infancy through the preschool years in the child care center, which developed the students' skills and knowledge while providing the center with staffing support.

The teachers and community members worked toward establishing partnerships in which community members took an active role in teaching and learning issues. Thus, the teacher leaders' agency promoted community members' agency in education. There were other benefits as well to promoting community connections. Three Queenstown community partners observed that school-community partnerships raised the school's and the students' status in the community. In the words of one partner,

> They [the students and school personnel] are a part of the community. And it makes them more a part of the community. You know,...interacting and working together and fulfilling the needs of the students, the teachers, the residents. It's just kind of a continuous interaction that benefits all.

Using Networks to Build Agency

The teacher leaders were acutely aware of students' needs and the impact of community conditions on the students and school programming. They also recognized the importance of assessing the broader social context, for it dictated the types of resources available. When they described approaching a potential partner, both educators and community members illustrated the value of networking. Participants reported establishing most of their partnerships through people with whom they or their colleagues were already socially or professionally associated. Thus, an interconnected web of associations was utilized to cultivate new ways of interacting (e.g., Capra, 1994; Morgan, 1997; Steiner, 2002).

Networking was seen as an essential component of partnering even before a partnership idea was formulated and a contact person was sought. It was necessary for educators who wanted partnerships to go to conferences, workshops, and the like to learn about resources and programs available to them in the community. "It brings [up] a lot people's names or services, or just ways we can access resources," according to history department head, Susan, and the teachers interviewed at Kincaid. Likewise, Marie observed of her professional relationships with community members,

> As you develop partnerships, then you develop that networking. That's how you learn more about what's available to you, because there is so much opportunity out there, in ways that our school and program could be supported, but teachers just aren't aware of them. For free. There's no cost involved in many of the partnerships that could be established.

Developing networks enabled the teachers to identify and approach potential partners, and to strategize ways of working together for mutual benefit.

Conversely, a lack of networks or the ability to make connections with a broad range of individuals was a substantial impediment for partnership development. The teachers reported that failed attempts to develop a desired partnership were often due to not knowing someone in an organization socially or professionally, and that such a connection was often necessary to facilitate partnership establishment.

Building Structures for Collaboration

Most study participants believed that the most effective strategy for developing partnerships was to promote the benefits of the partnership in the early stages of the relationship. Even before they met with potential partners, most of the teachers had a clear idea of what benefits the community member could provide, as well as what the school and students could contribute to the collaborative effort that would benefit the community organization. For relationships proposed by community members, the same onus was placed on the initiator to make the benefits for the school personnel and students clear.

Marie observed that the first contact with a potential partner was often not in person but through voice or electronic mail messages. Consequently, Marie noted the need for any partnership proposal to be clear and strong from this initial contact; it was important to state the benefits up front from the beginning because potential partners were busy. Similarly, Kincaid's community-based education[3] department head, Tom, found that because time constraints were problematic for any business, educators needed to be clear and concise in presenting partnering requests. Several community members agreed that schools did indeed need to advertise their goals and the benefits prior to partnership development, as they themselves did. According to a local grocery store owner, while not every citizen was interested in partnering, a failure to address the benefits and potential positive outcomes might impede partnership development. This was corroborated by some of the teachers' failed attempts to establish partnerships.

Teachers such as Gloria and Bob reported that they met with community representatives a number of times to define the nature of their partnerships and come to a mutually satisfying agreement. As Mosdell's partner, the college radio broadcasting program coordinator, noted,

> We can get something out of this, they can get something out of it, both parties are happy, it's a win-win situation. So why not put the time in to get it happening?... The meetings there and here were ... partly filled with...faculty experiences teaching kids, and I think that that was a commonality that started the ... conversation.... I think that [creating the partnership] was not very difficult *at all.*

Marie used the opportunity of meeting with partners to maximize the resources that could be provided by the community group. Similarly, Gloria entered into negotiations with a best outcome in mind. For her partnership with the college, she wanted access to college resources and a certain number of places reserved in the college broadcasting program for graduating Mosdell students in exchange for the college's access to the school's radio station; however, she was prepared to compromise. "Now, we wanted more than one spot, we didn't get it," she said. "We had to compromise. We wanted two or three spots, they wouldn't give us them. That would have been our ideal." Regardless, both parties were sensitive to the other's needs and organizational guidelines, and they worked together until they were satisfied with the terms of the partnership.

This was also the case for more structured school-community partnerships. For the community-based education teachers, the parameters of partnerships were prescribed by the Ontario Ministry of Education (see Flessa & Grégoire, Chapter 7, this volume). Yet, within the established boundaries of the partnership, there was room for negotiation in terms of the students' activities or duties. According to Tom at Kincaid:

> It depends on what fits for the kid, it depends on what fits for the business. It's very flexible. I'm open to suggestions. [It's] all negotiation. It has to make sense for the student, it has to be safe, has to be educational. Always we're asking, "Is the student going to learn here?"

Ongoing Negotiation to Sustain Partnerships

In addition to stressing the role of negotiation in the initial development of partnerships, teachers discussed the need for compromise and personal flexibility during the implementation of collaborative activities. One of Mosdell's partners observed that a partnership needed flexibility to evolve:

> If we were to set up something and not ever look at it or adjust it, we might be missing the boat or doing a disservice to some of the students or doing a disservice to ourselves or to [Mosdell]. And I think by ... discussing things, leaving some [partnership terms] vague and some ... open, ... then we can make modifications if we have to.

Whether or not the partnerships had a formal agreement associated with them, the teachers and their partners assessed their ability to address their needs over time, and they made any required adjustments.

Teachers as Leaders of Community Partnerships

Research on distributed leadership points to the need for interaction between two dimensions: organizational capacity and a culture that supports a distribution of responsibility and collaboration and the agency of those in leadership positions (Ritchie & Woods, 2007; Woods, Bennett, Wise & Harvey, 2004). Similarly, scholars of school reform note the importance of the influence of structures, cultures both within the school and in the surrounding community, and the agency of all constituents affected by education issues when implementing initiatives (see, for example, Datnow et al., 2002).

This chapter has highlighted the central role of teachers as leaders in creating school-community partnerships and of principals in establishing a culture of support for partnerships. As in Sanders and Harvey's (2002) study of community partnerships, a warm, open, and receptive school environment combined with principal support were central components of community collaboration. The principals played a pivotal role in partnership-building primarily through facilitating teacher leadership. Like administrators supporting teacher leadership in other areas, the principals encouraged teachers' leadership activities by valuing their work, enabling risk-taking (Katzenmeyer & Moller, 2001; Ritchie & Woods, 2007), and enhancing access to needed resources (Crowther et al., 2002). They facilitated collaborative activities, were available to support their faculty, modeled leadership, and provided verbal and technical support (Birky et al., 2006).

As we have seen, the teachers in this study took the primary role in partnership-building in order to meet student needs that could not be addressed by on-campus resources. This is consistent with several dimensions of teacher leadership and partnerships in the literature. Teachers are responsible for the "translation of the principles of school improvement into the practices of individual classrooms" (Harris, 2003, p. 316). They have both the expertise and knowledge to judiciously select additional assistance required (Harris, 2003; Ritchie & Woods, 2007). Like the "emissaries" who crossed organizational borders to form partnerships in Cordeiro and Kolek (1996), they were "armed with a purpose, with permission to seek out others with whom to form linkages, with the authority to act as leaders, and with the imperative to interact across levels and organizations" (p. 13).

This chapter has shown the role of teachers in various steps of the partnership process, from identifying needs and approaching potential partners to negotiating terms. As in York-Barr and Duke's (2004) description of teacher leadership, these teacher leaders initially assessed needs and set goals to meet them. Teachers drew on their social and professional networks to match needs to potential partners and make initial contacts. Networking has likewise been shown to be useful for addressing difficulties in instruction (Lieberman & Miller, 2005) and promoting teacher voice and professional development in school improvement efforts (Lambert, 2003). Both teachers and community members agreed that outlining the benefits of collaboration clearly and concisely when first approaching partners was an effective strategy for garnering support. Negotiating the terms of partnerships through dialogue was important for both school personnel and community members, as in Sanders and Harvey (2002). Similarly, Mawhinney's (2002) study of the social capital yielded by partnerships observed that the partnership process required flexibility and capacity-building in educators' responsiveness to community members' needs.

While principals facilitated teachers' ownership and responsibility over partnership initiatives, the structure of most of the teachers' workdays did not allow for the time needed to consult with community members and develop relationships. Teachers in this study typically worked on partnerships during their preparation periods, lunch breaks, or outside of school hours. Similarly, Sanders (1999, 2001) found that educators had limited time to identify, contact, and meet with community members, constituting a challenge to developing partnerships. Murphy (2005) observes that time for teachers to learn, converse with one another, procure resources, and to reflect are all foundational elements of teacher leadership; a lack of time is a substantial impediment to teacher leadership (LeBlanc & Shelton, 1997). While the teachers in this study successfully established most of their desired partnerships because they viewed them as essential, a lack of dedicated time for partnership development created potential challenges for them.

Interestingly, there was no evidence in this study that school personnel wished to engage community groups in education for ethical or philosophical reasons (e.g., Pushor & Ruitenberg, 2005). Rather, partnerships stemmed from a pragmatic understanding that community partnerships were necessary to provide students with the learning experiences and support they needed to succeed in school and beyond. As such, it was considered part of the teachers' responsibility as educators to seek out resources both within and outside of the school. This may be why there were no specific structures established at the schools to facilitate partnership development, such as a steering committee or a work schedule with dedicated staff time.

These findings highlight the reciprocal nature of partnerships and their impact on both the school and community theorized by scholars (see Banathy, 1992; Datnow et al., 2002; Hargreaves & Fullan, 1998; McLaughlin & Talbert, 1990; Morgan, 1997). In addition to the direct benefits yielded to students, collaborative activities had broader implications for school-community relations. They enabled students, school staff, and community members to interact with and get to know one another in new contexts. Student access to community facilities and organizations is enhanced and knowledge for the success of all students is fostered "by building dense sets of networks" of relationships between schools and communities (Mawhinney, 2002, p. 251). Some community partners in this study considered partnering with the school as a step toward improved relations within the community, and more broadly, the society. Thus, teacher-led partnerships provided opportunities to promote the agency of teachers, students, and community members beyond the contexts in which they usually operated.

Implications for Research and Practice

These findings have implications for further research, policy, and practice. Future studies may benefit from an examination of school practices for establishing community partnerships in other settings, such as large urban centers. In this way, comparisons of the partnership cultivation process across different community types could be investigated, and a greater understanding of contextual influences could be derived. Additionally, studies that include student voice in partnering are needed. The participants identified only two strong partnerships that involved students in the development stages, despite an acknowledgment by participants that it was necessary to involve all stakeholders in the process. More research is needed to identify the specific ways in which students of all ages in a broad range of communities would like to be involved with the community and the partnership development process.

The most successful partnerships reported in this study, as in others (Cordeiro & Kolek, 1996; Hands, 2005), were those voluntarily established by partners rather than those established by legislation or mandates for collaboration. This suggests that authentic school-community partnerships are best developed in a grassroots manner, based on the perceived needs and wishes of those directly involved in establishing them. In this study, the characteristics of the community shaped the needs of the students and the schools, and informed the collaborative activities the teachers and their community partners developed; the potential resources and partners available to the schools were specific to those communities (cf. Lin, 1999). District-, provincial-, or state-level policy to promote partnering without dictating the nature of the collaborative activities or the types of partnerships to be developed is likely to be more effective at supporting the partnership activities across diverse school settings.

It is clear that not all educators who want to develop community partnerships have been able to do so effectively (Sanders, 1999). Research on schools that have not been successful at partnership-building in comparison to those that have would also yield insight into the partnership process. The critical components necessary for partnership establishment could then be determined. For example, contrary to existing research that identifies action teams as essential in determining partnership goals and initiating the relationships (Epstein,

1995, 2001; Sanders, 1999, 2001; Sanders & Harvey, 2002), this study found no evidence that action teams were necessary. This factor points to the need for further research to identify the relative impact of partnership-building features that impede or facilitate partnership establishment.

The findings highlighted in this chapter illuminate a lesser-known aspect of teacher leadership as well as educators' experiences in establishing community links. Therefore, they may prove to be informative for practitioners considering developing their own partnerships. Administrators interested in community partnerships have options besides pursuing these on a schoolwide basis by themselves; they can share leadership for instigating and sustaining them with teacher leaders. To do so efficiently, administrators would do well to seek out human resources, scheduling alterations, or other organizational structures to provide teachers with the necessary time for partnership work. Collaboration with community groups can help meet the needs of students and school programs that might not otherwise be addressed, so teachers might wish to cultivate opportunities to learn about resources and potential partners available in the community through building their personal and professional networks. In this way, teachers build their leadership capacity to harness valuable resources for their schools.

In order to promote the importance of school-community relations among educators, universities and school districts should present partnering as an integral aspect of the teaching profession through preservice and in-service programs. If partnership-building is considered a core element of education and a fundamental means of community involvement in schooling, it is more likely that all children in our communities will have access to what they need to learn to fully and constructively participate as citizens in their society, which is, as one teacher observed, "what we are educating kids for."

Notes

1. The names of all individuals, schools, and communities are pseudonyms.
2. *First Nations* is a term applied to Canada's Aboriginal or Native North American people.
3. Community-based education staff in Canadian schools arrange for students to work in the community for a semester, with goals similar to those of experiential projects in service learning or community service. In Ontario, students must complete 40 hours of community service to graduate.

References

Anyon, J. (2005). *Radical possibilities: Public policy, urban education, and a new social movement.* New York: Routledge.

Auerbach, S. (2010). Beyond coffee with the principal: Toward leadership for authentic school-family partnerships. *Journal of School Leadership, 20*(6), 728–757.

Banathy, B. H. (1992). *A systems view of education: Concepts and principles for effective practice.* Englewood Cliffs, NJ: Educational Technology.

Birky, V. D., Shelton, M., & Headley, S. (2006). An administrator's challenge: Encouraging teachers to be leaders. *NASSP Bulletin, 90*(2), 87–101.

Blanchard, K. (1996). Turning the organizational pyramid upside down. In F. Hesselbein, M. Goldsmith, & R. Beckhard (Eds.), *The leader of the future* (pp. 81–86). New York: Drucker Foundation.

Bryk, A., & Schneider, B. (2002). *Trust in schools: A core resource for improvement.* New York: Russell Sage Foundation.

Buckner, K. G., & McDowelle, J. O. (2000). Developing teacher leaders: Providing encouragement, opportunities, and support. *NASSP Bulletin, 84*(616), 35–41.

Campbell, D. E., Steenbarger, B. N., Smith, T. W., & Stucky, R. J. (1980, September). *The ecological-systems approach in community psychology: Four implications for program evaluation.* Paper presented at the annual meeting of the American Psychological Association, Montreal, Quebec, Canada. (ERIC Document Reproduction Service No. ED201931)

Capra, F. (1994). *Ecology and community.* Retrieved from http://www.ecoliteracy.org/pages/publications.html.

Cordeiro, P. A., & Kolek, M. M. (1996, Winter). Boundary crossings: Educational partnerships and school leadership. *New Directions for School Leadership, 2,* 1–14.

Crowther, F., Kaagen, S. S., Ferguson, M., & Hann, L. (2002). *Developing teacher leaders: How teacher leadership enhances school success.* Thousand Oaks, CA: Corwin Press.

Datnow, A., Hubbard, L., & Mehan, H. (2002). *Extending educational reform: From one school to many.* New York: RoutledgeFalmer.

Davies, D. (2002). The 10th school revisited: Are school/family/community partnerships on the reform agenda now? *Phi Delta Kappan, 83*(5), 388–392.

Donaldson, G. A., Jr. (2006). *Cultivating leadership in schools: Connecting people, purpose, and practice* (2nd ed.). New York: Teachers College.

Epstein, J. L. (1995). School/family/community partnerships: Caring for the children we share. *Phi Delta Kappan, 76*(9), 701–712.

Epstein, J. L. (2001). *School, family, and community partnerships: Preparing educators and improving schools.* Boulder, CO: Westview Press.

Epstein, J. L., & Sanders, M. G. (1998). What we learn from international studies of school-family-community partnerships. *Childhood Education, 74*(6), 392–394.

Evans, M. P. (2011). Learning to organize for educational change: One CBO's efforts to influence educational policy. In C. M. Hands & L. Hubbard (Eds.), *Including families and communities in urban education* (pp. 139–160). Charlotte, NC: Information Age.

Forster, E. M. (1997). Teacher leadership: Professional right and responsibility. *Action in Teacher Education, 19,* 82–94.

Gilley, J. (2000). Understanding and building capacity for change: A key to school transformation. International *Journal of Educational Reform, 9*(2), 109–119.

Hands, C. (2005). It's who you know and what you know: The process of creating partnerships between schools and communities. *The School Community Journal, 15*(2), 63–84.

Hands, C. M. (2010). Parent engagement in school decision-making and governance. In D. Hiatt-Michael (Ed.), *Promising practices to support family involvement in schools* (pp. 97–127). Charlotte, NC: Information Age.

Hargreaves, A., & Fullan, M. (1998). *What's worth fighting for out there?* New York: Teachers College Press.

Harris, A. (2003). Teacher leadership as distributed leadership: Heresy, fantasy or possibility? *School of Leadership & Management, 23*(3), 313–324.

Harvard Family Research Project. (2002). *Concepts and models of family involvement.* Retrieved from http://www.gse.harvard.edu/hfrp/projects/fine/resources/case_study/intro.html#top.

Henderson, A. (1987). *The evidence continues to grow: Parental involvement improves student achievement.* Columbia, MO: National Committee for Citizens in Education.

Henderson, A. T., Mapp, K. L., Johnson, V. R., & Davies, D. (2007). *Beyond the bake sale: The essential guide to family-school partnerships.* New York: New Press.

Hubbard, L., & Hands, C. M. (2011). The role of leadership in forging family-school-community relationships. In C. M. Hands & L. Hubbard (Eds.), *Including families and communities in urban education* (pp. 41–68). Charlotte, NC: Information Age.

Hubbard, L., Mehan, H., & Stein, M. K. (2006). *Reform as learning: School reform, organizational culture, and community politics in San Diego.* New York: Routledge.

Kahrs, J. R. (1996). Principals who support teacher leadership. *New Directions for School Leadership, 1,* 19–40.

Katzenmeyer, M., & Moller, G. (2001). *Awakening the sleeping giant: Helping teachers to develop as leaders* (2nd ed.). Thousand Oaks, CA: Corwin Press.

Kotter, J. P. (1995). What leaders really do. In J. T. Wren (Ed.), *The leaders companion* (pp. 114–123). New York: Free Press.

Lambert, L. (2003). Leadership redefined: An evocative context for teacher leadership. *School Leadership & Management, 23*(4), 421–430.

LeBlanc, P. R., & Shelton, M. M. (1997). Teacher leadership: The needs of teachers. *Action in Teacher Education, 19,* 32–48. Retrieved from http://vnweb.hwwilsonweb.com.myaccess.library.utoronto.ca/hww/results/results_fulltext_maincontentframe.jhtml?url=results_single_ftPES.jhtml&_DARGS=/hww/results/results_single_fulltext.jhtml

Leonard, P. E. (1999). Examining educational purposes and underlying values orientations in schools. In P. T. Begley (Ed.), *Values and educational leadership* (pp. 217–235). Albany, NY: State University of New York Press.

Lieberman, A., & Miller, L. (2005). Teachers as leaders. *The Educational Forum, 69,* 151–162.

Lin, N. (1999). Building a network theory of social capital. *Connections, 22*(1), 28–51.

Mawhinney, H. B. (2002). The microecology of social capital formation: Developing community beyond the schoolhouse door. In G. Furman (Ed.), *School as community: From promise to practice* (pp. 235–255). Albany, NY: State University of New York Press.

McLaughlin, M. W., & Talbert, J. E. (1990). The contexts in question: The secondary school workplace. In M. W. McLaughlin, J. E. Talbert, & N. Bascia (Eds.), *The contexts of teaching in secondary schools: Teachers' realities* (pp. 1–14). New York: Teachers College Press.

Merriam, S. B. (1998). *Qualitative research and case study applications in education.* San Francisco, CA: Jossey-Bass.

Merz, C., & Furman, G. (1997). *Community and schools: Promise and paradox.* New York: Teachers College Press.

Morgan, G. (1997). *Images of organization* (2nd ed.). Thousand Oaks, CA: Sage.

Muncey, D., & McQuillan, P. (1996). *Reform and resistance in schools and classrooms: An ethnographic view of the coalition of essential schools.* New Haven, CT: Yale University Press.

Murphy, J. (2005). *Connecting teacher leadership and school improvement.* Thousand Oaks, CA: Corwin.

National Network of Partnership Schools. (n.d.). *Type 6: Challenges and redefinitions for collaboration.* Retrieved from http://www.csos.jhu.edu/p2000/challenges/type6cha.htm.

Neuman, M., & Simmons, W. (2000). Leadership for student learning. *Phi Delta Kappan, 82,* 8–12.

Paulu, N., & Winters, K. (1998). *Teachers leading the way: Voices from the National Teacher Forum.* Washington, DC: U.S. Department of Education.

Pushor, D., & Ruitenberg, C., with co-researchers from Princess Alexandra Community School. (2005, November). *Parent engagement and leadership* (Research report, project #134). Saskatoon, SK: Dr. Stirling McDowell Foundation for Research into Teaching.

Ritchie, R., & Woods, P. A. (2007). Degrees of distribution: Towards an understanding of variations in the nature of distributed leadership in schools. *School Leadership & Management, 27*(4), 36–381.

Sanders, M. G. (1999). Schools' program and progress in the National Network of Partnership Schools. *The Journal of Educational Research, 92*(4), 220–232.

Sanders, M. G. (2001). The role of "community" in comprehensive school, family, and community programs. *The Elementary School Journal, 102*(1), 19–34.

Sanders, M. G., & Harvey, A. (2002). Beyond the school walls: A case study of principal leadership for school-community collaboration. *Teachers College Record, 104*(7), 1345–1368.

Schein, E. H. (1995). Defining organizational culture. In J. T. Wren (Ed.), *The leader's companion: Insights on leadership through the ages* (pp. 271–281). New York: Free Press.

Sheldon, S. B. (2005). Testing a structural equation model of partnership program implementation and parent involvement. *The Elementary School Journal, 106*(2), 171–187.

Spillane, J. P., & Diamond, J. B. (2007). Taking a distributed perspective. In J. P. Spillane & J. B. Diamond (Eds.), *Distributed leadership in practice* (pp. 1–15). New York: Teachers College Press.

Spillane, J. P., Halverson, R., & Diamond, J. B. (2001). Investigating school leadership practice: A distributed perspective. *Educational Researcher, 30*(3), 23–28.

Statistics Canada. (2001a). *2001 Community profiles.* Retrieved from http://www12.statcan.ca/english/profil01/CP01/Details/Page.cfm?Lang=E&Geo1=CSD&Code1=3519028&Geo2=PR&Code2=35&Data=Count&SearchText=Vaughan&SearchType=Begins&SearchPR=01&B1=All&Custom=

Statistics Canada. (2001b). *2001 Community profiles.* Retrieved from http://www12.statcan.ca/english/profil01/CP01/Details/Page.cfm?Lang=E&Geo1=CSD&Code1=3519070&Geo2=PR&Code2=35&Data=Count&SearchText=Georgina&SearchType=Begins&SearchPR=01&B1=All&Custom=

Steiner, F. (2002). *Human ecology: Following nature's lead.* Washington, DC: Island Press.

Stone, M., Horejas, J., & Lomas, A. (1997). Commonalities and differences in teacher leadership at the elementary, middle and high school levels. *Action in Teacher Education, 19,* 49–64. Retrieved from http://vnweb.hwwilsonweb.com.myaccess.library.utoronto.ca/hww/results/results_fulltext_maincontentframe.jhtml?url=results_single_ftPES.jhtml&_DARGS=/hww/results/results_single_fulltext.jhtml

Wohlstetter, P., Malloy, C. L., Smith, J., & Hentschke, G. (2003). *Cross-sectorial alliances in education: A new approach to enhancing school capacity* (Working paper). Los Angeles: Rossier School of Education, Center on Educational Governance, University of Southern California.

Woods, P. A., Bennett, N., Harvey, J. A., & Wise, C. (2004). Variabilities and dualities in distributed leadership: Findings from a systematic literature review. *Educational Management Administration & Leadership, 32*(4), 439–457.

Yin, R. K. (1994). *Case study research: Design and methods* (2nd ed.). Thousand Oaks, CA: Sage.

York-Barr, J., & Duke, K. (2004). What we know about teacher leadership: Findings from two decades of scholarship. *Review of Educational Research, 74*(3), 255–376.

PART IV

New Contexts and Challenges in Leadership for Partnerships

11

TARGET, STRATEGIC PARTNER, CRITICAL FRIEND?

Relationships between School Leaders and Community Organizing Groups

Sara McAlister, Heinrich Mintrop, Seenae Chong, and Michelle Renée

Around the nation, parents and students are coming together to use their collective power to demand real change in their schools and more equitable education policies in their districts and states. Going beyond traditional parent or community involvement, these groups of organized parents and students in the nation's most underserved schools have become a formidable force for school reform over the past two decades. One recent estimate puts the number of community organizing groups engaged in education reform at 500 nationally (Warren, 2010). A scan of the six states that make up New England found more than 30 community organizing groups with active education campaigns (Renée, McAlister, & Potochnik, 2011).

Community organizing is having a real impact on the quality of education available to low-income students and students of color. Parents and community members working through established organizing groups have won new school buildings, new district-level resources and staff for community outreach, and equitable access to qualified teachers and rigorous courses (Gold, Simon, & Brown, 2002; Lopez, 2003; Mediratta, Shah, & McAlister, 2009a; Shirley, 2009; Warren, 2010). For example, they have established a districtwide small schools policy in Oakland, California (see Auerbach, Chapter 13, this volume) and a statewide program to train paraprofessionals and parent leaders as teachers for hard-to-staff schools in Illinois (Mediratta et al., 2009a).

Organizing can also be a powerful vehicle for building authentic, mutually accountable relationships between educators and parents and community residents (Gold et al., 2002; Mediratta et al., 2009a; Shirley, 1997, 2002; Warren, 2010). These relationships have been hard to achieve in traditional school contexts and particularly in urban schools. Parent participation in education is often limited to voluntarism, fundraising, and "involvement" activities in which the school informs parents about school activities or imparts advice about how to help students at home (Henderson, Johnson, Mapp & Davies, 2007). Principals often view parents—especially parents of color and low-income parents—as an external pressure to minimize rather than as partners. Status dynamics between professional, typically middle-class educators and lower-socioeconomic parents, in particular, have produced deficit models that posit that low-income and minority parents devalue education and have little to contribute to their children's achievement (Crozier, 2000; Delgado-Gaitán, 1994; Noguera, 2001; Valencia, 1997). Relationships between principals and parents are also influenced by accountability regimes that shift blame for low achievement to principals and teachers, discounting the impact of systemic disinvestment in public education and framing parents as consumers who hold public schools accountable by exercising choice (Mintrop & Sunderman, 2009).

One of the central projects of education organizing is to transform this dynamic, and engage parents as active participants at the school, district, state, and national level. Organizing posits that systems and institutions work best when those most directly impacted by them have a say in shaping them. Organizing provides a different paradigm of democratic, collective relationships between educators and parents. While organizing groups are often imagined as angry and confrontational and educators have often been hesitant about collaborating with community organizers (Fabricant, 2010; Shirley, 2009), community organizing for public education has been characterized by a marked emphasis on collaboration (Mediratta et al. 2009a; Warren, 2010).

At the same time, though, school leaders' apprehension about working with community organizing groups is not unfounded. Unlike parent-teacher associations and other groups that involve parents, organizing groups are autonomous from schools, set their own agendas, and wield power. They train parents to examine school data and ask hard questions about achievement and resources. They seek to hold public institutions accountable for serving communities well and equitably. And when negotiation and collaboration fail, they are not afraid to resort to contentious public action in the service of their demands.

This chapter looks specifically at forces that have shaped relationships between school leaders and community organizing groups and how organizing is a strategy for overcoming historic obstacles to collaborative, coempowered relationships. We begin with a review of the literature on principals' role in facilitating relationships between parents and schools and its implications for organizing. We then offer several examples of principals' role in community organizing for school improvement and analyze the benefits and challenges of relationships between principals and organizing groups. We draw from the research literature on school leadership and community organizing and on data from a national Annenberg Institute for School Reform study of community organizing for school improvement supported by the Charles Stewart Mott Foundation (Mediratta et al., 2009a).[1]

Leadership Perspectives on Parent Involvement and Organizing

When we examine the relationship between school leaders and community organizing groups from a school leadership perspective, we do so from a very small body of empirical research and almost no theorizing. We therefore need to extrapolate from literature on school leadership, parent involvement, and community organizing to stitch together some theoretical frames that make the relationship more intelligible.

Organized parents, be they represented by community leaders or directly interacting with the school their children attend, are by definition political actors; that is, actors who want to influence the course of action of an organization by projecting power. They want to be heard where they may have been ignored. They want to influence decision-making where they may have been silent. The act of organizing is by itself a political expression of interest articulation. It communicates to a school that the ordinary channels of parent influence (Schutz, 2006), such as parent-teacher associations, parent-teacher conferences, and school councils, are not considered sufficient in voicing parent concerns.

Despite sharing in the goal of educating children and sharing in the responsibility of enabling children's learning, it has long been recognized that parents and educators pursue these commonalities from different perspectives (Todd & Higgins, 1998). In her text on the relationship between families and schools, Sarah Lawrence-Lightfoot (1978), drawing from Parsons's classic formulation, delineates parents as having particularistic expectations which seek individual recognition and special attention for their child whereas educators have a universalistic perspective, which maintains a professional obligation to consider the academic development and welfare of all students and fair and objective assessments according to societally regulated performance. Educators, as a result, may perceive parents as attempting to undermine their professional charge when parents advocate for their own child at the expense of other children (Crozier, 2000). In contrast, teacher professionalization often places the teacher in the role of expert, discounting the wealth of knowledge that parents have about their own children (Bauch & Goldring, 1998). Organized parents, however, have already undergone a process of interest aggregation which in all likelihood has distilled some interests common to all involved parents. Thus, they stand in a different relation to schools than parents engaged in individualistic forms of advocacy.

While teachers are internally oriented, principals are the boundary spanners of their organizations. Principals attend both to the internal affairs of the school and a myriad of external demands such as district, state, and federal educational policy or pressures from parents and community members (Crow, Hausman, & Scribner, 2005; Shipps & White, 2009). As boundary spanners, they move between the school and the external environment (Goldring, 1990). As such, it is mostly the principal with whom organized parents will interact.

The literature describes principals as negotiating the external environment with a mix of buffering activities, which strategically limit external actors' access to core functions of the organization, and bridging activities, which engage with external actors. Both bridging and buffering are attempts of principals to maintain internal goals and missions in a fluid and contested environment (Honig & Hatch, 2004). Principals may try to buffer against parents and community members because they fear loss of authority and control over their vision of the school, and in some cases, loss of their job (Shirley, 1997). Sometimes buffering occurs not only because principals want to preserve their authority, but because teachers expect to be protected from undue external influences and want disruptions of the learning process minimized (Bauch & Goldring, 2000). Particularly the current strong focus of schools on official guidelines (standards, assessments, performance targets) within high stakes accountability systems may compel principals to buffer external interests or influences that detract from the school's core concern (cf. Rogers, Freelon, & Terriquez, Chapter 4, this volume).

Principals' buffering activities may also increase in situations that affirm or amplify status differentials between professionals and parents. Goldring's (1990) study of the influence of socioeconomic status on Israeli principals' relationships with parents found that principals parceled parent involvement activities along income lines. High-income parents were expected to be resource providers whereas low-income parents were expected to merely support the educational goals of the schools. Thus, the respect afforded to middle-class parents by school authorities is often not extended to low-income parents, and efforts of low-income parents are buffered (Noguera, 2001). Class and status differences between teachers and low-income parents, as well as the perception that lower class communities are less supportive of the school's educational mission, may educe negative value judgments about parents' lack of formal education and commitment to ambitious educational goals (Crozier, 2000). As organized parents actively challenge these status assumptions, conflicts may ensue.

On the other hand, it has been widely recognized that schools have a vital interest in parent involvement (Epstein, 2001) and that the educational mission of a school benefits from active parents who are more likely to promote pro-school attitudes and contribute to their children's school work (e.g., Epstein, 2001; Fan & Chen, 2001; Hoover-Dempsey & Sandler, 1997; Jeynes, 2005). Complaints about a lack of parent involvement from teachers in schools serving low-income communities are ubiquitous. Community organizing may mobilize parents to become more active participants in their children's education. Demanding recognition politically and contributing to the school-family relationship educationally may be two sides of a coin. Educators in schools can engage in the micropolitics of their district but as street-level bureaucrats embedded in a hierarchy, they cannot politically advocate in an overt way for the interests of their school (Lipsky, 1980). By contrast, organized parents can be particularly well-positioned political actors that also act in the interest of educators. Thus, mobilization for multiple purposes is the strongest asset that community organizing may bring to the table. With organized parents in the picture, principals are likely to see parents as legitimate stakeholders in the educational process (Shipps & White, 2009). But the relationship is an act of gamesmanship in which principals will strategically balance the interests of the school with the interests of organized parents (Griffith, 2001).

Personal views, ideologies, and orientations on leadership often predicate the principal's tendencies to approach parents as partners. Case studies of individual principals who are considered successful in their work with parents highlight various personal attributes and perspectives which can include an ethic of care, seeing the parents as partners in the education process, and an ability to create a relationship built on trust (Bryk & Schneider, 2002; Johnson, 2007; Sanders & Harvey, 2002). Principals can also indirectly influence collaborative bridging relationships by encouraging teacher relationships with parents. When work environments were perceived as supportive and caring and parents volunteered, teacher-parent relationships were more strongly developed as well (Bauch & Goldring, 2000). These are probably characteristics that apply whether parents are organized or unorganized.

Principals can impute the relationship with parents with either an "enablement" or "empowerment" perspective (Nakagawa, 2003). An enablement role supports parent participation in the education program by seeking to increase parents' ability to help their child succeed in school whereas empowerment positions parents as participants in school reform and change (Nakagawa, 2003). Empowerment perspectives are particularly conducive to relationships between principals and organized parents. One resource uniquely available to low-income parents to move beyond an enablement role toward empowerment is the power of collective action. Through education organizing, low-income parents are able to build power by accumulating social capital (Warren, 2005). Organized parents do not advocate for their children only, but advocate for educational change that benefits a broad base of children (Noguera, 2001). Thus, empowerment perspectives help principals to use politics to their advantage.

Some authors go as far as envisioning a synergy that could flow from an empowerment perspective. One example of such a synergy comes from Bauch and Goldring's (1998) model of parent-teacher participation in school governance. In what they term the *partnership/communal mode* in their typology, Bauch and Goldring articulate a type of participation that rejects notions of parent as expert or teacher as expert and instead recasts parents and teachers as members of a larger community with particular spheres of influence that derive from their respective roles. Both parties are considered responsible for the same outcomes but in ways that respect and empower the resources unique to the actor's role in the community. At the heart of such relationships is the concept of relational trust as put forward by Bryk and Schneider (2002). Relational trust requires the enacting of particular expectations and obligations associated with a given role. If parents and school leaders are both cast as equally responsible parties but with different resources that contribute to the educational success of the child, an educative relationship that minimizes self-interest and political struggles may be conceivable. School leaders can then foster the values that are integral to the initiation and development of educative relationships that emphasize the mutual responsibility of all parties involved in the educational success of the child. It is, however, not clear how such harmonious interest accommodation could occur when parents articulate as organized political actors.

Based on the slim literature and the resulting theorizing, it appears that gamesmanship is the most likely option for principals when faced with organized parents. Even in research that explores more collaborative relationships, the tone is set by the principal's own motivations; while more caring and likely marked by relational trust, these relationships still serve to support the principal's vision of a collaborative community. It is not clear, however, how the political dimension of organizing changes the dynamics between low-income parents and principals. As education organizing increases its impact on school reform, it is important to understand the factors that encourage or constrain principals' abilities to chart new relationships with organized parents. We next discuss foundations of organizing and examples of collaboration between educational leaders and community organizing groups.

Community Organizing as a Vehicle for Reciprocal Relationships

Foundations of Education Organizing

Community organizing proposes that through collective action based on shared self-interest, traditionally marginalized groups can shift the balance of power and demand fair treatment from public institutions (Anyon, 2005; Oakes & Rogers, 2006). Saul Alinsky elaborated the basic tenets and strategies of community organizing in Chicago in the 1930s, applying labor organizing tactics to press for better social and economic conditions in working-class neighborhoods. Over the years, community organizing models have come to emphasize social capital and relationship-building as the basis for power, emphasizing the capacities of community members and democratic, consensus-based norms of decision-making (Chambers, 2003; Delgado, 1997). The power of organizing groups depends on their ability to develop indigenous leaders with the skills and knowledge to act on shared needs (Delgado, 1997).

Organizing follows a cycle of relationship-building, research, and action (Gold et al., 2002; Mediratta et al., 2009a; Warren, 2010). Through individual meetings called "one-on-ones" and small group meetings often called "house meetings," organizers develop relationships with community members and elicit stories about their aspirations and needs. Through these conversations, organizing groups recruit new members, identify potential leaders, and target issues that are broadly shared. The group then researches the issue, exploring potential solutions and developing concrete demands for change. Next, the group mounts an action campaign to win their demands. This phase can include building alliances, negotiating with targets, circulating petitions, testifying at public meetings, and holding rallies and protests.

Member recruitment and leadership development are ongoing. Some organizing groups draw on existing institutions—primarily religious congregations—to build their membership, while others directly recruit individual neighborhood residents. Regardless of membership model, community organizing groups draw their strength from the social and political capital of a broad membership base with the skills to act in its own self-interest. Throughout the organizing cycle, leaders develop new skills in facilitating meetings, reaching out to new members, understanding data, using research, speaking publicly, and negotiating with officials (Mediratta et al., 2009a). While professional organizers provide crucial training and support, decisions are made and carried out by members and leaders, in contrast to advocacy organizations in which professionals represent a constituency's interests and act publicly in its behalf (Evans, 2009).

Facilities and safety are common issues for organizing groups entering the education arena. Overcrowded classes, crumbling buildings, and dangerous walks to school are visible and concrete to parents, and present readily actionable demands like increased safety patrols or building repairs. As parents and community members experience success in campaigns focused on these concrete issues, they begin to identify new issues that focus on more core issues of instructional quality, such as qualified teachers, services available to English learners, the rigor of courses, and teacher interactions with parents (Gold et al., 2002; Mediratta, 2004; Warren, 2010).

Collaboration with School Leaders

There is no single rule that defines the relationship between community organizing groups and school leaders. While some might assume that principals are the target of education organizing, there is evidence that more often principals and school leaders are strategic allies. For example, both Mediratta et al. (2009a) and Warren (2010) explain that while many organizing groups began by identifying issues in the school and demanding action from the principal, they quickly learned that targeting principals often ended their access to schools and earned the distrust of teachers. As organizing groups have delved more deeply into education issues, they have for the most part come to see principals as allies in the struggle for equity and improvement.

Likewise, whereas principals might first react to organizing with the traditional strategy of buffering the school and system from organizers, many come to see education organizing groups as important critical friends or allies in the struggle to educate children (Mediratta et al., 2009a; Shirley, 1997, 2002). The focus of organizing groups on larger systems of structural inequality allows them to see failing schools as the product of concentrated poverty, segregation, neglect, and vastly unequal education spending (Oakes & Rogers 2006; Renée, Welner, & Oakes, 2010). Unlike many other policy actors in the current paradigm, they often recognize that principals work in this context of structural inequality and are constrained by policies and bureaucratic norms that limit their decisions (Mediratta et al., 2009a).

Educational change is complex, slow, and easily derailed by competing and shifting priorities (Coburn, 2003). In order to access the data and knowledge to shape effective campaigns and ensure that changes are well-implemented, organizing groups must build long-term relationships with educators, researchers, and decision-makers. Education organizing has been shown to be characterized by a reliance on collaborative tactics (Warren, 2010). Both organizing groups and school and district administrators benefit from the collaboration. Warren (2010) noted that schools and districts in low-income communities are often starved of resources and expertise and lack the capacity to respond on their own to demands for improvement. By engaging over the long term as partners, organizing groups bring the power and attention needed to secure resources for underserved schools and districts. Warren (2010) characterized this approach as one that builds "relational" power, in contrast with the "unilateral" power in mobilizing large numbers of people to embarrass public officials into action. This relational power nicely complements Bryk and Schneider's (2002) model of relational trust. Importantly, the extensive work that organizing groups do at the school level to improve relationships between teachers and parents and create meaningful avenues for parent participation prioritizes collaboration and trust.

Still, the power of community organizing rests in part in the implied threat that the group can take public action when collaboration and negotiation fail. Organizing groups are ultimately accountable to their members' demands, not to school or district leaders' priorities. They do, when necessary, turn to protest and the media, often armed with data and research to back their claims (Fabricant, 2010; Gold et al., 2002; Mediratta et al., 2009a). On occasion, organized parents have pressed to have principals removed from schools when the parents felt that the principals were unresponsive to reasonable requests or complacent in the face of educational failure (see Fabricant, 2010). Even when contentious action is aimed at winning new resources or programs, such actions can be threatening to principals who are accustomed to a more bureaucratic, hierarchical culture.

The relationship between school leaders and community organizing groups varies across time, location, and campaign. It is shaped by the approach to school reform taken by a particular organizing group, local context and history, as well as school leaders' priorities, beliefs and disposition to community engagement. We next explore examples of these dynamics and strategies for collaboration, highlighting differing benefits and challenges to school leaders and organized parents.[2]

Organizing Groups as School Advocates and Allies

Harnessing Collective Power to Gain Resources

In contrast to blaming teachers and principals as the source of low achievement as in the current accountability regime, organizing groups place failing schools in a larger context of poverty, disinvestment in inner cities, and race and class effects on access to public services (Oakes & Rogers, 2006; Renée et al., 2010). The emphasis within organizing on building the power of marginalized groups predisposes them to such an analysis, which is then often reinforced by their research on campaign issues. As parents and organizers delve into problems with facilities, curriculum, and teacher quality, they quickly discover that these issues are shaped by policies beyond the control of individual schools. For example, when parents involved with Chicago ACORN became concerned about dramatic teacher turnover at a local school, they soon learned that all schools in the neighborhoods where ACORN organized were struggling with vacancies and relying on uncertified teachers; by contrast, new selective schools were opening across the city with full complements of highly qualified teachers. The parents turned their attention to district hiring practices and later waged a campaign for a statewide teacher pipeline (McAlister, Mediratta, & Shah, 2010).

Organizing also provides a counternarrative to the view of parents as consumers who hold individual schools and the educators in them accountable for poor performance by exercising choice and exit, as in the highly publicized Students First (2011) agenda. Rather than training parents to better advocate for their own children, organizers train parents to act on behalf of all children in a school or community. Rather than choice and competition, organizing groups focus on resources and support for schools that have been starved of both. Collective action based on shared self-interest is the source of power for underserved parents who otherwise have very little real power or choice. When they are able to mobilize a broad base of parents and community members, organizing groups prove to be formidable allies for school leaders and teachers who are constrained by bureaucratic norms and systemic inequities.

The following analysis from a parent leader and organizer with Eastern Pennsylvania Organizing Project (EPOP) demonstrates how some organizing groups harness the political power of parents:

> How do they have power? As parents. They're sending their children in there for services. And sometimes the principal can see this as a bridge because the principal has to deal with the district. He can request things… but [principals] have to go through the same process and it's backlogged, so you have to wait until it's your turn. But parents, on the other hand, don't have to worry about how they look or stepping on any toes. They're not working for the district.

She went on to explain that parents succeeded by working collectively to move the system: "[O]ne person complaining is not really going to be heard. Now, if you have 60, 70, 100, 200 parents complaining about the same thing, and then demanding, you are going to see results." Principals generally valued the group for its ability to effect concrete improvements. "As long as you're doing work around the building and bringing in resources, you are loved," according to the organizer. "You are seen as a blessing."

Renée et al. (2010) describe how a coalition of parent organizers and legal advocates used a similar logic for the *Williams v California* lawsuit (2004). The organizers and advocates began by documenting the terrible conditions in some California schools, taking photographs of broken bathrooms and crumbling buildings and documenting students' experiences of trying to learn without textbooks or qualified teachers. Rather than argue that as consumers they should be able to choose a better school, organizers argued that all children should have access to the resources (teachers, learning materials, and safe facilities) they need to learn. The result was a settlement that included almost $1 billion to support the 19 lowest performing schools in the state, and the creation of a new statewide accountability system in which parents, students, and teachers can file complaints about inadequate resources and the district and state are required to fix the problem.

Relationships between School Leaders and Community Organizers

The work of People Acting for Community Together (PACT), a congregation-based organizing group in Miami, provides an example of the dynamic nature of the relationships between community organizers and school leaders. PACT turned its attention to education when public school parents shared concerns about their children's low reading achievement in parish meetings. Rather than confront individual schools and demand that they raise achievement, the parents and community members formed an education committee and began researching early literacy. They learned of a program called Direct Instruction (DI) that had been used successfully in schools with large immigrant and English Learner populations, similar to the local schools in PACT's neighborhoods. Because the district approved of a list of literacy curricula from which schools could choose, PACT mounted a long and successful campaign to include DI on the list (Mediratta et al., 2009b).

Working with sister organizations across the state, PACT won a legislative appropriation to pay for reading coaches to support DI schools. It also trained parents and congregation members as liaisons who met with principals and teachers regularly and relayed their concerns to district officials (Mediratta et al., 2009b). Through its advocacy, PACT was able to influence at least one principal hiring decision to ensure that the school could continue with DI. A principal in a school using DI valued PACT's ability to apply pressure to district officials:

> Dade County supports and listens to the community. When they [community members] get active and they get involved to prevent anything major from happening, they realize that they have more access to media than we would at the school. And of course, being an employee of the system, you have to put up with … what you're told to do.

This sort of action recasts low-income parents and parents of color as concerned, knowledgeable and capable allies of schools. Through organizing, parents analyzed data, conducted research, and met with experts to shape campaigns. They became capable public speakers and savvy strategists who could mobilize a large constituency of parents to demonstrate broad support for their demands. Principals recognized PACT leaders' professionalism and knowledge. For example, a Miami principal described how parents trained by PACT identified solutions to problems of mutual concern:

> They actually organize the frustrations and the things these parents would like to see changed here. "We have seen this and we think that something like this should [happen]. What is it that you're able to do? I think we'd like to see changes because of this." And then when they invite me in, it's when they have all the issues ready.… Then they present these issues in a forum, like here in like the cafeteria with about 40 or 50 parents and [the organizer] will be here and then I start going into questions. For me, it makes my job a little easier.

In this way, organizing facilitates the bridging or boundary-spanning role of school leaders by providing a structured methodology for parents to identify shared concerns, develop potential solutions, and negotiate with principals.

The alliance of school leaders and organized parents in pressing for new resources or policies is not without tension. Organizers and parents have found that principals are sometimes reluctant to share data that could strengthen campaigns. Organizing groups use careful data collection and analysis to bolster their claims for equitable policies and resources (Renée, 2006; Renée et al., 2010). For school-level educators who bear the brunt of high-stakes accountability systems and their attendant sanctions, publicizing data that reflects schools' struggles can be understandably uncomfortable and can be received as a challenge to educators' autonomy and competence.

The political nature of organizing can also be intimidating to school leaders and teachers who are immersed in a more bureaucratic culture. One common tactic is a public "accountability session," in which the organizing group demonstrates its power and broad support by turning out hundreds or thousands of members and inviting public officials to "sign on" to the group's demands. Often, leaders have negotiated the demands in advance with public officials, and the session serves in part as an opportunity for the officials to demonstrate their receptiveness to community concerns. Many organizing groups have used this tactic to build public momentum for education demands, often with teachers and principals participating (Fabricant, 2010; Mediratta et al., 2009a, 2009b; Shirley, 1997, 2002).

PACT leaders and organizers recounted an accountability session at a DI school where the director of transportation for the district had been invited to respond to parent demands for buses after two children had been hit by cars while walking to school. The parents presented evidence of the need for buses, and asked questions of the director. An organizer explained that the parents were following a methodology for public actions that PACT had carefully developed through trial and error, treating the director "with respect, but we were treating him firmly because we know how these guys will be." But the "idea of us taking on the director of transportation was just too much" for the principal, according to the organizer. Even though the principal was an enthusiastic supporter of Direct Instruction and had spoken publicly about the support that PACT provided for her school, she seemed uncomfortable with parents controlling the meeting and making demands of the official. She took the microphone and chastised the facilitators of the session for not letting the director speak. The clash of cultures evident at the meeting did no real damage to the long-term partnership but it highlighted the complexity of community organizations as critical friends holding leaders accountable.

Organizing for School-Level Change

While organizing groups often work at the state or district level to increase resources and change policies, they recognize that reforms are ultimately implemented in classrooms. Many organizing groups theorize that long-term engagement with local schools is necessary to build the capacity for real improvement (Warren, 2010). Organizing builds the power of parents to develop their own agendas for school improvement and act on them. Parent leaders involved in organizing groups have a base of power that is autonomous and separate from schools. They learn to identify problems and to formulate solutions based on their own experiences and their research. For example, an EPOP organizer described how parents trained with EPOP in Pennsylvania went on research visits to the Cross City Campaign for Urban School Reform to "look at best practices in other cities and make recommendations," bringing valuable information back to their school. Through such training and experiences, organizing works to neutralize the power differential between parents and educators, to allow them to approach each other as equals.

Fabricant (2010) illustrated this potential in a study of CC9, an education organizing collaborative formed by six community-based organizations in the South Bronx that organized Family-School Partnership committees at local schools. The committees recruited parents at each school, introduced them to community organizing skills, and led activities to build relationships between families and educators. CC9 came to an agreement with local district officials and the teachers union to set aside professional development time for community tours led by parents. The tours, which CC9 hoped would improve teacher retention by connecting new teachers more deeply with their students' neighborhood, introduced teachers to local resources like libraries and cultural centers, as well as the challenges that students faced outside of school. By framing parents as instructors, Fabricant (2010) explained, the tours contributed to "the development of more equal and reciprocal relationships" (p. 93). A youth organizing group connected to CC9 adopted the tours, being sure to include the sites of their earlier education victories, and used them as the basis for conversations with teachers about how youth leaders could shape school improvement. By positioning parents and students as experts with knowledge that can directly benefit schools, these organizing groups were able to disrupt the status dynamics that privilege teachers' professional expertise.

Despite organizing groups' efforts to position themselves as capable allies, tensions often arise as parents shift their attention from safety, textbooks, and facilities to issues that more directly impact teaching and learning. In one Pennsylvania school, EPOP has led a decade-long fight, with the support of several successive principals, for a new building to replace the school's unsafe 100-year-old building (McAlister et al., 2009). In other schools where EPOP organized, however, parents' demands for increased access to teachers and changes to school practices have led school leaders to "kick out" EPOP, at least temporarily.

EPOP's experience at one elementary school in Philadelphia encapsulates shifting dynamics between educators and organizing groups. Organized parents were first seen as a resource for addressing safety problems, then resented for their personnel demands, and later welcomed by a new principal. Students at the school had been forced to walk past several known drug houses on the way to school, and gunfire often kept them inside their houses in the afternoons. EPOP organizers trained parents on whom to approach about public safety and won a commitment from the city for increased police patrols in the neighborhood surrounding the school. The fledgling group soon secured funding for a new roof for the aging school building and later for a full-day kindergarten at a nearby community center (McAlister et al., 2009). Relations changed when organizers and parent leaders began to advocate for better access to teachers and more bilingual staff; though the school was nearly 100% Latino, only one teacher and two office staffers spoke Spanish. EPOP leaders demanded that the school provide a bilingual reading teacher and fill any vacancies in the school with Spanish-speaking teachers.

The parents' increased interest in teaching and learning created tensions with school staff. Some teachers felt attacked by EPOP's criticism of school practices. Parents told the *Philadelphia Daily News* that the principal had blamed low test scores on the students' lack of preparation at home; the principal denied this. When the new superintendent praised the energy and engagement of the EPOP parents after a public meeting at which he agreed to hire a bilingual reading teacher, teachers told reporters that EPOP parents were troublemakers in search of headlines (Mezzacappa, 1995; Moran & Laker, 1995). Over the summer, the principal left the school, and the teachers saw EPOP as antagonists who had "organized out a principal," according to the principal who took over the school.

The new principal, the first Latino principal the school had ever had, moved to meet teachers' needs, to rebuild trust between organized parents and teachers, and to rebuild productive relationships with EPOP leaders. When teachers told him that they did not have a good relationship with the EPOP organizer, he asked EPOP to switch organizers. He met informally with EPOP parent leaders, and asked what they wanted to see happen at the school. They asked for basic things, like teachers to meet their classes outside in the morning so that parents had a chance to speak with them. He agreed with the parents' insistence that their children needed bilingual teachers, and worked quickly to fill four vacancies with bilingual candidates. With these efforts, the principal said, the culture of the school shifted:

> And then what ended up happening is that we were addressing issues with kids, we were meeting the needs of parents as well and of the children in the community and kids started going home and saying, "Look, things are a really different...." [W]e set the frame and environment where teachers could teach and kids could learn.

By working together, EPOP and the new principal were able to create the space for relational trust and power. On a very tangible level, parents gained more access to the people educating their children, as well as increased power in making decisions about who those people were. The principal likewise gained access to the power of the community, could communicate when there was a problem, and ultimately was able to use the presence of the community at school to create a climate more conducive to learning and teaching. EPOP's engagement with schools demonstrates the careful investments of trust, time, and power that go into creating reciprocal, authentic relationships.

Conclusion

Education organizing differs from traditional forms of parent engagement in that it seeks to directly disrupt the status and power dynamics that marginalize low-income parents and parents of color from important decisions about school policy and practice. Schools' traditional efforts to increase parent involvement often take the form of one-way communication about how schools would like parents to behave in either assisting or advocating for their own children. In contrast, education organizing focuses on building the collective power to assist and advocate for all children. By definition, then, relationships between education organizing groups and principals are different from relationships between parents and principals generally.

This chapter has synthesized implications of the existing literature alongside data from a national study of community organizing to highlight key lessons on building educative relationships between school leaders and organized parents. At the center of these relationships is a commitment to carefully earning and building trust over time. Also important is that the relationships focus on the power and resources each group brings to the table while understanding their limitations. Educative relationships do not mean that principals need to lead a public protest, or that community organizers should take charge of every school policy. Rather, they mean that each group uses its power to work toward better educational opportunities for all students, while respecting the unique power and role of the other entity.

This chapter documents emerging evidence that both education organizers and school leaders benefit from forming educative relationships. Through their unique position outside the hierarchical education system, community organizing groups are able to fight for and secure new resources and create the public pressure needed to implement equitable policy. Organized parents can also serve the role of critical friend, bringing problems to the attention of school leaders and pushing for change. Similarly, school leaders can contribute significantly to the success of education organizing. On a very practical level, they can infuse a campaign or debate with knowledge about the unique school context, as well as district, state, and national policies. This knowledge can be critical to shaping a campaign and its demands to address problems of concern to parents and students. School leaders also have the opportunity to increase access for organizing groups to classrooms and teachers, as well as to decision-making tables. In this way, school leaders can serve a boundary spanning role, using their own social and political capital to connect education organizers to the rest of the education system.

While there are many benefits to each party, educative relationships between school leaders and organizing groups are not without challenge. At a most basic level they challenge the traditional understanding of how leaders and parents should interact and what an appropriate role is for each party. They also require lots of time, trust, and patience—resources that are at times even more limited than money in the current polarized education reform context. Educative relationships also require both parties to operate in uncomfortable places and share hard earned power. These challenges are often worth the benefits. At the end of the day, school leaders go to work and parents send their children to school because they all hope to give young people the opportunity to learn and become productive, successful people. By working together, school leaders and organized parents increase the numbers and power of people striving to create a more equitable American education system.

Notes

1. Quotes from principals, organizers, and parent leaders in this chapter are drawn from interview data collected as part of the national study of community organizing funded by the Charles Stewart Mott Foundation and carried out by researchers with the Annenberg Institute for School Reform from 2002 to 2009. For a description of the study methodology, please see www.annenberginstitute/wedo/Mott.
2. The relationships that lend themselves most obviously to relationships between organized parents and school leaders are formal, long-term partnerships centered on transforming school culture, like those of the Industrial Areas Foundation's Alliance Schools. Because the Alliance Schools have been extensively and capably studied (Gold et al., 2002; Murnane & Levy 1996; Shirley, 1997, 2002; Warren, 2001) and because the deep embedding of organizing into school culture at the heart of the model is not broadly representative, we do not focus on the IAF's work here.

References

Anyon, J. (2005). *Radical possibilities: Public policy, urban education, and a new social movement.* New York: Routledge.

Bauch, P. A., & Goldring, E. B. (1998). Parent-teacher participation in the context of school governance. *Peabody Journal of Education, 73*(1), 15–35.

Bauch, P. A., & Goldring, E. B. (2000). Teacher work context and parent involvement in urban high schools of choice. *Educational Research and Evaluation, 6*(1), 1–23.

Bryk, A. S., & Schneider, B. L. (2002). *Trust in schools: A core resource for improvement.* New York: Russell Sage Foundation.

Chambers, E. T. (2003). *Roots for radicals: Organizing for power, action and justice.* New York: Continuum.

Coburn, C. (2003). Rethinking scale: Moving beyond numbers to deep and lasting change. *Educational Researcher, 32*(6), 3–12.

Crow, G. M., Hausman, C. S., & Scribner, J. P. (2005). Reshaping the role of the school principal. *Yearbook of the National Society for the Study of Education, 101*(1), 189–210.

Crozier, G. (2000). *Parents and schools: Partners or protagonists?* Sterling City, VA: Trentham.

Delgado, G. (1997). *Beyond the politics of place: New directions in community organizing in the 1990s.* Oakland, CA: Applied Research Center.

Delgado-Gaitán, C. (2001). *The power of community: Mobilizing for family and schooling.* Lanham, MD: Rowman & Littlefield.

Della Porta, D., & Diani, M. (1999). *Social movements: An introduction.* Oxford, England: Blackwell.

Epstein, J. L. (2001). *School, family, and community partnerships: Preparing educators, and improving schools.* Boulder, CO: Westview Press.

Evans, M. (2009). *Inside education organizing: Learning to work for educational change* (Unpublished doctoral dissertation). Boston College, Chestnut Hill, MA.

Fabricant, M. B. (2010). *Organizing for educational justice: The campaign for public school reform in the south Bronx*. Minneapolis, MN: University of Minnesota Press.

Fan, X., & Chen, M. (2001). Parent involvement and students' academic achievement: A meta-analysis. *Educational Psychology Review, 13*(1), 1–22.

Gold, E., Simon, E., & Brown, C. (2002). *Strong neighborhoods, strong schools: Successful community organizing for school reform*. Chicago, IL: Cross City Campaign for Urban School Reform.

Goldring, E. B. (1990). Principals' relationships with parents: The homogeneity versus the social class of the parent clientele. *The Urban Review, 22*(1), 1–15.

Griffith, J. (2001). Principal leadership of parent involvement. *Journal of Educational Administration, 39*(2), 162–186.

Henderson, A. T., & Berla, N. (1994). *A new generation of evidence: The family is critical to student achievement*. Washington, DC: National Committee for Citizens in Education.

Henderson, A. T., Johnson, V., Mapp, K. L.M., & Davies, D. (2007). *Beyond the bake sale: The essential guide to family/school partnerships*. New York: New Press.

Honig, M. I., & Hatch, T. C. (2004). Crafting coherence: How schools strategically manage multiple, external demands. *Educational Researcher, 33*(8), 16–30.

Hoover-Dempsey, K. V., & Sandler, H. M. (1997). Why do parents become involved in their children's education? *Review of Educational Research, 67*(1), 3–42.

Jeynes, W. H. (2005). A meta-analysis of the relation of parent involvement to urban elementary school student academic achievement. *Urban Education, 40*(3), 237–269.

Johnson, L. (2007). Rethinking successful school leadership in challenging U.S. schools: Culturally responsive practices in school-community relationships. *International Studies in Educational Administration, 35*(3), 49–57.

Lawrence-Lightfoot, S. L. (1978). *Worlds apart: Relationships between families and schools*. New York: Basic Books.

Lipsky, M. (1980). *Street-level bureaucracy: Dilemmas of the individual in public services*. New York: Russell Sage Foundation.

Lopez, M. E. (2003). *Transforming schools through community organizing: A research review*. Cambridge, MA: Harvard Family Research Project, Harvard Graduate School of Education.

McAlister, S., Mediratta, K., & Shah, S. (2010). Improving teacher quality through public engagement in Chicago. In M. Orr & J. Rogers (Eds.), *Public engagement for public education* (pp. 201–226). Stanford, CA: Stanford University Press.

Mediratta, K. (2004). *Constituents of change: Community organizations and public education reform*. New York: Institute for Education and Social Policy, New York University.

Mediratta, K., Shah, S., & McAlister, S. (2009a). *Community organizing for stronger schools: Strategies and successes*. Cambridge, MA: Harvard Education Press.

Mediratta, K., Shah, S., & McAlister, S. (2009b). *Building a campaign for reading reform in Miami*. Providence, RI: Annenberg Institute for School Reform, Brown University.

Mezzacappa, D. (1995, May 31). Parents call for bilingual reading specialist. *Philadelphia Inquirer*, p. B1.

Mintrop, H., & Sunderman, G. L. (2009). Predictable failure of federal sanctions-driven accountability for school improvement and why we may retain it anyway. *Educational Researcher, 38*, 353–364.

Moran, E., & Laker, B. (1995, May 30). Staying power. *Philadelphia Daily News*, p. 6.

Murnane, R. J., & Levy, F. (1996). *Teaching the new basic skills: Principles for educating children to thrive in a changing economy. New York: Free Press.*

Nakagawa, K. (2003). Parental and community empowerment: The Chicago model. In L. F. Miron & E. P. St. John (Eds.), *Reinterpreting urban school reform: Have urban schools failed, or has the reform movement failed urban schools?* (pp. 209–228). Albany, NY: State University of New York Press.

Noguera, P. A. (2001). Transforming urban schools through investments in the social capital of parents. In S. Saegert, J. P. Thompson, & M. Warren (Eds.), *Social capital and poor communities* (pp. 189–212). New York: Russell Sage Foundation.

Oakes, J., & Rogers, J. (2006). *Learning power: Social inquiry, grassroots organizing, and educational justice.* New York: Teachers College Press.

Renée, M. (2006). *Knowledge, power, and education justice: How social movement organizations use research to influence education policy* (Unpublished doctoral dissertation). University of California, Los Angeles.

Renée, M., McAlister, S., & Potochnik, T. (2011). *Community organizing & engagement for education reform: A directory of New England organizations.*

Renée, M., Welner, K., & Oakes, J. (2010). Social movement organizing and equity-focused educational change: Shifting the zone of mediation. In A. Hargreaves, A. Lieberman, M. Fullan, & D. Hopkins (Eds.), *International handbook of educational change* (2nd ed., 153–168). New York: Springer.

Sanders, M., & Harvey, A. (2002). Beyond the school walls: A case study of principal leadership for school-community collaboration. *Teachers College Record, 104*(7), 1345–1368.

Schutz, A. (2006). Home is a prison in the global city: The tragic failure of school-based community engagement strategies. *Review of Educational Research, 76*(4), 691–743.

Shipps, D., & White, M. (2009). A new politics of the principalship? Accountability-driven change in New York City. *Peabody Journal of Education, 84*(3), 350–373.

Shirley, D. (1997). *Community organizing for urban school reform.* Austin, TX: University of Texas Press.

Shirley, D. (2002). *Valley Interfaith and school reform: Organizing for power in South Texas.* Austin, TX: University of Texas Press.

Shirley, D. (2009). Community organizing and educational change: A reconnaissance. *Journal of Educational Change, 10,* 229–237.

Students First. (2011). *Policy agenda: A challenge to states and districts: Policies that put students first.* Washington, DC: Author. Retrieved from www.studentsfirst.org/policy-agenda

Todd, E. S., & Higgins, S. (1998). Powerlessness in professional and parent partnerships. *British Journal of Sociology of Education, 19*(2), 227–236.

Warren, M. R. (2001). *Dry bones rattling: Community building to revitalize American democracy.* Princeton, NJ: Princeton University Press.

Warren, M. R. (2005). Communities and schools: A new view of urban education reform. *Harvard Educational Review, 75*(2), 133–173.

Warren, M. R. (2010). Community organizing for school reform. In M. Orr & J. Rogers (Eds.), *Public engagement for public education* (pp. 139–172). Stanford, CA: Stanford University Press.

Williams v. State of California, 312236 (City and County of San Francisco Superior Court 2004).

12

DYNAMICS OF PARENT INVOLVEMENT IN URBAN CHARTER SCHOOLS

Parents' Perceptions, Principals' Expectations, and Student Achievement

Marc L. Stein, Ellen Goldring, and Claire Smrekar[1]

School choice is frequently referred to as a powerful engine for creating the constitutive elements of the parent-school community (Bryk, Lee, & Smith, 1990; Smrekar & Goldring, 1999). For example, much charter school research reveals higher levels of parent satisfaction and parent involvement compared with traditional public schools (Bifulco & Ladd, 2005; Bulkley & Fisler, 2003). This is consistent with the theory that charter schools will be more responsive to parents because they are accountable to them as "consumers." Charter schools also have more flexible school structures that should mitigate the barriers large bureaucracies often build between parents and schools (Seeley, 1993).

While it is quite common for academics and the general public to speak of charter schools as a monolithic entity, charter schools vary greatly in terms of their mission, organization, and instruction. By definition, charter schools are supposed to promote innovation and differentiation (Lubienski, 2003). Thus, it is likely that there is variability in the nature and extent of parent involvement across charter schools. Research has documented that the organizational and institutional environments of schools are important for understanding parents and their willingness to become involved. For example, using reports from teachers and principals, Bifulco and Ladd (2005) found that efforts by schools to promote parent involvement generated higher levels of parent participation in charter schools than in traditional public schools. The first goal of this chapter is to explore variability among charter schools in terms of parents' perceptions of the extent to which schools invite their participation, based on part of Hoover-Dempsey and Sandler's (1995, 1997) model of parents' motivation for school involvement.

Although the research that links parent involvement and student outcomes is well documented, much less is understood about the factors that motivate or explain parents' willingness to become involved and the subsequent relationship between these factors and student achievement. Thus, the second purpose of this chapter is to explore the relationship between parents' perceptions of school invitations for involvement and gains in student achievement in charter schools.

Lastly, we expand upon the findings regarding parent involvement and student achievement in charter schools by explicating the role principals play in supporting the home-school relationship. Prior research has indicated that the principal's role and perspectives on parent involvement are paramount in terms of setting expectations and policies for robust, meaningful parent-school relationships (Auerbach, 2009). There may even be a stronger case for the centrality of the principal in charter schools since they are more autonomous and independent in their roles and must rely on parent choice and satisfaction to maintain student enrollment.

In this chapter we report on a mixed methods study of urban charter schools in Indianapolis that focused on three questions: (a) What are parents' perceptions of the invitations from schools and teachers to be involved in charter schools? (b) To what extent are the levels of school and teacher invitations for involvement related to gains in student mathematics achievement in charter schools? (c) What role do school principals play in supporting the home-school relationship in charter schools? As the number of charter schools grows, it is important to explore these questions to better understand the extent and dynamics of school-family partnerships in these relatively autonomous contexts.

Parents and Charter Schools

Three possible mechanisms explain the way that charter schools and other schools of choice may support higher levels of parent involvement: the act of choice itself, the parent-school fit or match, and the nature of school organization and role of the school principal. First, parents normally make a conscious decision to choose a particular school of choice, although it may be only a single alternative to the neighboring public school (Goldring & Shapira, 1993). In so doing, there is the possibility for greater cooperation between the school and families in the education of the student. The act of a family choosing a school, being selected by the school to attend, and deciding to enroll assumes at least the basis of a partnership or community (Hausman & Goldring, 2000). Thus, under choice arrangements, teachers and principals may be more open to working with students and their families and families more open to working with the school.

Second, the focused program or purpose of many schools of choice may increase the possibility of greater congruence between what families want for their children and what the school purports to provide, thereby proposing a "good fit" between home and school. Earlier literature on effective schools (e.g., Brookover & Lesotte, 1979; Goldring & Shapira, 1993) and on restructuring emphasized the need for goal consensus (e.g., Elmore, 1990). School choice attempts to resolve conflicts over goals through voluntary membership (Bryk, Lee, & Holland, 1993; Raywid, 1985). Bifulco and Ladd (2005) discuss the "parent-school match" in charter schools, which led families to feel a heightened comfort level and willingness to be involved.

Third, schools of choice may embody certain communal-organizational characteristics that enhance home-school relationships. Schools of choice are generally thought to consist of decentralized mechanisms of control, enabling them to operate less bureaucratically than traditionally organized public schools (e.g., Chubb & Moe 1990; Raywid, 1985) while simultaneously providing teachers and principals with autonomy. Bifulco and Ladd (2005) found higher levels of staff autonomy in charter schools, such as influence over school programs and policies, and these levels of autonomy were associated with higher levels of parent participation. In theory, charter schools should alter the traditional roles of all stakeholders involved in the education of children, including principals (Chubb & Moe, 1990; Hausman & Goldring, 2000). Changes in principals' roles are predicted to stem from more permeable boundaries, reduced bureaucracy, heightened autonomy, and increased responsiveness and accountability (Crew & Anderson, 2003).

Davies (1995) noted that "families, communities and schools hold shared and overlapping responsibility for the healthy development and the social and academic success of all children" (p. 267). Principals play a key role in setting policies and expectations for parent involvement, including building bridges between the cultures of home environments and the school; empowering parents to engage in school; helping parents support their children's academic and social learning; and building a school culture of school-family communication and collaboration (Crowson, Goldring, & Haynes, 2010). Principals "model community collaboration for staff, establish norms about the importance of parent connections, and provide opportunities for staff to develop the collaborative skills needed to work effectively with parents" (Murphy, Elliott, & Goldring, 2006, p. 34). Auerbach (2009), for example, in profiling principals who were proactive and directly involved in family engagement, found that they implemented unique programs and activities to meet the needs of their particular communities rather than relying on traditional forms of parent involvement. The relationship between schools and parents is not just one way, from the school outward to the community. Effective leadership also ensures that expectations, information, and interests from parents and the community are part of the school's goals, culture, and decisions (Murphy et al., 2006).

Zimmer et al. (2003) suggest that opportunities for parent involvement are greater in charter schools; this in turn may lead charter school parents to participate more than parents in traditional public schools. Partly this is due to the nature of choice itself, as noted above. Partly it is also due to the pervasive use in the charter school sector of parent contracts whereby parents promise to support student learning at home, ensure students attend school on time, and complete a set number of volunteer hours at the school, among other things (Becker, Nakagawa, & Corwin, 1997). Zimmer et al. (2003) reported that 80% of charter schools in California required contracts between parents and the school compared to 68% of a matched set of traditional public schools; however, only charter schools can require volunteer hours. Bifulco and Ladd (2005) attributed the increased parent participation in charter schools to organizational and institutional characteristics such as smaller enrollments and higher levels of principal and teacher influence on school policies.

Zimmer and Buddin (2007) are among the few researchers to study the link between parent involvement and student achievement in charter schools. In a study of all California charter schools and a matched set of traditional public schools, they reported that parent involvement had a positive effect on elementary and middle charter school students' reading and math scores. Achievement in matched traditional public schools, however, was not positively affected by parent involvement. After examining many operational and structural indicators that could impact student achievement, Zimmer and Buddin (2007) determined that the school feature that most reliably affected student academic outcomes was the level of parent involvement as reported by principals.

The Parent Involvement Model

Our study examined the manner in which parents perceive general school and specific teacher invitations to get involved in their children's charter school. We applied the Hoover-Dempsey and Sandler (1995) model, which suggests that, if positive, parents' perceptions of invitations to involvement catalyze actual parent participation in schools. Ultimately, this model suggests links between parent involvement and positive educational outcomes.

Hoover-Dempsey and Sandler (1995) explored the positive influence of parent involvement on academic outcomes by investigating the sources of parents' motivations to get involved, acts of involvement, and the effects of the process on student academic achievement. Their model theorized five key reasons that parents become involved in their child's education: (a) role construction (the belief that parents might hold that it is their duty to be involved); (b) efficacy (the belief that their involvement will help their child); (c) parents' perceptions of invitations to get involved from the school; (d) parents' perceptions of invitations to get involved from the teacher; and (e) parents' perceptions of invitations to get involved from the child. This model implies that if they perceive invitations for involvement from the school and the teacher as welcoming, meaningful, and frequent, parents will engage in the education process. While we drew upon the model developed by Hoover-Dempsey, Sandler, and colleagues (Green, Walker, Hoover-Dempsey, & Sandler, 2007; Hoover-Dempsey

& Sandler, 1995; Hoover-Dempsey, Walker, & Sandler, 2005) to develop measures for this study, we focused only on the two motivations for involvement that address parents' perceptions of general invitations from the school to get involved and parent perception of invitations from the teacher to get involved.

The model states that: "General school invitations include broad school attributes or activities that convey to the parent that his or her involvement is welcome and useful in supporting student learning and success" (Walker, Wilkins, Dallaire, Sandler, & Hoover-Dempsey, 2005, p. 94). These general invitations provide for the opportunity for parents to become involved. While the presence of general school invitations may not be "necessary nor sufficient conditions for the occurrence of parent involvement," they may lay the groundwork for the emergence of active parent involvement (Hoover-Dempsey & Sandler, 1995, p. 316).

However, not all involvement is at the school level; often parents develop relationships with individual teachers who encourage them to participate in school activities. Many parents have more firsthand knowledge and experience with their child's school at the classroom level through interactions with teachers. Thus, the extent to which teachers solicit and invite parents to be involved is an important institutional factor associated with levels of parent involvement. "Teacher invitations are influential in part because they underscore the teacher's valuing of parent contributions to student's education success," according to Green and colleagues (2007, p. 533). Research suggests that interventions that improve teachers' invitations for parent participation can influence the levels and types of parent involvement at school (Epstein & Van Voorhis, 2001).

We hypothesized that parents in charter schools will perceive that schools and teachers reach out to them with invitations for involvement. This is likely for two reasons. The first is related to the nature of school choice and charter schools; parents have made a conscious decision to enroll their child in a particular school and therefore may be more likely to perceive invitations for involvement. In addition, charter schools and teachers are likely to be compelled to reach out to parents due to pressures to maintain and increase enrollment. Second, if teachers individually and together are given more autonomy, discretion, and control in conducting their work in charter schools, they will feel a greater sense of ownership and responsibility for student outcomes. This suggests that charter schools teachers might give priority and time to engaging in in-depth interactions with families.

Indianapolis Charter Schools in Context

Indiana passed initial legislation authorizing charter schools in the state in 2001, with revisions in 2007. Many charter school advocates consider the Indiana charter law one of the "strongest" or most "friendly" in the nation to the creation of charter schools (Center for Education Reform [CER], 2008). This designation stems from provisions in the law for multiple authorizers, funding formulas on par with traditional public schools, and automatic waivers from state and district regulations and policies. The Indiana charter school law was also unique in that at the time of the study, it was the only law in the United States to give a mayor the power to authorize charter schools. This brought both attention and funding to the Indianapolis charter initiative. The first mayoral charter schools opened in the 2002-2003 school year with approximately 500 students. By the 2006-2007 school year a total of 16 charter schools had been approved and were in operation in Indianapolis[2] serving approximately 4,000 K-12 students (Read, 2008).

When examining charter schools and public school choice it is important to remember that there is no standard form to a charter school and there is wide variation within the sector in terms of organizational forms and in educational missions. Parents in Indianapolis who considered enrolling their children in a mayoral charter school had a variety of options ranging from schools that focused on a "back-to-basics" curriculum of math and reading, the arts, technology, college preparatory curriculum, or experiential learning. Some charter schools were run by national networks, such as Knowledge is Power Program (KIPP), or were associated with school reform groups, such as the Big Picture Company, while others were developed by local philanthropists and community groups with particular target populations, such as at-risk students or those with limited English.

Methodology

Data and Sample

This chapter is based on a mixed methods study of mayoral charter schools in Indianapolis. Anchored in work by Caracelli and Greene (1993) and Tashakkori and Teddlie (1998) on mixed methodology, we present the results of parent surveys, student achievement data, and qualitative interviews with school principals. Our approach utilizes the results generated by one analytical method (quantitative analyses of surveys and student achievement data) as the basis for collecting or analyzing new data using the other analytical method (qualitative analyses of interviews with charter school principals).

In the spring of 2007, we administered surveys to all parents from all of the 16 mayoral charter schools in operation in Indianapolis. Parents of first year students were excluded from the survey since their involvement and engagement with the school was too new and could be too rose-colored. Parents were offered a $15 gift card if they returned the survey and the class (homerooms) received a $200 gift card if 80% of the classroom returned the survey. These procedures resulted in 84% of parents responding, for a total of 2,493 parents. We further collected school-level demographic information (enrollment, charter age, indicator of mandatory parent involvement through school contracts, and the percentage of minority students enrolled in the school) for the 2006-2007 school year from either the school's Web page or through telephone inquiries directly to the school.

We also obtained school-level mean mathematics[3] achievement gains (the average gain for all students who had remained in and had been tested in the same charter school for both the fall 2006 and spring 2007 test administrations) from the Northwest Evaluation Association (NWEA), which contracts with states, districts, and schools to provide interim student assessments. We were unable to compute a mathematics gain score for two schools that did not contract for testing for one of the two testing points. Another school was dropped from the study because of its unusual mission and school population,[4] bringing the total of charter schools in the sample to 13.

After excluding the three schools from the analysis, 2,066 parents remained in the sample. Of these remaining parents a small number (n = 49, 2.4%) did not respond to some of the items on the survey that are of interest to this study and were removed from the data, resulting in a final analytic sample of 2,017 parents with complete data. Table 12.1 indicates key demographics of the parent respondents and schools in the analytic sample. Overall, 79% of parents

TABLE 12.1 Analytic Sample Descriptive Statistics of Parents, Schools, and Outcomes of Interest

Variable	*M*	*SD*	*Min.*	*Max*
Parents[a]				
Minority	0.79	0.41	0	1
White	0.21	0.41	0	1
Parental SES	-0.01	0.85	−1.91	2.00
Level of Income	3.61	1.59	1	6
Highest Level of Education	2.95	1.01	1	5
Schools[b]				
Charter Age	2.82	1.24	0.83	5.08
Total Enrollment	252.69	150.85	98	609
Percent Minority	69.77	31.27	12	100
Math Gain	5.86	5.25	−4.20	13.48
Mandatory Parent Volunteer Hours	0.38	0.51	0	1
Parent Perceptions of Invitations for Involvement[a]				
School Level	5.07	0.83	1	6
Teacher Level	3.16	1.48	1	6

[a] n = 2,017
[b] n = 13

responding were minorities, with African American parents representing the largest group (69%). Based on a measure of parents' socioeconomic status (SES) that is a composite of their reported highest level of education and range of family income, parent respondents on average had completed some college and reported a family income of approximately $30,000 per year. Although all the schools were located in an urban center, there was considerable variability in the SES levels of parents with children enrolled in the charters. About 9% of the parent respondents reported they earned less than $10,000 a year, while 19% earned over $50,000. Furthermore, 10% of parents did not graduate from high school, while 23% had earned a bachelor's or an advanced degree.

The average age of the charter schools in the sample was approximately 3 years in operation, with a range from new start-ups to 5 years. The schools in the sample ranged in size from approximately 100 to 600 students with an average enrollment of approximately 250. Minority enrollment in these charter schools was on average quite high, representing approximately 70% of the total student population. However, there was a wide range between schools in the minority percentage of total enrollment from a low of 12% to a high of 100%. Mandatory parent volunteer hours were required by 38% of the charter schools in this sample.

Survey Measures

We measured parents' perceptions of general (school) and teachers' invitations to involvement on two scales, Parents' Perceptions of General Invitations to Involvement from the School (α = .89) and Parents' Perceptions of Specific Invitations from the Teacher (α = .88). These measures were developed by Hoover-Dempsey, Sandler, and colleagues (1997, 2005) and have undergone extensive psychometric development and testing. The first involvement scale reflected the parents' perceptions of general outreach and invitations from the school. The scale was formed by seven survey items that gathered information about the level of agreement with statements about the overall perception of parent outreach from the school (e.g., This school offers activities for parents, The school's staff contacts me quickly about any problems, I feel welcome at this school). The second scale was formed by six items focusing more on the perception of parents about the invitations of the teacher of "my child" that "have happened since the beginning of the school year" (e.g., My child's teacher asked me to help out at the school, My child's teacher contacted me, My child's teacher asked me to attend a special event at school).

Quantitative Analytic Approach

In order to investigate the relationships between charter school characteristics, parents' perceptions of invitations for involvement from schools and teachers, and student mathematics achievement gains, we constructed a series of OLS models where parents' perceptions were modeled as functions of individual level demographic characteristics (minority parent and socioeconomic status) as well as the characteristics of the charter school in which the student or child was enrolled (percentage minority enrollment, total enrollment, charter age, mandatory parent volunteer hours, and school average mathematics gain). We accounted for the inherent hierarchical nature of educational data by using adjusted standard errors that account for the nesting of parents in schools. While hierarchical linear modeling techniques would have been our preferred method of analysis, limitations in the number of higher level units (i.e., total of only 13 schools) precluded our using these techniques.

Qualitative Interviews and Analysis

As part of the larger study of mayoral control of charter schools, we conducted qualitative case studies of four purposely selected charter schools (see Smrekar, 2009). In this chapter we draw from in-depth, semistructured interviews with four charter school principals to supplement the survey and achievement analyses. The research team sought to include contrasting schools in the case studies in an effort to capture variability in the roles principals may play in the charter school context. We considered academic achievement records, student demographics, grade distribution, school size, type of charter school (independently operated or operated by a charter management organization), and responses to the parent surveys, along with student achievement results and adequate yearly progress (AYP) status. Below are brief sketches of each of the four schools.[5]

> Tisdale Charter School was a college preparatory school serving grades 6 through 12 that had consistently met state targets under NCLB. Its student population was nearly 100% African American. Tisdale's instructional program required students to earn college credit in 11th and 12th grade and there were an extended instructional day and Saturday program to support these efforts.
>
> Carroll Academy was also a small school of approximately 240 K-6 students (99% African American, 87% eligible for free or reduced price lunch). It was located in a historic African American neighborhood with close ties to a nonprofit community organization. At the time of our interviews the school was undergoing a period of transition between the founding and incoming administrators.
>
> Lane Academy, one of the first mayor-authorized charter schools, enrolled 410 students in a K-8 grade structure. The student population was quite balanced racially (32% African American, 29% Hispanic, 39% white) and was also high poverty (86% free or reduced price lunch). The school had

> high academic achievement on state testing and had a locally designed program that focused on arts, global education, and lifelong learning.
>
> Capital Academy was part of a national network of nonprofit charter schools and enrolled 489 students in grades K–8. The school's curriculum focused on the arts, core academic subjects, and character education. Like Lane Academy, the student population was also diverse (58% African American, 8% Hispanic, 34% white) and mostly high poverty (84% free or reduced price lunch). At the time of the study Capital had low performance on the state accountability tests.

At each of the schools, we conducted semistructured interviews with principals and other instructional leaders (e.g., assistant principals, directors of instruction). We focused on such questions as: What do parents expect when they choose this school? What do they expect of you and the teachers? What is the nature of parent involvement and engagement at this school? The research team used digital recorders to record the on-site, face-to-face interviews. The interviews were analyzed using a "grounded theory" approach (Strauss & Corbin, 1998), an inductive approach in which the categories used for analysis are derived from the data rather than preceding them. Initial analysis focused on fully understanding each participant's responses (Glaser & Strauss, 1967). As noted, we were interested in patterns and themes from the principal interview data that augmented and explicated the findings from the survey and achievement analyses.

Results

Variation in Parents' Perceptions of Involvement Invitations

The descriptive statistics of our two scales of parents' perceptions of invitations for involvement are presented in Table 12.1 above. They indicate that there was variation among charter school parents in their perceptions of the extent to which schools and teachers attempted to involve them in the school and in their child's education. Parents on average rated general invitations from their schools quite high with a mean response of 5.07 on a 6-point Likert scale, with the majority rating their schools between 4.0 and 6.0 (sd = 0.83). Parents appeared to be more varied in their perceptions of teacher levels of invitations for involvement (mean = 3.16, sd = 1.48). The average parent indicated that they had received invitations for involvement from teachers approximately three to five times over the course of the school year, but the range of parents' perceptions was substantial from parents feeling that teachers never extended invitations to them to the opposite extreme of perceiving daily invitations from teachers.

Table 12.2 presents the results of our analytic models investigating the variation in parents' perceptions of involvement invitations from schools and teachers. We proceeded in a stepwise fashion by first introducing parent char-

TABLE 12.2 OLS Regression Estimated Effects of Parent and School Characteristics on Parents' Perception of Invitations for Involvement

	Invitations for Involvement			
	School Level		*Teacher Level*	
	Model 1	*Model 2*	*Model 3*	*Model 4*
Parent SES	−0.079** (0.029)	−0.069*** (0.021)	0.035 (0.035)	0.028 (0.028)
Minority Parent	−0.013 (0.123)	−0.015 (0.071)	0.473*** (0.063)	0.303*** (0.084)
School Average Mathematics Gain		−0.032** (0.014)		−0.064*** (0.008)
School Percent Minority		0.003 (0.003)		0.007** (0.003)
Total Enrollment		−0.001** (0.000)		0.000 (0.000)
Charter Age		0.03 (0.053)		−0.004 (0.050)
Mandatory Parent Volunteer Hours		−0.241 (0.132)		−0.066 (0.084)
Intercept	5.082*** (0.127)	5.359*** (0.210)	2.788*** (0.049)	2.952*** (0.176)
R-squared	0.036	0.065	0.174	0.194
F	4.29**	9.85***	28.01***	41.85***
n	2017	2017	2017	2017

Note. All models include grade fixed effects and standard errors adjusted for clustering of parents in schools. Standard errors are in parentheses. SES = socioeconomic status
* $p < .10$. ** $p < .05$. *** $p < .01$

acteristics only in columns 1 and 3; then we added school level characteristics variables as a block in columns 2 and 4. F-tests of the joint significance of the independent variables in the models were all statistically significant at or below the conventional .05 level (see Table 12.2).

School-Level Invitations for Involvement

Of our two parent characteristics (Table 12.2, Model 1), only the SES of the individual parent was statistically significantly related to perceptions of school-level invitations for involvement. A one unit increase in parent SES was predicted to a .079 decrease (-0.10 standard deviation units) in the parent's perception of school-level invitations. While overall, parents' perceptions of charter school invitations for involvement were high, this finding indicates that at lower SES levels, parents were more likely to perceive that charter schools were attempting to get them involved.

With the introduction of school-level characteristics, we see that the relationship between parent SES for the school as a whole and perceptions of school-level invitations (Table 12.2, Model 2) remains significantly negative, but is reduced in magnitude (-.069; -.08 standard deviation units). As noted above, schools serving lower SES families appeared to be reaching out more to them to become involved than schools serving higher status families. At the school level, there was also large variability of parent social class. One school for example, served parents who, on average earned $42,000 while another charter school's parents earned almost half that on average.

Of the school-level characteristics, both the school average mathematics gain and the size of the school's enrollment were statistically significant negative predictors of parents' perceptions of school-level invitations for involvement. For example, an increase of one point in school average mathematics gain predicted a decrease in parents' perceptions of school-level invitations by .03 points. Thus, the higher the mathematics gain, the less likely parents were to perceive strong invitations for involvement. While the magnitude of this finding appears to be small, it is quite intuitive. We might expect that charter schools that have higher student achievement gains would be less likely to feel pressure from their external accountability environments (i.e., NCLB targets for adequate yearly progress) as well as their internal accountability to their customers (parents), thereby obviating partially the pressure for such schools to reach out to parents as a strategy for raising achievement.

We also found that as the size of the charter school increased, parents' perceptions of school-level invitations decreased; so that an increase of 100 students to the charter school's enrollment would predict a statistically significant decrease in parents' perceptions of invitations by .1 points (.12 standard deviation units). This is consistent with charter school research and theory that smaller charter schools will be better able to provide more individualized educational experiences for parents and students. This may, in turn, be driving the finding that parents in larger charter schools perceived fewer invitations for involvement.

Teacher-Level Invitations for Involvement

In relation to teacher-level invitations for involvement, we found no statistically significant relationship between parent SES level and parents' perceptions (Table 12.2, Models 3 and 4). However, we estimated a statistically positive relationship between the minority status of the parents and their perceptions of invitations from teachers. We see in Model 4 (controlling for school characteristics) that a minority parent was predicted to have perceptions of teacher invitations for involvement that were .303 points (.20 standard deviation units) higher than those of nonminority parents. It may be that teachers were responding to charter school missions that seek to better serve minority or previously underserved populations and were therefore making a more concerted effort to reach out to minority parents.

As with school-level invitations, we also estimated a predicted decrease in parents' perceptions of teacher-level invitations for involvement as the average mathematics gain score for the school increased (Table 12.2, Model 4). For a one point increase in school average mathematics gain we would predict a .064 point decrease in parents' perceptions of teacher-level invitations. Again this finding is quite intuitive in that we would expect teachers in schools with higher average student mathematics achievement gains to be less likely to reach out to parents.

Finally, we see that as the percentage of minority students in a school increases, we would predict an increase in parents' perceptions of teacher-level invitations for involvement, mirroring our finding that minority parents reported more invitations from teachers for involvement. For example a 10% increase in the percentage of minority students would predict a .07 point increase in parents' perceptions of teacher invitations.

Principals' Role in Involving Parents

Several themes emerged from our interviews with charter school principals and instructional leaders in Indianapolis charter schools that support, extend upon, and help to explain our survey findings. First, accountability pressure from outside of the school to the mayor's office and to the state was a real and daily concern while the need to maintain or increase enrollment led to direct efforts to reach out to current and potential parents. Second, increased organizational flexibility allowed principals and their staff to reach out to parents in unique ways that may not be present in traditional public schools. Third, as charter schools matured and became perceived as successful, either through performance on state tests or word of mouth among parents, the nature of parent involvement changed. Below we develop each of these themes in more detail.

External and Internal Accountability Pressures. Principals and other instructional leaders in the study were highly aware of and concerned about their school's performance on external accountability measures. This concern was twofold. First, as public schools they were accountable for student performance on state tests and had to make adequate yearly progress under NCLB like any other public school. Second, as mayoral charter schools they had to also show improved or "good" student performance to retain their charters and were subject to regular reporting to the Mayor's Office. These accountability pressures resulted in principals being aware of the importance of actively engaging parents in the daily workings of the school and their belief that this engagement would lead to better student outcomes. As the principal of Tisdale stated:

> [The key is] a parent coming in, having an interaction with the teacher, the teacher and the parent coming to terms on some issues.... We just want you in the building, because that connection does it. And all the research says despite parents' educational attainment level, socioeconomic status, [when] they're very involved in school, kids will learn.

Another principal summarized a similar expectation for parents as "be supportive and be involved. I think that the more parents are involved, the more their children will be."

The principals interviewed shared another pressure that was common to them all: In order for their schools to be viable, they had to be actively engaged in recruiting new parents/students and retaining their currently enrolled parents/students. This pressure also led these principals to reach out to parents. As the school leader of Lane Academy recognized,

> Word of mouth is the number one reason why parents come here. They speak to a family that is having a negative or indifferent experience somewhere else, and they come here. So we work really hard at those relationships and that has some carryover [into maintaining enrollments and recruiting new students].

The need to build and maintain relationships with parents led this principal to be attentive to the "messages" sent to parents about "the types of results that we are getting and the varied experiences that our students are getting and how that is then helping them to become better students."

The principals also recognized that in many cases, parents had special circumstances and needs that should be recognized by the school and that it was the responsibility of the school to be responsive to these needs in order for their students to succeed. They reported that many families in these schools needed help with economic stability, public services, parenting skills, and educational skills. For one charter that was associated with a community outreach center, the school could

> refer a parent over [to the community center] for some need, we can do that.... That is part of the school ...[to help with] a light bill, a gas bill, any human need, food, clothing, shelter. And if parents don't have the money, they [the center] may be able to do a referral or whatever is necessary.

For this principal, the ability of her school to help families find and receive needed social services was one of the ways that parents found out about the school and chose to enroll their children there. At Lane Academy, responsive outreach took the form of ensuring that there were people on staff that spoke Spanish so that Hispanic parents could communicate with the school and the school could communicate with the parents. According to the principal,

> We cater to [the Hispanic] population group and they recognized it. And then through word of mouth, people say, "I never had that problem [communicating in Spanish] at Lane. And why would I want to keep going to a school where nobody can speak to me, [where] I never get the newsletter in language I can read [and where] I can't go to my child's conference because there is no one to translate?"

The principals we interviewed highlighted the fact that many of their families were headed by single parents or parents who often worked multiple jobs with schedules at odds with school hours. Several principals noted that they had forged relationships with after-school care providers in or close to their students' neighborhoods where working parents could send their children after school at low cost. The schools' bus routes were organized so that these centers were accessible to the students. Recognizing that it was not always easy for parents to come to the school for parent-teacher conferences, two schools made regular home visits to check on families when students failed to turn in homework, misbehaved at school, or had other potential issues that came to the attention of the school. One principal felt that these home visits helped parents to feel valued and that someone cared about them; this helped potentially reticent parents to become more involved in their child's education and the school.

Organizational Flexibility. Many of the principals indicated that the flexibility in organization and budgeting allowed them as a result of being charter schools permitted them to reach out to parents in unique and authentic ways that may not occur in traditional public schools in the community. As one principal stated, "I think it is really [about] being proactive in reaching out to those parents and letting them know that we are here for you." In this school it was a job responsibility for all faculty and staff to reach out to parents. For example, all parents received "welcome" calls from their child's teacher, the director of instruction, and other staff upon enrollment. During the school year teachers were required to make regular contact with parents either through phone calls or letters home. The principal noted that while this practice was not uncommon in her previous traditional public school, teachers were not contractually obliged to communicate regularly with parents and as a principal it was hard to compel the practice. However, in the charter context she had the power to enforce the practice among her teachers. Lane Academy similarly used its budgetary flexibility to pay an incentive to teachers to make home visits during the school year.

Capital Academy had a specifically designated marketing budget that was spent on parent recruitment and retention. For example, the school reached out to families during the summer by giving teachers a stipend to come into school and make phone calls to families to "see how they are doing" and if "there is anything that we can do for you." Further, the marketing budget allowed the school to have Backpack Night where parents came in before the beginning of the school year to get busing information and a backpack full of school supplies. The school also allocated resources for a staff member to act as a parent liaison, among other duties. The liaison, who also drove one of the buses for the school, greeted students and families in the morning as students came to school. From these interactions she created an "agenda" of "any problems that may have occurred on the bus or in the neighborhood or maybe some families [that] are in need of different services," which was communicated to the principal every morning. These agenda items often became the impetus for calls and visits to the home.

The Changing Nature of Parent Involvement. Some principals noted that the nature and intensity of parent involvement had changed as their charter schools grew both in enrollment and the number of grades served. For example, in the early years of operation, one school regularly had over 150 parents attend biweekly parent meetings. However, over time, the number of parents who attended these nights regularly dwindled to a handful of "regulars." In the words of the principal of Tisdale,

> The more comfortable parents are with your program, the less likely they are to come in and watch what you're doing.... When we were brand new, and nobody knew us from a hole in the wall...we had parents here all the time.... [We] wouldn't have had to call parents on the phone. You would have been tripping over them in the hallway.... And so, the better we've gotten, the more parents kind of say, "I'll drop you off at the door....You're in a safe place."

While this change in attendance was a consequence of the school's academic success, the principal and board of trustees viewed it as a potential problem and continued to look for new ways to actively engage their parents in the school (cf. Auerbach, Chapter 13, this volume).

Discussion and Conclusion

In this chapter, we used Hoover-Dempsey and Sandler's model and data from Indianapolis mayoral charter schools to examine parents' perceptions of invitations from charter schools and teachers for parents to become involved, the relationship between levels of invitation and gains in mathematics achievement, and the role of principals in support of parent involvement. We found that on average, parents perceived more invitations for involvement from the school than from their child's teachers. In addition, as may be expected, there was much more variability in parents' perceptions of invitations from teachers than perceptions of invitations from the school. Our findings suggest that parents of students who are considered to be more at-risk—that is, minorities of lower

SES who attended schools with smaller academic gains in mathematics—were more likely to perceive that the schools and the teachers were reaching out to them (communicating quickly when there was a problem, scheduling activities at times they could attend, asking for help in the classroom, and asking them to assist their child with homework).

We also found that parents' perceptions of invitations from both the school and their child's teacher were associated with a decrease in students' mathematics scores between the fall and the spring semesters. The consistent direction of the findings suggests that parents perceived their charter school was reaching out to them more in cases where students were less academically successful. It may also be the case that schools that had students who were not gaining in mathematics achievement were reaching out to parents.

We learned that principals were acutely aware of the accountability pressures that they faced externally from the mayor's office and the state and internally from the parents who chose to enroll their children in the charter school. These accountability pressures in part led principals to be very proactive in attempting to involve parents in the daily functioning of the school as the principals believed that active involvement of parents was foundational to the success of their school and students. Principals leveraged the flexibility afforded them as charter school leaders to be creative in their use of budgets and staff to support and reach out to parents.

On the face of it, the results suggest that charter schools are responding to both market driven and bureaucratic/legal accountability systems (see Adams & Kirst, 1999) in their approach to parents. From a bureaucratic/legal perspective, charter schools may be trying to meet the demands of NCLB in part through enlisting parents to help them raise student achievement on state tests. According to parents surveyed, schools that were achieving the least were reaching out the most to parents as they strove to be accountable. Similarly, parents were defining their needs as consumers by choosing charter schools for academic reasons. Leaders of those schools that served lower achieving students knew they must reach out to parents and invite their participation in order to achieve results; that is, to improve achievement and continue to attract parents—since the market is supposed to work based on the performance of the school,

One obvious limitation of this work is that we do not have a comparison sample of parents and schools from traditional public schools in the district. We are left with the "compared to what" question. We do not know without comparison schools if this pattern is unique to charter schools or holds for other schools in the district. In any case, the direction of the findings suggests that reaching out to parents may be, at least in part, a response to accountability pressures by charter schools. A second limitation of this research is that we do not know if reaching out from schools and teachers to parents also translates to parents reaching in to assist and support the school and their children's learning.

Despite these limitations the results of this study suggest that charter school principals responded to accountability demands and used the autonomy afforded to them by engaging with parents, especially in schools with students from lower SES and lower achievement levels. Requiring parent involvement as part of teachers' contracts and incentivizing teachers to engage with parents were unique aspects of the flexibility of charter school principals, who individually negotiate teacher contracts. Flexibility and creativity in terms of partnering with social service agencies and altering bus routes were other examples of how these principals used their autonomy to better serve families and promote positive home-school relations. In these examples we see evidence that charter school policies do support their intended purpose of using their autonomy to implement programs and actions that support their mission. The school leaders in our study were proactive in their approach to parent engagement. They knew their communities well, developed creative strategies to meet the needs of a diverse group of parents, and connected with other agencies—key strategies in leadership for partnerships (Auerbach, 2009).

Notes

1. The study reported in this chapter was supported by the National Center on School Choice, which is funded by a grant from the Institute of Education Sciences, U.S. Department of Education [R305A040043].
2. All schools are located within Marion County, Indiana which has a unitary government structure with the City of Indianapolis.
3. We also obtained achievement gain scores in reading. Models using reading individually and in combination with mathematics do not add substantively to the analysis and we therefore only present analyses using mathematics.
4. This school serves students who are suffering from alcohol or substance abuse.
5. All school names are pseudonyms.

References

Adams, J., & Kirst, M. (1999). New demands and concepts for educational accountability: Striving for results in an era of excellence. In J. Murphy & K. Seashore Louis (Eds.), *Handbook on research on educational administration* (pp. 463–490). San Francisco, CA: Jossey-Bass.

Auerbach, S. (2009). Walking the walk: Portraits in leadership for family engagement in urban schools. *The School Community Journal, 19*(1), 9–32.

Bifulco, R., & Ladd, H. F. (2005). Institutional change and co-production of public services: The effect of charter schools on parent involvement. *Journal of Public Administration Research and Theory, 16*(4), 553–576.

Brookover, W. B., & Lezotte, L. W. (1979). *Changes in school characteristics coincident with changes in student achievement.* East Lansing: Institute for Research on Teaching, College of Education, Michigan State University.

Bryk, A. S., Lee, V. E., & Smith, J. B. (1990). High school organization and its effects on teachers and students: An interpretive summary of the research. In W. Clune & J. Witte (Eds.), *Choice and control in American education: Vol. 1. The theory of choice and control in American education* (pp. 135–226). Philadelphia, PA: Falmer Press.

Bryk, A. S., Lee, V. E., & Holland, P. B. (1993). *Catholic schools and the common good.* Cambridge, MA: Harvard University Press.

Bulkley, K., & Fisler, J. (2003). A decade of charter schools: From theory to practice. *Educational Policy, 17*(3), 317–342.

Caracelli, V. W., & Greene, J. C. (1993). Data analysis strategies for mixed-method evaluation designs. *Educational Evaluation and Policy Analysis, 15*(2), 195–207.

Center for Education Reform (CER). (2008). *Charter school laws across the states: Rankings and scorecard 2008.* Washington, DC: Center for Education Reform.

Chubb, J. E., & Moe, T. M. (1990). *Politics, markets, and America's schools.* Washington, DC: Brookings Institution.

Crew, R. E., & Anderson, M. R. (2003). Accountability and performance in charter schools in Florida: A theory-based evaluation. *American Journal of Evaluation, 24*(2), 189–212.

Crowson, R., Goldring, E., & Haynes, E. (2010). *Successful schools and the community relationship.* Richmond, CA; McCutchan.

Davies, D. (1995). Commentary. In L. Rigsby, M. Reynolds, & M. Wang (Eds.), *School-Community Connections* (pp. 267–280). San Francisco, CA: Jossey-Bass.

Elmore, R. (Ed.). (1990). *Restructuring schools: The next generation of educational reform.* San Francisco, CA: Jossey-Bass.

Epstein, J. L., & Van Voorhis, F.L. (2001). More than minutes: Teachers' roles in designing homework. *Educational Psychologist, 36*(3), 181–193

Glaser, B. G., & Strauss, A. L., (1967). *The discovery of grounded theory.* Chicago, IL: Aldine.

Goldring, E. B., & Shapira, R. (1993). Choice, empowerment, and involvement: What satisfies parents? *Educational Evaluation and Policy Analysis, 15*(4), 396–409.

Green, C. L., Walker, J. M., Hoover-Dempsey, K. V., & Sandler, H. (2007). Parents' motivations for involvement in children's education: An empirical test of a theoretical model of parent involvement. *Journal of Education Psychology, 99*(3), 532–544.

Hausman, C., & Goldring, E. (2000). Parent involvement, influence and satisfaction in magnet schools: Do reasons for choice matter? *The Urban Review, 32*(2), 105–121.

Hoover-Dempsey, K. V., & Sandler, H. M. (1995). Parent involvement in children's education: Why does it make a difference? *Teachers College Record, 97*(2), 311–330.

Hoover-Dempsey, K. V., & Sandler, H. (1997). Why do parents become involved in their children's education? *Review of Educational Research, 67*(1), 3–42.

Hoover-Dempsey, K., Walker, J., & Sandler, H. (2005). Parents' motivations for involvement in their children's education. In E. Patrikakou, R. Weisberg, S. Redding, & H. Walberg, (Eds.), *School-family partnerships for children's success* (pp. 40–56). New York: Teachers College Press.

Lubienski, C. (2003). Innovation in education markets: Theory and evidence on the impact of competition and choice in charter schools. *American Educational Research Journal, 40*(2), 395–443.

Metz, M. (1993). Teachers' ultimate dependence on their students. In J. Little & M. McLaughlin (Eds.), *Teachers' work: Individuals, colleagues and contexts* (pp. 104–136). New York: Teachers College Press.

Murphy, J., Elliott, S. N., Goldring, E., & Porter, A. C. (2006). *Learning-centered leadership: A conceptual foundation.* New York: Wallace Foundation.

Raywid, M. A. (1985). Family choice arrangements in public schools: A review of the literature. *Review of Educational Research, 55*(4), 435–467.

Read, T. (2008). *Early investment jump-starts change: Lessons from the Annie E. Casey Foundation's strategic support of Indianapolis Mayor Bart Peterson's Charter Initiative.* Retrieved from http://www.innovations.harvard.edu/cache/documents/859/85901.pdf.

Seeley, D. S. (1993). A new paradigm for parent involvement. In N. F. Chavkin (Ed.), *Families and schools in a pluralistic society* (pp. 229–234). Albany, NY: State University of New York Press.

Smrekar, C. (2009). *Taking charge of choice: How charter school policy contexts matter.* Paper presented at the invitational conference School Choice and School Improvement: Research in State, District and Community Contexts, Vanderbilt University, Nashville, TN.

Smrekar, C., & Goldring, E. B. (1999). *School choice in urban America: Magnet schools and the pursuit of equity*. New York: Teachers College Press.

Strauss, A., & Corbin, J. (1998). *Basics of qualitative research. Techniques and procedures for developing grounded theory* (2nd ed.). Thousand Oaks, CA: Sage.

Tashakkori, A., & Teddlie, C. (1998). *Mixed methodology: Combining qualitative and quantitative approaches*. Thousand Oaks, CA: Sage.

Walker, J. M. T., Wilkins, A. S., Dallaire, J. R., Sandler, H. M., & Hoover-Dempsey, K. V. (2005). Parental involvement: Model revision through scale development. *The Elementary School Journal, 106*(2), 85–104.

Zimmer, R., & Buddin, R. (2007). Getting inside the black box: Examining how the operation of charter schools affects performance. *Peabody Journal of Education, 82*(2–3), 231–273.

Zimmer, R., Buddin, R., Chau, D., Daley, G., Gill, B., Guarino, C., ... Brewer, D. (2003). *Charter school operations and performance: Evidence from California* (Monograph No. MR-1700). Santa Monica, CA: RAND Corporation.

13

CONVERSATIONS WITH COMMUNITY-ORIENTED EDUCATIONAL LEADERS

Edited by Susan Auerbach

This chapter brings the voices of educational leaders directly into the conversation with excerpts from telephone interviews on their views of leadership for partnerships. Five U.S. school and district leaders from urban, suburban, and rural communities in the Northeast, Southeast, Midwest, and West were chosen based on referrals from book contributors and others; while not a scientific sample, they represent a thoughtful mix of perspectives from a variety of contexts. The opinions expressed are those of individuals and not necessarily those of their institutions.

The Speakers

Michele Brooks has been assistant superintendent for family and student engagement in the Boston Public Schools since 2008, one of a small number of leaders in such cabinet-level positions. She was previously a school board member, consultant, and director of the Boston Parent Organizing Network. The urban district of 56,400 students is 37% African American, 9% Asian, 39% Latino, and 13% White, with 74% eligible for free or reduced price meals and 21% English Learners.

Dr. Nancy Golden has been superintendent of the Springfield Public Schools in Springfield, Oregon, since 2003. She has been an educator for over 30 years, including directing and teaching in the administrator licensure program at the University of Oregon. The suburban/rural district of 11,000 students is 2% African American, 2% American Indian, 2% Asian, 17% Latino, and 74% White, with 65% eligible for free or reduced price meals and 3% English Learners; the Latino population has increased dramatically in recent years.

Dr. Deborah Hoffman is principal of Lincoln Elementary in Madison, Wisconsin, with 15 years of administrative experience. Her grade 3-5 school's population of 365 students is 29% African American, 14% Asian, 32% Latino, 2% Native American, and 24% White, with 71% of students eligible for free or reduced price meals and 38% English Learners.

Hae-Sin Thomas was an administrator in the Oakland Unified School District in California until 2007, serving as director of the New Schools Development Group and New School Network, as well as principal and assistant principal. She is currently an educational consultant. Oakland is an urban district of 46,500 students that is 35% African American, 15% Asian and Pacific Islander, 37% Latino, and 7% White, with 68% eligible for free or reduced price meals and 31% English Learners.

Dr. Aaron Woody is principal of John R. Lawrence Elementary in Archdale, North Carolina, with eight years of administrative experience. The mostly lower middle-class suburban pre-K-5 school of about 500 students is 11% African American, 3% Asian, 5% Latino, and 78% White, with 40% eligible for free or reduced price meals and 3% English Learners.

What does the word *partnerships* mean to you? What is your personal vision of what family and community partnerships should look like in schools?

Brooks: I like to make dating analogies. [Family] involvement is when you might have a casual date. [Family] engagement is when you're serious and learning what you have in common. Partnership is like marriage; it's really focused on a shared vision of what you're producing for the future, where people are equal partners. There's give and take, there's open communication, and the joy and the pain are shared equally. So with home-school partnerships, I think of schools that welcome families and see them as assets for educating children, that share the successes with families and the challenges, and partner with families to overcome the challenges either for individual students or for the whole school.

Golden: You're cocreating a vision of what you want for kids in your community, a pathway. What you want your students to see is that this is a great community because we all come together. If the kids see all these people are invested in their success, it becomes a culture—like our vision with the Springfield quality education model (see below). They [community partners] all come with different skill sets. So when a problem comes up, who are we going to partner with to work this out? You can multiply your ability to impact kids in a greater way.

Hoffman: My vision is that whether I see or hear from the parent or not, that they feel connected and comfortable being part of the school community at whatever level works for them and they feel their child is safe and happy when they are here. I don't feel every parent has to come up to the school to be part of the school. Lots of our parents work two jobs. I hope they know that we're a welcoming place—that's our reputation—and if they need something from us they'll ask. I want them to know we're here for them and supporting their student's work.

Thomas: I think it means that you view the family as an equal in the education of the child. I have found that when I am humble, respectful, thoughtful, and I come in as a learner, that I can embrace and bring the parents in as partners or allies. People say partnership and they really mean service, and then there's a power dynamic in the relationship. Part of the problem is that schools assume they have nothing to get from the parents or community. I go in with the perspective that I have a lot to offer but also that I have a lot to gain. The biggest thing to be gained is not that parents come in and volunteer or help you with managing the child. When you partner with parents and they feel respected, a lot of times they become strong advocates for schools and communities. You cannot have a high performing school without strong parent advocates. For me that's the voice that's missing [in urban schools]. We have created a power dynamic where we have written off parents and the community, operating under the assumption that they are the problem or that we don't think it's our responsibility to build capacity for parents to be able to advocate effectively for their child.

Woody: Partnership is where people have mutually exclusive roles but are working in tandem to see that students are getting the best out of their opportunities and creating a better community for everybody. The primary reason schools are here is for students to grow and mature and be nurtured in the quest for knowledge, and that happens through curriculum but also through all the teachable moments on campus and in the community. The vocabulary and behavior in the school changes, and everyone recognizes we are seeking to be a lighthouse to our community. It sounds very much like what a church should be doing, but I think it should be a significant part of what school is about. If you can develop democracy and cooperation and service and humility in a school, that helps develop a better larger community.

What are some ways your organization has pursued school-family or school-community partnerships? What has been your role in these efforts as an educational leader?

Brooks: We're constantly looking for opportunities and tools to build capacity. We do workshops with parents and teachers from the same school who meet separately and we ask them the same questions about expectations and beliefs around children and learning; then we bring them back together and share answers. There's generally not too much difference between what families say and what teachers say. It creates an environment for them to begin to talk about things where there are differences. Our School Engagement Action Teams focus on developing the family and student engagement plans; we have worked with [district staff] to make sure that for every instructional strategy a school identifies for its Whole School Improvement Plan, there is a family engagement strategy linked to that. We have a toolkit aligned to academic strategies that schools can use. We have a Family Learning Guide that breaks down what students should know and be able to do and gives parents tips for learning at home. Those have been the real levers for us. And we use a lot of community partners. We have a Parent University taking off like wildfire [series of classes for parents]; about 700 parents went through it last year.

[As a leader of partnerships] sometimes I'm the visionary, sometimes I'm the facilitator. I've got to be able to influence allies in this work, communicating clearly what the work is and mobilizing folks. I see my role as creating opportunities for people to embrace their role in [family] engagement and for coordinating the development of tools that make it easier for them to do that.

Golden: We used a community engagement process [with the Springfield Quality Education Model] to come up with what we needed to do. We are a community of 55,000 people; we talked to 11,000 people [through a series of community meetings]. We went to City Council meetings, Rotary meetings. We cocreated the big ideas we wanted to do [for a vision of quality education]. Like we had the idea of a magnet school, so we partnered with a downtown community group that was trying to revitalize an old theater; when the partnership with the school happened, they were able to raise enough money to get the theater open. We spent $300,000 to partially own this building. For the city, they know it's going to keep going; [the benefit] multiplies. Partnerships like that are so powerful. When we wanted to make sure we had our Latino families engaged, we said, "What would a meeting look like for you to want to be there and be comfortable?" They told us they don't like to be in a group where the majority is not Latino and you've got this weird [translation] machine on that makes you stand out when you already stand out. They just wanted to have their own meeting [in Spanish]. So it's making sure you are not creating forms that are comfortable for you and not for other people.

My job as superintendent is to galvanize the community, to understand the community's collective values. It's about getting clear about who you are leading the organization for. How do you bring people to a common place around values? I made a commitment to learning Spanish from the moment I got here. For the Latino community, that was very heartening. I'm not completely fluent but I can welcome them or help people who are struggling to talk. So they got to feel comfortable with me. I'm out every night at all the events and I see that as my opportunity to really talk to parents. Parents entrust their kids to us every day so it's critical that I get to know them and they get to know me. I can share the vision and they get to share their lives so that I can understand them.

Hoffman: At my first school [as principal] when we were restructuring with a service delivery model, we needed to make sure parents understood what it meant—how we were educating their children, how it would be different and how the same, and how we wanted to have a relationship with them. So we started groups that we called Parent Empowerment Groups. After the groups accomplished the initial goal, we found so many other benefits; we started having such a deeper understanding of what we wanted to build with parents. Those groups are still running today, even without grant money. Teachers felt they were so meaningful; if they were going to volunteer their time that was where they were going to do it. These are veteran teachers that have always had Open House and parent conferences but when we started having these groups, the teachers felt it was very different. Traditional parent-teacher organizations I've been involved with have been really healthy and respectful but they're based a lot around fundraising, and the parents we were seeking to include were interested in other issues. So we have built a system where parents set the agenda and I find people to come in and speak. Different parent groups have different agendas. Some would say, "We want to know how to help our children in math at home," so teachers would design small lessons. We had everything from a school safety officer who talked about gangs to health care people coming to talk about access and immunizations and also hot topics of things happening in the community. [The agenda] wasn't always necessarily school-based. We really focus on the whole child and not just their academic math brain; the brain has to be happy and safe before they can do the math.

[As a leader] I have to set the stage here to make partnerships a possibility. Getting set up for getting parents being involved and feeling safe and happy, just like we want the students to feel, is a lot more work [than once things are running]—so that they know they will not be talked down to because they don't speak English or be made to feel uncomfortable because they're poor. We have supports in place and a common way of interacting with all parents. There's everything from the tone in the school office to having these elaborate meetings with food and child care and transportation so that everyone can get access. As a leader I have to set the tone for all of that. Teachers set the tone for parent conferences and set the expectation that we will have 100% participation.

Thomas: The community has a very negative history dealing with the district and you're going in there to try to close their schools; it was very important to work with a trusted community partner. We worked with Oakland Communities Organizations (OCO) to reach out to PI4 and 5 schools [that failed to meet targets under NCLB] to educate families about what it means to be PI4 and 5 schools and help them research school options. So when I became director of the New Schools Development Group, it was a natural alliance to work with OCO. They trusted me, I trusted them, so they trusted the new schools design group as a result. When we would pick a [new school] leader, we required that they do one-to-one meetings with church leaders, recreation center leaders, canvas the streets, find out who were the gatekeepers in the neighborhood where they were going to open or recreate schools. The first thing we made all those hot shot leaders do was literally eat humble pie and sometimes get yelled at and cursed out and go on in with the intent of building relationships with the community. Ninety percent of the time it worked well.

I created a new school development curriculum [for new leaders]. The first strand was know thyself, the second was know thy community. My role was both modeling my own leadership style, which was very community oriented, and holding the new leaders accountable for doing it. Those leaders were evaluated and coached for that.

Woody: We spent a lot of time reaching out to the neighboring businesses, invited them to come out for Principal Breakfasts. We held these quarterly, free breakfast and town hall meetings for people to come and ask questions. Those were really successful for connecting people. The meetings all had themes, like technology in the classroom. Parents were asking, "What are ways we could better support the school with technology?" So that led right into fundraising. We developed a committee, reached out to our parents and business partners, and in two years, we were able to purchase 24 Smartboards. That came right out of our Principal Breakfasts. Parents would ask questions about school safety or a decision that was made; there were good opportunities as well for critique. I tried as principal to foster a culture of civil disagreement. It's OK for people to disagree but let's disagree civilly, so that parents and community members have a voice.

What do you feel has been your greatest accomplishment as a leader of partnerships?

Brooks: My greatest accomplishment happens when I'm not there—when my colleagues ask [at district cabinet meetings], "How do we engage families around this? What is our strategy?" I feel like I've infiltrated. There's a lot of concrete things we have done, but I think the shift in thinking about family engagement is the greatest accomplishment. My goal is to work myself out of a job, when partnerships are the norm and a part of the fabric of who we are.

Golden: Cocreating a vision and getting everybody aligned to help our kids know and be everything they can be, to graduate career and college ready, to be good citizens—so that together, we're helping our kids be successful.

Hoffman: I'm most proud of how parents talk about me and the schools that I'm a part of. The word on the street is you can go talk to Deb, she's available, she shows up, she'll listen to you. Over time I've built a pretty positive relationship with the community. I'm super proud of what we've been able to do with our Parent Empowerment Groups, we're on year 12; obviously we have built a sustainable program. We have parents whose opinions haven't ever been counted before on school surveys; if we're having a parent group in Hmong [language], the specialist can read them the survey at the meeting and take down and translate their responses.

Thomas: I'm proud of the group of leaders who came out of that small schools development process. I think they are a different kind of leader than exists in most school systems as a result of our focus on visionary, transformative, community leadership. They feel accountable to the community and for empowering their community, including staff. The schools that we created have much flatter structures; it's easy to mobilize parents. Because we had a very thoughtful, community-based process, we were able to close a huge number of failing schools without too much controversy. That is what has sustained us through various changes and crises.

Woody: I like to think it is that the culture of our school has changed from a place that was driven by individual personal interest, indicative of an upper middle-class affluent school, to an emphasis on the greater good of our community, trying to promote that idea. We're making strides; we're not there yet.

What about your greatest challenge as a leader of partnerships?

Brooks: The greatest challenge is getting the resources to expand the work, not just finances but the human resources. We are seeing the shift with principals in the way that they are dealing with families but it's not moving fast enough. With budget cuts, we're now at 50% of our staffing. We have 137 schools and six [district] staff that focus on family engagement, so it really pushes us to figure out how to develop tools that schools can take and do themselves or with minimal support from our office.

Golden: Building the relationships so you really understand who your community is. My second year [as superintendent], we brought forward a diversity plan that people got upset about because I didn't understand some of the community. When you don't inform people, they jump to conclusions generated by their worst fears. We had 200 people at a board meeting, I listened and listened, and I said, "We've got to stay in conversation; if we start polarizing and fighting each other, students will not feel safe and respected." If I was to do it again, I would set up a ministerial group, call on churches to help understand the community.

Hoffman: Sometimes we don't get it right in the one-to-one relationships. I had a parent tell me she's leaving the school and cussed me out in the hallway. It makes me really sad every time that I don't make that connection. It's another time that a parent is not going to feel understood or welcome at school, and all of that baggage makes it a really hard climb for that child to be successful in school if their parent feels that negative about the system. So every time we lose one, it's a huge loss. Fortunately I don't think that has happened too often.

Thomas: I don't think there is a lot of value placed on engaging the community. Nobody funds it and superintendents, principals, boards—that's not something they talk about or emphasize. Parent involvement is often given lip service, but not really thoughtful parent leadership or advocacy or partnership with community-based organizations. The status quo is that most leaders were trained in a different school of thought and not held accountable to the community.

Woody: You can't do this work without being transparent and being vulnerable as a leader because that's how you're going to garner trust and help people make meaning. I want to be a real person, I don't want to be phony. So you have to have some tough conversations and walk the walk, not just talk the talk. If you stand up at PTA and say, "We want you to get plugged in," then people start coming, so you have to have a plan of how to plug these folks in; if you don't, they get disenchanted and tell other people. So you've got to be organized. Then you have to be able to deal with all these different personalities. Certain parents or organizations have certain characteristics that you don't especially love but you have to navigate that. A lot of times, businesses are looking at the bottom line, what's in it for me, but that's not what it's about; we're trying to make the school a better place. Maybe down the road that investment will pay rich dividends [for the community partner], but it's not a quick return.

What leadership capacities are needed to lead the kind of partnerships you envision?

Brooks: There is no other factor in my experience that impacts the level of engagement of families more than leadership styles. If a principal values the engagement of families, if a principal is collaborative and an inclusive leader and creates a space for the voices of those impacted by the work or those doing the work, engagement in those schools thrives. If the principal is a top-down leader, the engagement looks different. Even if they value their families, it's not as open or collaborative, not as welcoming and inclusive of families' voices, and there isn't space for working through conflict or differences. [Capacities needed are] patience, humility, not being afraid to share power with teachers, with families, and with the students themselves.

Golden: You have to not be scared to hire people that are better than you. Then you have to really empower them to have the authority, alignment around the values, and let them go. If you do that, you have a lot of time [as a leader] to be out in the community. If people trust me, I can move with the speed of trust; if not, everything is questioned. If you have the right group of people in the room, any problem can be solved. The greatest skill [for leading partnerships] is facilitation skills—having a sense of vision and really knowing how to facilitate [meetings] so people feel heard and believe that together we're stronger.

Hoffman: You have to care about all of your students. You have to really at your core values believe things can be different than they are right now. That's hard for a lot of my colleagues in terms of leadership because it's tiring to think that your work is never done, that it can always be better, that you will be abused in some way by many members of your organization. That tenacity to continue the work—I can't sustain it by myself. I need other people to give me feedback and be on my team; I need distributed leadership. It's also important to know how to respond to parents in a nonthreatening way where they're asking difficult questions, like about the overrepresentation of Black males in special ed. If you're a Black parent and didn't know this was a problem, it's easy to think, "Why is the system so racist?" So when you have parent meetings, you have to be prepared intellectually and emotionally to explain what the problems are and how we are trying to repair the system, and that we're all on the same team, trying to make this better for kids. If I don't recognize that there is a problem or if I blame the students or the parents, that's a whole group that's no longer going to be involved. So principals and teachers who set out to have more in-depth parent relationships need to be well-educated about their own biases, their own emotional response to some challenging issues in order to support parents' continued involvement.

Thomas: Cultural competence is a big one and community competency. The best principals are the ones who ask questions, model inquiry, and go into the community with a learner orientation. Leaders also have to have really strong interpersonal skills and be strong strategic thinkers. Sometimes crises happen quickly and you go into communities that have been oppressed for decades, so there's got to be a level of persistence and will around developing these relationships. The more you do it, the better you get at it. Often in situations when parents are frustrated, angry, or have had negative experiences with school folks, if you are willing to work through that and be disrespected initially and you persevere and present a different face, people start trusting you. You can become an advocate not just for the child but the family, which means ultimately that child does better.

Woody: You have to be a very effective communicator and take some risks. You have to put yourself out there and say, "We're going to build this together, I don't have it all figured out," making yourself transparent and vulnerable. You can only do that by being genuine and real. And if you're an effective communicator, you're going to build relationships, and out of them, you can become more organized and develop a vision. It's being able to work with all different kinds of people and build a collective vision and see things through.

Comments on partnerships with business and community organizations

Golden: We have something unique here, Team Springfield, where the CEO of the public utility, the city, Parks and Recreation, the schools—we each put money in a pool, we meet monthly, and set goals together. We [the district] got a 21st Century Learning Community grant for Parks and Rec for after-school programs; when that was running out, Parks and Rec went out for a bond. What's unique about us is we really try to take the infrastructure, things that are already at play [in the community] and use those to get farther.

Hoffman: We are part of Madison Schools Community Foundation with formalized adopt-a-school partnerships. We do Principal for a Day every year; out of that, St. Mary's Hospital adopted our school. If you're going to have that relationship [with a community partner], it needs to be organized, somewhat formal, and you need to build that relationship. I attend all the joint steering committee meetings. A lot of times, these partners are looked at as your sugar daddy, and they do give us a lot. But we're trying to make that a two-way thing. Just because our kids are poor, we still want to have them involved in community service; we have something to offer, too. Our choir went over and sang for the [hospital] patients; we color all of their birth announcement cards; we assisted in making a video with them with student emcees who did a tour of the hospital. So it's a very intertwined relationship.

Comments on parent and community participation in school governance

Thomas: I think the ongoing struggle in places like Oakland is that at the school level, there are means by which parents are allowed to govern, and most have to do with money and budgets; they don't have to do with teacher or principal selection or evaluation or decisions about programs for the most part. There's a delicate line here. There are specialists who have special training who should be doing this work. At the same time, as messy as this sounds, the community of parents should have a strong role in how schools and districts are governed. If you actually trained parents and community to cogovern, you would get a chance of maintaining some level of consistency in the approaches that schools and districts take. The small schools work in Oakland has stuck because we have empowered teacher communities but also because we have organized parents who understand the value of the work.

Comments on working with low-income or working-class versus middle-class/affluent communities

Brooks: For the last 5 to 6 years, Boston Public Schools has done a lot of different things to attract middle-class families back into our system. And we've done so by advantaging them over poor and working-class families in my opinion. When you have a wide variety of diversity in your school—you have middle-class families that have resources and the time to be very active, and you have poor and working-class families who work, don't speak the language, who've had horrible experiences in education or are just disenfranchised—schools tend to gravitate to those families that have resources and are engaged and say, "The other ones don't come." So we've been doing some cultural proficiency work with staff. Now we're getting ready to do it with families, with mostly White middle-class families who have asked [for help with School Site Council representation]. It's raising awareness of their belief system and how their attitudes impact others when they come into the same space. We've been working with a couple of principals at schools that have been brave enough to start those courageous conversations. You cannot apply a middle-class model of engagement when you have such a diverse population—PTA, raise funds, be the boosters and volunteer for field trips—because most of these [poor and working-class] parents cannot do that. You have to figure out ways for them to make contributions that are aligned to their values. You've got to really figure out how to reach your families where they are, when it's convenient for them, and provide them information that is relevant to them. We have a few schools piloting home visits and it has challenged teachers' assumptions about who these poor and working-class families are; it builds that relationship, that relational trust, so those parents are much more responsive now.

Woody: The challenges I have found in my current setting [mostly White lower middle-class population with some more affluent families] is there are real issues of power and entitlement. I'm a White male; some of the most influential people I deal with are White females, stay-at-home moms. These ladies are very connected; they have a lot of perceived power and you have to navigate that. Meanwhile, there are a lot of people in the school not being adequately represented. For example, at our Principal Breakfasts, by the third year, it was the same people showing up. So I started doing evening events directly connected to student events like the art show, concerts, and we'd feed everybody. You get to hear from a single mom or an African American male or a grandpa who is a first-generation immigrant. You find out that our school is bigger than just [that small group]. It's about finding ways to create space where everyone's voice can be heard.

Some in the field feel that true partnerships call for educators sharing power with parents and other stakeholders. How do you see this?

Brooks: Boston has been cutting edge with this. Site-based management has been standard here for the last 20 years. School Site Councils have decision-making authority over school policy, budget, instructional direction. We are partnering with Boston Teachers Union to provide training for school teams to make sure they are being effective in decision making. This is still a work in progress and just like with student achievement we have pockets of excellence, with family engagement we have pockets of excellence.

Hoffman: I don't believe that a school board or a parent that hasn't been to college should be telling me what curriculum I should be using. That just continues to deprofessionalize what we know based on research and practice. Parents should be involved but we need to all remember our roles. Teachers need to remember that parents are the most important relationship in students' lives. That relationship needs to be healthy and workable in the best interest of kids. Lots of our parents who are privileged are overassertive and teachers shut down, and that's not healthy. And we also have teachers that don't respect the parents because of issues in how they live their lives. Either way that goes, it's damaging for student achievement. We have to share power but we need to remember what our roles are and stay focused on students being happy, safe, and learning.

Thomas: The system is not designed to support cogovernance right now. That requires investment of resources and time to build structures and systems to engage parents and build their capacity. Even very educated folks on charter school or nonprofit boards do not know how to govern schools; there is very little training available. The biggest challenge continues to be that when stuff is bad, good folks will rise up and help manage but when things are going well, people are barely present. We had strong parent leadership teams at ASCEND [new small school]; they were the right hand for the principal when there was a lot to advocate for to get a new facility, etc. When things are going well and parents trust the school, they sort of check out. That's what's happened in some of our small schools. We had 95% parent participation in student-led conferences, student celebrations, literacy nights—but not as much when you need them to come in for hard budget decisions.

Woody: I think sharing power is meaningful but you have to be organized and have a clear vision. If you just open it up—schools exist for kids, not for adults to have jobs or to have their individual agenda. You're not going to be a collective community school if you're not including the voice of the people and you're not listening. The principal is not the one holding all the power and knowledge and truth. You have to be able to facilitate the bigger discussions about the vision for the school as a place that's ultimately more caring with deeper, more rich academics taking place. My school setting is pretty traditional, so as much as I have tried to release that [traditional model] and become a facilitator, there are still staff and parents who just want me to tell them what to do. It's a hard paradigm shift. You can't just demand it, you have to model it and communicate it.

What trends do you see in education today that affect partnerships or leadership for partnerships? For example, how does the accountability movement affect home-school relations?

Brooks: What gives me hope is that there is a lot of movement around family engagement as a lever for improving student outcomes. It's been a long time coming. I'm excited about the conversations happening at the federal level. If they bear fruit, then reauthorization of Title I will really have some ways to hold people accountable and some measures so people will know what engagement looks like. We've got a lot of energy around family engagement but what gives me pause is that some of that energy is grounded in the "fix the parents" kind of philosophy rather than partner with the parents.

Golden: We're in a great place [in Oregon] right now because we have a governor who really gets it. Our governor-elect really believes in an age 0–20 pathway for every kid and when you have a governor who is so insightful, you start thinking about deeper partnerships with Head Start or the Promise Communities. The governor's vision will cause people to work together.

Hoffman: The accountability movement in terms of the general public [understanding of the issues] is really damaging. We're a school that's in sanctions [under NCLB]. I'm living in a state that requires bilingual education and in a country that doesn't recognize that. If we teach a kid to read in Spanish, why would we expect them to pass a test in English? It affects home-school relations because it goes into the newspaper that we're a failing school. It doesn't say that we have two government institutions that are not in alignment. If parents don't know our school, why would they want to send their kid here?

Thomas: On the positive front, this big focus on data and school performance has been huge leverage for engaging parents. When you do not have information to tell parents if a school is good or bad, it's hard to build a conversation. When you have that data and walk through the school and do some minimal capacity building around a rubric—are you greeted warmly, what's displayed in the hallways, what's the general culture of the school?—none of it is stuff that parents and community people can't evaluate; it's not rocket science. There isn't a parent out there who wants to see their kid not go to college or who doesn't believe in rigor or high expectations, and they don't hate testing. Parents are allies of education reform, and when we don't use them as allies and we go in without their input, we create enemies and distrust.

Woody: With all the deep budget cuts coming right now, you limit the time and space you have to cultivate relationships and to have these deeper conversations. We're so driven by results, principals face an internal conflict. The first danger is to become so driven by the supremacy of the push for student achievement that we retreat from our emphasis on community building. The other challenge is to become so driven by community organizing that you allow student achievement to become underemphasized. A lot of districts don't allow the principal to stay vested long enough in their school to have these collaborative relationships that actually build community. Meaningful relationships take time; you can't cultivate this stuff quickly.

Do you have any recommendations for leadership preparation programs on how to develop capacity for leadership for partnerships?

Brooks: There's only so much you can learn from the books. It's about hands-on [experience], so internships, practicums, or observations in schools and having some guidelines to really analyze family engagement. [Harvard University professor] Karen Mapp does a class and we have her students come and do an analysis of family engagement in schools, and it's really transformative. To actually be able to observe and experience it helps [preservice educators] understand what engagement looks like and that it's doable.

Golden: If you think that facilitation is a core skill, [preparation programs could say] "Here's the 10 best facilitators in the area. We want you to go see how they facilitate a meeting." Instead of just general [field or practicum] experience for people, we could pinpoint the most important experience and say, "This is what we want you to stay focused on and keep looking for."

Hoffman: Having taught adjunct for University of Wisconsin, I know it's important to pay a lot of attention to research and practice, but we need more emphasis on practice. The failures [in leadership] I've come across have not been because of lack of research knowledge; they've been administrators' body language that turned off parents or not having the skill to run that meeting or not having enough understanding of my own racism and classism and the need to work toward being antiracist, and be honest with my parents so that they see I don't know it all. The equity and social justice work in preparing principals—if that's not done, I think almost everything is lost. I don't see any point in working in public education if you're not working to repair the damage that's been done by marginalizing people. Sometimes it's the all White or all privileged schools that need more antiracist leadership than a [diverse urban] school like the one I'm at right now.

Thomas: [Leadership] students could be going into communities, doing listening campaigns, doing research, and getting training on how the community has been at odds with the school system and with folks who come in from outside. Currently, training is going on in Oakland about privilege and how it is received; the more aware you are of how it is received, the more you can counter it. That's something you have to build into leadership programs and then force leaders to reflect on regularly. Leaders should be trained to want community feedback and build systems and ways to get community feedback—surveys, focus groups are not done enough at schools. All of this starts with knowing yourself: What is your leadership style, how do you respond to crisis, how do you deescalate conflict, what do you do when you're feeling attacked?

Woody: Maybe leadership preparation programs can work on how to navigate political structures. I took a course on power and politics in schools and that was very meaningful. You have to navigate those power structures and be able to connect people. It seems like it's manipulation and deception but it's not; you need everyone to make this work. Any work that preparation programs can do with a democratic focus would be very helpful for community organizing at the school level.

In closing, what advice do you have for aspiring or practicing administrators about leadership for family and community partnerships?

Brooks: Parents are your partners. Every single parent has hopes and dreams for their children and every day they give us their best. What they expect from us is to work with them to get those children to realize those hopes and dreams, and the best way I know to do that is to find ways to partner. If they don't come to you, go to them.

Golden: If you believe in partnerships, the resource pool [for education] automatically expands. It's not just about the school district, it's about the greater community. Then the ability to do what you need to do for kids is really endless.

Hoffman: The stamina and emotional centeredness that it takes to do this work is a challenge. There has to be a lot of rehearsal for the unexpected, not necessarily acted out but it needs to be intellectually practiced. It's when I'm caught off-guard or if I'm being personally attacked that I do the worst in my parent relationships.

Thomas: Especially if you are not from the community, make sure that you have community leaders that people respect as your allies. So if you are a White man going into West Oakland, you should have a strong African American leader who you meet with regularly and invite to give you feedback.

Woody: Get immersed in this topic [leadership for partnerships] because I believe this is the most important variable of your leadership; it's going to make or break your success. If families are connected, if the school has partnerships with all the influences that shape the larger community and the kids feel good about their experiences, there's going to be constant teachable moments as part of the curriculum and tests are going to take care of themselves. What's unfortunate is some of my peers are so driven to find a program for the best math scores that they have lost the soul of what school is really about. This is the most important opportunity to leave a meaningful legacy at the school that you work with, how you cultivate and develop democracy.

14

CONCLUSION

Susan Auerbach

The voices of the reflective leaders in Chapter 13 provide an inspiring, yet realistic insiders' view of the rewards and challenges of leadership for partnerships. They articulate many themes addressed in other chapters of this book, suggesting important links between research and practice. Among these points of overlap are perspectives on boundary spanning, accountability, power-sharing, and what Riehl in Chapter 2 calls "the emotional aspects of leadership practice," as well as recommendations for leaders and leadership preparation programs.

The practitioners in Chapter 13 are committed to boundary-spanning and bridging roles as a central part of their leadership practice, deliberately rejecting a buffering stance that distances schools from stakeholders. Leaders documented in other chapters are more likely to act as buffers, as in ignoring parents' requests to discuss a bilingual program or interfering in a mother's workplace to coerce her attendance at special education meetings (Chapters 5, 6). Principals need to honestly assess their practice to see if it is conducive to partnerships and the new opportunities that partnerships bring to students, families, and schools (Chapters 9, 10, 13). Chapter 11 suggests an emerging type of boundary-spanning role for school leaders as allies with community organizing groups and empowered parents. Far from the traditional boundary-spanning role as an agent of public relations, this model casts school leaders as agents of school change who work in common purpose with stakeholders and parent leaders.

Many parts of this book speak to the impact of external accountability pressures on partnership efforts, as well as the need for stronger internal accountability systems to promote partnerships. The press to raise student achievement has spurred some school leaders to reach out to families as partners in this task (Chapters 2, 3, 7, 9, 10, 11, 12, 13). But the same pressures have moved other leaders to relegate partnerships to lower priority or to engage in inequitable practices (Chapters 4, 5, 6, 13). Meanwhile, most school systems lack the clear policies and internal mechanisms needed to hold administrators accountable for promoting partnerships (Chapters 4, 7, 8).

Power-sharing remains a sensitive issue in leadership for partnerships, as seen in the range of perspectives among administrators in Chapter 13. Participatory governance structures are necessary but clearly not sufficient for meaningful parent and community involvement in decision-making (Chapters 1, 3, 4, 7, 8). Leaders need to demystify school policies, procedures, and terminology so as to include stakeholders more fully in decisions about individual students and school programs or operations (Chapters 4, 5, 8). Collaborations with community organizing groups offer opportunities for school leaders to work with informed, knowledgeable parents and disrupt traditional power relations with relational power (Chapters 3, 4, 11). Leaders should welcome community organizing groups as allies working toward common goals of equitable, high quality schools while being prepared to negotiate the tensions inherent in such alliances (Chapters 11, 13). Similarly, they should call on intermediary organizations as cultural brokers and support their work in parent leadership development, recognizing its potential to expand meaningful parent participation (Chapter 9).

Leadership for partnerships, as much of this book shows, is essentially about the skills of collaboration for building relationships (Chapter 3). Leaders need to enhance their political awareness, cultural competence, and interpersonal skills as they navigate complex individual and collective encounters with stakeholders (Chapters 5, 6, 9, 11, 13). Practitioners in Chapter 13 stress the need to be prepared for conflict and confrontation with stakeholders while being open to new learning and genuine in one's communications. They urge leadership preparation programs to focus more on developing candidates' listening, facilitation, and political skills.

Both researchers in this book and practitioners in Chapter 13 agree that effective leadership for partnerships begins with reflection, self-assessment, and dialogue. Leaders can combat prevalent deficit models of low-income communities and parents of color, as well as limited views of parent involvement, by first clarifying their own values, then initiating courageous conversations and inquiry with faculty and staff (Chapters 3, 5, 6, 9, 13). They can position themselves as learners alongside stakeholders as they come to better understand their community and themselves (Chapters 3, 5, 11, 13) in an instance of the two-way benefits of partnerships for leadership development (Chapter 2). Together with stakeholders, leaders can assess what is and what could be in efforts to engage families and community groups and pinpoint areas of common concern (Chapters 3, 9). They can recognize and seek opportunities to counteract the marginalization of bicultural parents by supporting parents' advocacy for their children who have been poorly served by the system (Chapters 5, 6). Rather than silencing parent advocates, school leaders can affirm and join with them to ensure that schools address the learning needs of all students (Chapters 5, 6, 11, 13).

Among this book's implications for future research is the need for conceptual models of leadership that give greater attention to leaders' role as boundary spanners and its integration with other aspects of leaders' work (Chapters 2, 3). Similarly, models of distributed leadership should acknowledge the importance of nurturing leadership among parents and other stakeholders rather than solely among educators (Chapters 2, 9, 11). We need more empirical studies that open up the black box of schooling to investigate how administrators actually engage with and interact with families and community groups, including larger scale quantitative investigations (Chapters 2, 4).

Future studies could address new questions raised by this collection, such as: Under what policy mandates, structures, leadership, and social-political contexts does meaningful parent participation in school governance occur? To what extent are charter schools fulfilling their potential as small learning communities of choice to create new types of relationships with parents? For example, how do rules about mandatory parent volunteer hours play out in these settings and shape the climate for partnerships? Are female school leaders more likely than their male colleagues, on average, to collaborate and share power with community stakeholders and if so, why? How widespread is the shift in community organizing to a less adversarial, more collaborative stance toward school leaders, as documented in Chapter 11?

This book also has implications for the hundreds of educational leadership preparation programs in American universities. Imagine what those programs (and their graduates) would be like if they featured panel discussions with community-oriented leaders like those in Chapter 13 as role models. Imagine the difference it would make if preparation programs redesigned fieldwork with opportunities to shadow, interview, and intern with such administrators, as well as community leaders and community organizers. "Teachers and administrators must learn, in concrete ways, how communities can and have been engaged and empowered,..." observes Schutz (2006), "or most are unlikely to believe it is even possible" (p. 729).

Preparation programs need to move away from the traditional public relations approach in school-community relations courses to a focus on the interpersonal, moral, and political dimensions of building authentic partnerships. This dimension of their role should be emphasized as leadership candidates craft their personal leadership platforms. Indeed, programs should reinforce the connection between leadership for partnerships and leadership for equity and social justice that has been evident throughout this book. As Osterman and Hafner (2009) point out in their review of preparation programs' curricula, leadership for social justice involves developing skills for working with diverse families and creating welcoming school climates, as well as cultivating the disposition to share power. Preparation programs must push students beyond their comfort level if they are to "develop in potential leaders a passion for public concerns" and be part of building a socially just order in democratic schools (Hoff, Yoder, & Hoff, 2006, p. 246)

What are the prospects for a broad-based movement toward leadership for authentic partnerships, rather than a small number of "wizards" in isolated cases? Two hopeful signs may be not only the growth of community organizing in education but of small, equity-oriented schools where educators know students and families well. As Deborah Meier (2010) explains:

> Teachers are far more internally vulnerable than many professions because part of being good at our work is the degree to which we expose ourselves, making authentic connections with kids and families. It may be one reason schools used to keep parents away. Without sufficient time for building relationships with both our students and their families, misunderstandings are the norm, not the exception.
>
> *(paras 8–9)*

Meanwhile, it is heartening to see a greater emphasis on advocacy, parent leadership, and power issues in recent textbooks on partnerships and standards for parent involvement (e.g., Henderson, Mapp, Johnson, & Davies, 2007; National PTA, n.d.; Sanders & Sheldon, 2009). And some scholars see an opening for more collaborative leadership with new generations of school leaders, especially women and people of color, who may have an affinity with marginalized groups, feminist beliefs, and relational power (Cooper, Riehl, & Hasan, 2010; Henry, 1996; Warren, Hong, Rubin, & Uy, 2009). Thus, we may soon see more administrators leading by example to counter deficit thinking and create inclusive school cultures, in part by striving for more authentic partnerships with families and communities.

References

Cooper, C. W., Riehl, C. J., & Hasan, L. (2010). Leading and learning with diverse families in schools: Critical epistemology amid communities of practice. *Journal of School Leadership, 20*(6), 758–788.

Henderson, A. T., Mapp, K. L., Johnson, V. R., & Davies, D. (2007). *Beyond the bake sale: The essential guide to family-school partnerships*. New York: New Press.

Henry, M. E. (1996). *Parent-school collaboration: Feminist organizational structures and school leadership*. Albany, NY: State University of New York Press.

Hoff, D. F., Yoder, N., & Hoff, P. S. (2006). Preparing educational leaders to embrace the "public" in public schools. *Journal of Educational Administration 44*(3), 239–249.

Meier, D. (2010, October 7). Beyond anger lies hope? Bridging differences blog. Retrieved from http://blogs.edweek.org/edweek/Bridging-Differences/

National PTA. (n.d.). PTA's national standards for family-school partnerships. Retrieved from http://www.pta.org/national_standards.asp

Osterman, K. F., & Hafner, M. M. (2009). Curriculum in leadership preparation: Understanding where we have been in order to know where we might go. In M. Young, G. M. Crow,

J. Murphy, & R. T. Ogawa (Eds.), *Handbook of research on the education of school leaders* (pp. 269–317). New York: Routledge.

Sanders, M. G., & Sheldon, S. B. (2009). *Principals matter: A guide to school, family, and community partnerships.* Thousand Oaks, CA: Corwin Press.

Schutz, A. (2006). Home is a prison in the global city: The tragic failure of school-based community engagement strategies. *Review of Educational Research, 76*(4), 691–744.

Warren, M., Hong, S., Rubin, C. L., & Uy, P. S. (2009). Beyond the bake sale: A community-based relational approach to parent engagement in schools. *Teachers College Record, 111*(9), 2209–2254.

NOTES ON THE CONTRIBUTORS

Susan Auerbach (Editor) is an associate professor in the Department of Educational Leadership and Policy Studies at California State University, Northridge. She received her doctorate in Urban Schooling from the University of California, Los Angeles in 2001 and has published on parent involvement, school-community partnerships, leadership for partnerships, urban education, and college access in *Harvard Educational Review, Educational Administration Quarterly, Journal of School Leadership, Teachers College Record, Urban Education, Latino Education, School Community Journal, Journal of Research on Leadership Education*, and elsewhere. She served as chair (2007-2010) and other positions with the American Educational Research Association Family-School-Community Partnerships Special Interest Group (SIG).

Seenae Chong is currently a doctoral student in the Policy, Organizations, Measurement and Evaluation program of the Graduate School of Education at the University of California, Berkeley. She studies the ways that policy dictates how neighborhoods, communities, and schools interact and how students experience and engage with these intersections. She received a master's in education from Harvard Graduate School of Education and a bachelor's degree in psychology and social welfare from UC Berkeley.

Janet H. Chrispeels is professor emeritus of Education Studies, University of California, San Diego, and currently serves as executive director of Transformative Inquiry Designs for Effective Schools and Systems (TIDES), a nonprofit organization working with school districts in redesigning their systems to meet 21st century learning needs. Her educational career has ranged from parent volunteer and activist to coordinator of school improvement initiatives at a county office of education to 17 years as a faculty member at UC Santa Barbara and UC San Diego. She has authored numerous books and articles on school-family partnerships, school effectiveness, district and school reform, and school leadership teams.

Joseph Flessa is an associate professor in the Department of Theory and Policy Studies at the Ontario Institute for Studies in Education (OISE) at the University of Toronto. A former teacher and principal in the United States and Mexico, Flessa now teaches in the undergraduate program in teacher education and the graduate program in educational administration at OISE. A scholar of urban educational leadership and reform, Flessa has published work in both academic and professional venues that examines the connections and disjunctures between schools and communities.

Rhoda Freelon is a doctoral student in the Urban Schooling Division of the University of California, Los Angeles's Graduate School of Education and Information Studies. She also works as a Graduate Student Researcher for UCLA's Institute for Democracy, Education, and Access (IDEA) and the University of California All Campus Consortium on Research for Diversity (UC/ACCORD), where she monitors and creates state and national indicators for analyses of educational equity and opportunity. Her research explores parent engagement and the intersectionality of race- and class-based educational inequality.

Ellen Goldring is Patricia and Rodes Hart Chair and Professor of Education Policy and Leadership and chair of the Department of Leadership, Policy and Organizations at Peabody College, Vanderbilt University. Her research interests focus on school improvement with particular emphases on school choice and school leadership. Her recent books, with coauthors, include *Leading with Data: A Path to School Improvement* (Corwin Press), *From the Courtroom to the Classroom* (Harvard Education Press), and *School Choice and School Improvement* (Harvard Education Press). She is a coauthor of the *Vanderbilt Assessment of Leadership in Education,* an instrument to assess the effectiveness of the learning-centered leadership of school principals.

Molly F. Gordon is a research associate at the Center for Applied Research and Educational Improvement at the University of Minnesota. She received her master's degree in educational policy studies from the University of Wisconsin-Madison and her doctorate in educational policy and administration at the University of Minnesota-Twin Cities. Her recent research has focused on leadership in educational settings, parent and community engagement, school reform and improvement, educational policy contexts, and how education leaders in diverse settings create college-going cultures in their schools to help underrepresented students prepare for postsecondary education.

Hélène Grégoire is a senior policy advisor in the Community Partnerships Unit of the Ontario Ministry of Education, where she provides strategic advice to promote school-community partnerships in the province. Previously, with the Parent Engagement Office of the same Ministry, she provided advice to create conditions to support parent engagement in the education of their children and in the education system. She previously worked in community-based settings, including as a research and evaluation coordinator at a community health center in Toronto, where she led community-university research partnerships. She received a doctorate in adult education from Cornell University. Her earlier studies were in international development and sociology, with a focus on community development.

Catherine M. Hands is an instructor in educational administration and leadership at Brock University in Ontario, Canada. Prior to her current appointment, she was an assistant professor in the Leadership Studies Department at the University of San Diego. Catherine has been an elementary school teacher, as well as a researcher and educational consultant in Canada, where she worked with administrators in independent schools as well as with district- and school-level administrators in the public school system. Her research interests and publications are in the areas of school-family-community relations, educational leadership, professional learning communities, school reform, and social justice issues in schooling.

Sara McAlister is a research associate with the Annenberg Institute for School Reform. She is a coauthor of the *Organized Communities, Stronger Schools* case study series documenting the findings of a Charles Stewart Mott Foundation-funded research study on the impacts of community organizing for school reform. She is also a coauthor of *Community Organizing for Stronger Schools: Strategies and Successes*, published by the Harvard Education Press. She conducts research on community and youth organizing for school reform and provides research, policy analysis and tool development support for education organizing efforts. She holds a master's degree in public administration from New York University, Wagner.

Heinrich Mintrop is associate professor of Policy, Organization, Measurement and Evaluation at the University of California, Berkeley. His research explores how educational policies form institutional structures that in turn shape teaching and learning in schools. In recent years, his work has turned to the issue of school accountability, particularly in low-performing schools. He is the author of *Schools on Probation: How Accountability Works (and Doesn't Work)* published by

Teachers College Press. He was a teacher in both the United States and Germany before he entered into his academic career. He received a master's degree in political science and German literature at the Freie Universität Berlin (1978) and a doctorate in education from Stanford University (1996).

Edward M. Olivos is associate professor in the Department of Education Studies at the University of Oregon. He received his doctorate in education jointly from San Diego State University and Claremont Graduate University. His research interests include Latinos and education, bicultural parent involvement, policy studies, bilingual education, and critical pedagogy. He is the author of *The Power of Parents: A Critical Perspective of Bicultural Parent Involvement in Public Schools* (2006) published by Peter Lang. He is a former San Diego elementary school teacher, where he taught in bilingual education settings for more than 10 years.

Michelle Renée is a senior research associate at the Annenberg Institute for School Reform and assistant clinical professor in the Urban Education Policy Program at Brown University. She led a scan of New England community engagement and organizing; serves on the team providing support to the Nellie Mae Education Foundation and the research team for the College Readiness Indicator Systems project; and is a core staff member of the new Center for Education Organizing, which provides research and strategic support to education organizing groups around the United States. Prior to joining the Institute, Michelle was a postdoctoral fellow at the University of California, Los Angeles's Institute for Democracy Education and Access. She holds a bachelor's degree from University of California, Santa Cruz, and a doctorate in education from UCLA.

Carolyn Riehl is associate professor in the Department of Organization and Leadership at Teachers College, Columbia University. She is a sociologist of education with special interests in organizational dynamics in schools and school systems, leadership for equity and diversity, and public engagement in education. She earned a master's degree in school organization and administration from New York University and a doctorate in sociology and education from Teachers College, Columbia University. She has been a high school English teacher and has held faculty appointments at the University of Michigan, Eastern Michigan University, and the University of North Carolina at Greensboro.

John Rogers is an associate professor in the University of California, Los Angeles's Graduate School of Education and Information Studies and Director of UCLA's Institute for Democracy, Education and Access (IDEA). He also serves as the faculty codirector of UCLA's Principal Leadership Institute. He is the coauthor of *Learning Power: Organizing for Education and Justice* (2006) and the coeditor of *Public Engagement for Public Education: Revitalizing Democracy and Equalizing Schools* (2010). He received his doctorate in education from Stanford University and his bachelor's degree in public policy and African American studies from Princeton University.

April Ruffin-Adams earned a master's degree in social work in 2001. She is completing her doctorate in cultural studies from the University of North Carolina at Greensboro. Her research interests relate to African American mothers, critical race theory, and parent involvement in special education. She has presented papers related to mentoring, special education advocacy, and African American mothers' advocacy at national conferences. Her passion for improved collaborative partnerships with African American mothers stems from her previous work as a school social worker as well as her role as the mother of a young son.

Claire Smrekar is associate professor of Public Policy and Education at Vanderbilt University. She earned her doctorate in education policy at Stanford University. She conducts qualitative research studies related to the social context of education and public policy, with specific reference to the intersection of desegregation plans and choice policy on families, schools, and neighborhoods. She is currently involved in a study of public housing reform and neighborhood schools. Her work has been funded by the U.S. Department of Education, the Danforth Foundation, the Spencer Foundation, the W.T. Grant Foundation, and Peabody College.

Marc L. Stein is an assistant professor in the Department of Teacher Leadership and Development at the Johns Hopkins University School of Education. Broadly, his research interests lie in understanding the social contexts surrounding schools and schooling and the role that these contexts play in the enactment of educational policy. More specifically this includes research on the social and policy implications of school choice for students, parents, and schools, as well as investigation of neighborhood and school effects on summer learning loss and programs and policies that can support student learning outside of school.

Veronica Terriquez is an assistant professor of sociology at the University of Southern California. She received her doctorate in sociology from the University of California, Los Angeles, a master's in education from UC Berkeley, and a bachelor's degree in sociology from Harvard University. Her research focuses on educational inequality, civic engagement, and immigrant integration.

Camille M. Wilson (previously published under Camille Wilson Cooper) is an associate professor in the Department of Educational Leadership and Cultural

Foundations at the University of North Carolina at Greensboro. Her research and teaching focuses on school-family relations, transformative leadership, and equity-oriented reform that integrates critical, culturally relevant, and gendered perspectives. She has published numerous journal articles and book chapters and is currently writing a book tentatively titled *Motherwork in Schools: The Politics and Pedagogy of African Mothers' Educational Activism.*

INDEX

Page numbers in bold refer to tables.